THE KIMBERLEY

Alasdair McGregor, 'Wet season, Mitchell Plateau' (oil on canvas, 152 x 122 cm).

THE KIMBERLEY

horizons of stone

ALASDAIR McGREGOR &
QUENTIN CHESTER

Including photography by
Rob Jung, Alasdair McGregor &
Quentin Chester

NEW HOLLAND

Published in Australia in 1999 by
New Holland Publishers (Australia) Pty Ltd
Sydney • Auckland • London • Cape Town

14 Aquatic Drive, Frenchs Forest NSW 2086, Australia
1A/218 Lake Road, Northcote Auckland, New Zealand
24 Nutford Place, London W1H 6DQ, United Kingdom
80 McKenzie Street, Cape Town 8001, South Africa

First published in 1992 by
Hodder & Stoughton (Australia) Pty Ltd

National Library of Australia Cataloguing-in-Publication Data

McGregor, Alasdair, 1954–
The Kimberley: horizons of stone

Bibliography
Includes index

ISBN 1 86436 533 1

1. Natural History — Western Australia — Kimberley.
2. Wilderness areas — Western Australia — Kimberley.
3. Kimberley (W.A.). 4. Kimberely (W.A.) — history.
I. Chester, Quentin, II. Jung, Rob. III. Title.

333.784099414

Reproduction: DNL Resources
Printer: Times Printers, Malaysia

Photographic Acknowledgments

Photograph positions: t = top; b = bottom; l = left; r = r.

BATTYE LIBRARY: Pages 103 (photo 65026P), 110 (photo 65199P), 125 (photo 816B/B6106), 126t (photo 816B/B6101), 126b (photo 816B/B6105), 176r (photo 25949P), 181 (photo 65194P). **Q. CHESTER:** Pages 26t, 32b, 37l, 39b, 40t, 48tr, 66t, 91tr, 105b, 121, 122t, 134, 152, 169b, 196tr, 199. **P. GREEN:** Page 2. **R. JUNG:** Pages 19t, 20t&b, 24, 32t, 34t&b, 37t&r, 39t, 42, 45, 46, 48b, 49, 55t, 60t, 63tr, 64t&b, 65, 68, 69, 79t, tr&bl, 80t&br, 83l&tl, 84t, 99t, 105t, 118r, 132t, 136, 137, 138t, 145b, 147t&b, 149t, 150b, 154, 158t, 162t&b, 166b, 172t&r, 174t&b, 178t&r, 187b, 189t, 190t&b, 193t&l, 196tl&b, 200t.
A. McGREGOR: pages 10, 13, 15, 19b, 21b, 26b, 28, 31, 48tl, 51, 53t&b, 55b 58, 60b, 63tl, bl&br, 66b, 71t&b, 72, 76, 77, 79tl&br, 80l&t r, 83b r, 84l&r, 86, 88, 91tl&br, 94, 96, 99t&b, 101t&b, 107t&b, 109, 111t&b, 116, 118t&l, 120t&b, 122t, 124t&b, 128, 130t&b, 132b, 138b, 140, 142, 144, 145t, 158b, 159, 161t&l, 164, 166t, 172l, 185, 189b, 191, 193r, 194, 200b.
MITCHELL LIBRARY, STATE LIBRARY OF NEW SOUTH WALES: Pages 168, 171, 176l. **J. SCHMIECHEN:** Pages 21t, 40b, 114, 169t, 178l, 187t. **S. TREMONT:** Pages 83t, 149b, 150t, 161r. **D. WEST:** Pages 92, 100. **J. WOODFORD:** Pages 91bl, 157.

For Morea and Robyn

Such savage and scarlet as no green hills dare
Springs in that waste, some spirit which escapes
The learned doubt, the chatter of cultured apes
Which is called civilisation over there.

A.D. Hope
'Australia'

This ravine, in the luxuriance of its vegetation and the great size of the trees, as well as in its rapid stream, at times leaping in cascades, or foaming in rapids, resembled those we had before seen in the sandstone ranges, but it differed from them in the greater height of the surrounding hills and cliffs, which being overshadowed with hanging trees and climbing plants, presented as rich a painting as the eye could behold: and as these grew golden with rays of the setting sun, or were thrown into deep and massive shadows, I could not but regret that no Claude of the tropics had arisen, to transfer to canvas scenes which words cannot express.

George Grey
Journals of Two Expeditions, 1841

Contents

Acknowledgements

One of the pleasures of researching and writing this book has been the opportunity of making new friends and sharing memorable times with old. So many people have helped in a multitude of ways: advising, reading, listening and encouraging.

Travelling back and forth to the Kimberley from Sydney is the quickest way to gain an appreciation of the immense scale of our country. Covering such enormous distances has involved considerable cost, so we are greatly indebted to a small group of sponsors.

Ansett Australia generously provided return fares to Darwin for our final research trip. Fuji Australia (Hanimex Industries) and Goodmans Photographics assisted with film stock. (The majority of images were taken on Fuji film, in particular the outstanding 'Velvia'.) Paddy Pallin Pty Ltd, enthusiastic supporters of our travels, kindly provided essential items of outdoor equipment.

Of the many people with whom we roamed the Kimberley, Joc Schmiechen and Rob Jung deserve special thanks. In every sense, both were integral parts of our team.

In 1986 Joc helped lead the first canoe descent of the Drysdale River in the northern Kimberley as part of Operation Raleigh's world-wide program for young adventurers. From that time on he became one of the region's staunchest advocates. Joc's passion for the country, its original inhabitants and rock art, was the bridge we crossed to reach the Kimberley. We are forever indebted to Joc for his generosity as an organiser, guide and unequalled bush cook. But most of all we thank him simply as faithful companion and friend.

Similarly Rob Jung's contribution far exceeds his role as a key photographic contributor. In the field, his sensitivity to the wild landscapes he loves to explore was an inspiration, as was his dedicated and creative quest for subject matter. Rob's enthusiasm does not wane in an urban setting. His research assistance and thoughtful comments on our progress were invaluable.

Others who shared in the efforts and rewards of being bush include: Pat Batters, Ray Firth, Tony Flaherty, Ian Greenwood, Chris Henderson, Sally Hildred, Laura Hodan, Michael Hoffman, Neil Keech, Ian McNicol, Joanne Mynor, Bob Pascoe, Ian Roberts, Robert Tiley, the Welch family and David West. Without their companionship our experiences would have been very much the poorer.

Our times in the Kimberley were immeasurably enriched by the hospitality and co-operation of many generous people who call the place 'home'. We extend our gratitude to the following individuals and organisations across the north-west.

Kununurra: George and Elaine Gardiner, Nicky Chetwin at the Kimberley Court Motel, and Chris Done, Regional Manager of the Department of Conservation and Land Management (CALM).

Derby: the Gulingi Nangga Aboriginal Corporation, its Planning Co-ordinator David Madiros, Kim Keevil of Buccaneer Sea Safaris, Leah Douglas at the Derby Tourist Bureau, Tony Gravranich, and Leighton and Paula from the West Kimberley Lodge.

Kalumburu: the Kalumburu Aboriginal Corporation, Chairman Les French and Project Officer Chris Casey, Hector, Austin and Robert Unghango, Mary Pandilo and John Maraldtadj. The Kalumburu Mission, its Administrator Jan Martin and in particular, the unforgettable Father Anscar McPhee who freely gave of his time, experience and humour, very much to our benefit.

On the Kimberley cattle stations: Roy Wilson and Eric Cooper at Carson River Station, John and Anne Koeyers at Drysdale River Station, Peter and Pat Lacey at Mt Elizabeth Station and William Burrell of El Questro Station. A number of stations were crossed in the course of our travels. We appreciate the co-operation of Theda, Mt Pierre, Noonkanbah, and Go Go stations.

Thanks to Ian Roberts and Clare Robertson and Bob and Anne Pascoe in Darwin and David Wagland in Perth for their splendid hospitality en route. Bob Pascoe made our final trip possible. A skilled pilot, at home in the wet–season skies of the north, Bob was always happy to meet our requests.

Away from the excitement of actually being there, many people were enormously helpful. Rob Jung, Diarmid Ross, Geoff Sainty, Joc Schmiechen, Robert Tiley, Steve Tremont, David West and James Woodford all made their photographs available for inclusion. Jonathan Chester gave us the run of his photographic studio and happily loaned camera gear, whilst Ian Gibson kindly placed photocopiers and a portable computer at our disposal. Norm McKenzie of CALM's Wildlife Research Centre advised on mammals, and Kevin Kenneally of the Western Australian Herbarium identified several troublesome plant species. Pauline English searched out a bounty of information on Kimberley geology, and Grahame Walsh gave helpful guidance on rock art early in the project.

We particularly appreciated comments on various stages of the draft manuscript from Dr Val Attenbrow, Professor Ralph Buckley, Chris Done, Pauline English, Ray Firth, David Headon, Rob Jung, Neil Keech, Margrit Koettig, Norm McKenzie, Father Anscar McPhee, Lin Onus, Joc Schmiechen and David Wagland.

The Benedictine Community at New Norcia, the Western Australian Museum, the Royal Western Australian Historical Society, the Battye Library in Perth and the Mitchell Library in Sydney readily gave permission for the inclusion of historic photographs. Thanks to Father Placid Spearritt and to Carmel McRobert of the Library and Information Service of Western Australia for making the necessary arrangements on our behalf in Perth.

Collins/Angus & Robertson consented to the publication of an extract from the poem 'Australia' by A.D. Hope from his *Collected Poems* © A.D. Hope, as did Allen & Unwin for the excerpts from *Fighters and Singers: The Lives of Some Australian Aboriginal Women*, edited by I. White, D. Barwick and B. Meehan.

Fundamental to the whole project has been the help from the team at Hodder and Stoughton. In particular we are indebted to the Publishing Director, Bert Hingley, for taking the initial leap of faith.

Finally, Dale Arnott and Morea Grosvenor supported us in more ways than can ever be thanked.

ALASDAIR McGREGOR AND QUENTIN CHESTER

Prologue

The way forward is unmarked and best approached on foot. After bumping along in the vehicle through so much woodland, it is both a shock and a relief to walk quietly through the vegetation that crowds the river. We drop down a steep bank, down through canegrass that rattles high around our ears. The air is dry with the smell of warm straw and peppered with bulldust scuffed up by our feet. Ahead the fronds of pandanus stand sharp in the tropical afternoon light. Beyond the native pines and cadjeputs, the escarpment rises.

We push on through more bristling grass. Cattle have eroded the flood banks, trampling pathways into the soft earth. We descend to wide lanes of amber sand. These flood-courses are bordered by islands of river gums. Even the stoutest specimens lean rakishly downstream. Debris borne by wet-season stormwaters lies tangled at the base of most trees: branches, twisted roots and hanks of bark. In places the debris is wedged in tree forks two body lengths overhead. Now, midway through the dry season, the river flows placidly in the shadow of the trees, and the oily-green water is fringed with pandanus.

On the other side of the river, a scree of black boulders rises steeply through a tangle of figs and vines to a cleft in the escarpment. Deep overhangs on the cliff hold the last of the day's light.

This is wild country, though not quite wilderness. A few kilometres downstream, another long day of mustering has just ended. In a narrow lagoon, away from the river and the crocodiles, we wash the dust and travel from our bodies. The mud at the water's edge is gouged with cattle hoof-prints. As we prepare for our first night out, these are reminders that it will take several days of travel on foot before we can be claimed by the true Kimberley wilderness.

In the stillness of the following afternoon we scramble up the blackened boulders on the other side of the river. Vines and figs grasp the rocks with their tentacle roots. The blinding heat makes any shade a prize. Near the crest of the scree we enter clusters of Elephant-ear Wattle and fragrant native pine. The understorey is crowded with prickly stemmed hibiscus and spinifex.

We enter a valley flanked by crags of burnished rock. On a terrace ahead, a wallaby springs away out of sight. Higher, through a swathe of canegrass, we find shelter in a jagged overhang of stone, where wasps dart and hover. The sun dips low, penetrating the filigree of palms, vines and wattles at the entrance to the overhang. A faint breeze stirs this veil of vegetation, throwing patterns of light onto the walls around us.

In the midst of this shadow play, other images stir. Tiny red figures run at full stretch across the uneven stone surface with marvellous vivacity. Though some paintings have faded beyond recognition, others are clear and complete, immaculately preserved as oxide stains in the outer few microns of sandstone. Beguiling figures, transfixed in time.

After the clinging humidity of the vine thicket, the shelter's cool shade is a tonic. We scan the ceiling and recesses, excited by the possibility of piecing together some understanding of a distant time from the mass of cryptic paintings and marks.

We had been lured into the Kimberley and guided to this shelter by an old friend, Joc Schmiechen. For him this was a return to a place he had first located some three years earlier. Like Joc we find ourselves captivated by the presence of these spritely figures and their links with another world. The stimulus of the art, and its inseparable relationship to the surrounding environment, was to become the vital spark of our experience in the wild north-west. With each surprising encounter the imprint of the Kimberley's sublime essence deepens.

From a ledge on a giant rock slab we gaze across the valley to where the overhangs are aglow. Black Cockatoos split the air with their cries. The day is slipping away but there is just enough light to look along a great stretch of river that hugs the escarpment. From where we sit the sun becomes eclipsed by a solitary palm at the cliff-edge. The last burst of full sun catches the palm fronds, forming a penumbra of golden-green light.

Opposite: The deciduous dry season, El Questro Station.

Prologue

The river below, and the expanse of country its presence implies, has a resounding, undisturbed quality. There is a temptation to speculate about the images on the walls and the people who created them: how they lived with the land and the pendulum of the seasons. But it is also enough to marvel at the concert of it all: the flamboyant vegetation, the natural stone sculptures, the art and the profusion of life. As we sit here the past appears as though it is illuminated from behind, casting its light forward to different times.

Authors' Note

Common names for species appear in the text with capital letters when a specific animal or plant is the subject of discussion, e.g. Fern-leaved Grevillea, Elephant-ear Wattle, Great Bowerbird or Short-eared Rock-wallaby.

Scientific names (in italics) follow the usual conventions, e.g. *Grevillea pteridifolia* and *Acacia dunii*. When the *genus* is referred to in a specific context, e.g. *Grevillea* or *Acacia*, capitals are also employed.

Collective common names for species appear in the lower case; e.g. cadjeput, rock-wallaby and bowerbird could all refer to a number of species. Even if the name has a scientific origin, e.g. pandanus, eucalypt, acacia or grevillea, when used in a general collective context, the word appears in lower case.

Opposite: Alasdair McGregor, 'Vine scrub and kangaroo, Drysdale River' (gouache on paper, 50 x 38 cm).

1

A place apart:
Impressions ancient and modern

Big mobs country

Napier Broome Bay, on the very northern rim of the Western Australian coast, shines silver in the early morning April light. Low scrubby hills enfold this impressive body of water, stretching in fine blue-grey arms towards the Sir Grahame Moore Islands and the Timor Sea beyond. Horizons of stone, thinly clad in their sparse north Kimberley woodland garb, strike inland. They run unchallenged, destined for exhaustion in the desert, 500 kilometres to the south. Directly in front of us is a crescent-shaped beach, tied at each end with thickets of mangroves. The beach is about as close to populous Asia as anywhere in Australia, yet this expansive coast, and the hinterland it defines, remain remote, sparsely populated and undeveloped, tinged with mystery. [1]

The bulky silhouette of an ungainly looking craft rides at anchor close to the beach, its presence uneasy against the natural tranquillity of the bay. An early attempt at luxury tourism in the Kimberley, this large catamaran had been built as a floating grandstand for the fuss and fizz of the 1987 America's Cup defence. It now plies the coast from Broome on the southern edge of the Kimberley, to Wyndham in the north-east, probing the bays, inlets and harbours, sniffing the edge of the country. Five-star luxury on a five-star coast.

Its presence, like some flotsam of twentieth-century culture on a prehistoric shore, seems decidedly incongruous. Despite the pleasures of fine food and service, the vessel's captive passengers look slightly bored. Physically isolated from the landscape and cocooned by air-conditioning, their 'Kimberley experience' appears more vicarious than actual. The real Kimberley, if such a thing can ever be defined, certainly has little to do with such embellishments and inhibitions of modern life.

Behind the beach near our camp, a small group of old Aboriginal men has also spent the night, accompanied by a research student in anthropology. Together, they have just returned from the Mitchell Plateau and Admiralty Gulf to the west, where the group was recording aspects of traditional Aboriginal culture.

The early morning fire dies, is rekindled and dies again as we sit on the ground in conversation with the men, big enamel mugs of tea in hand. They talk of their country. 'Good country', they say, with intense pride and belonging. It is a pride they seem anxious to share. They want us to understand, to know, to 'learn' their country. Each one refers to 'big mobs [lots of] country' accompanied by appropriate expansive gestures. It is a phrase used repeatedly to describe their world.

The description 'big mobs' is one that has passed into the vernacular of northern Australia, both black and white. Constantly used to emphasise so many aspects of life in the region, it is not just a delineation of scale. Its colloquial simplicity seems to be an outward manifestation of part of that much talked of and little understood relationship of Aboriginal people to their land, their 'good country'.

We have barely started to 'learn' the old men's country. It seems slightly presumptuous to even think it possible to ever understand this strange and fantastic landscape. The old men's knowledge and bond with the country is theirs and theirs alone, born not just of a life-time but of endless generations. But hopefully, with a willingness to observe and absorb, we might at least be able to penetrate past the view of the Kimberley as mere scenery.

Unfortunately, those confined to the other side of the safety glass and panoramic port-holes aboard the luxury catamaran anchored in the bay were probably destined for only that. Their incongruous conveyance symbolised everything alien to the Kimberley. It is a vessel fixed in the late twentieth century, yet the society to which the old Aboriginal men belong is not confined to any era or time.

In one sense though, there is nothing new about an alien craft probing the Kimberley coast. The first immigrants to take up permanent residence on the Australian continent, the ancestors of our old men, may have landed on a silver morning at a place just like Napier Broome Bay. Successive waves from the nearby north have followed, each isolated by great gulfs of time. And in the last few centuries, no more than a fragment in the life of

Opposite:-Sunset over stone country, Drysdale River.

The Kimberley region, Western Australia

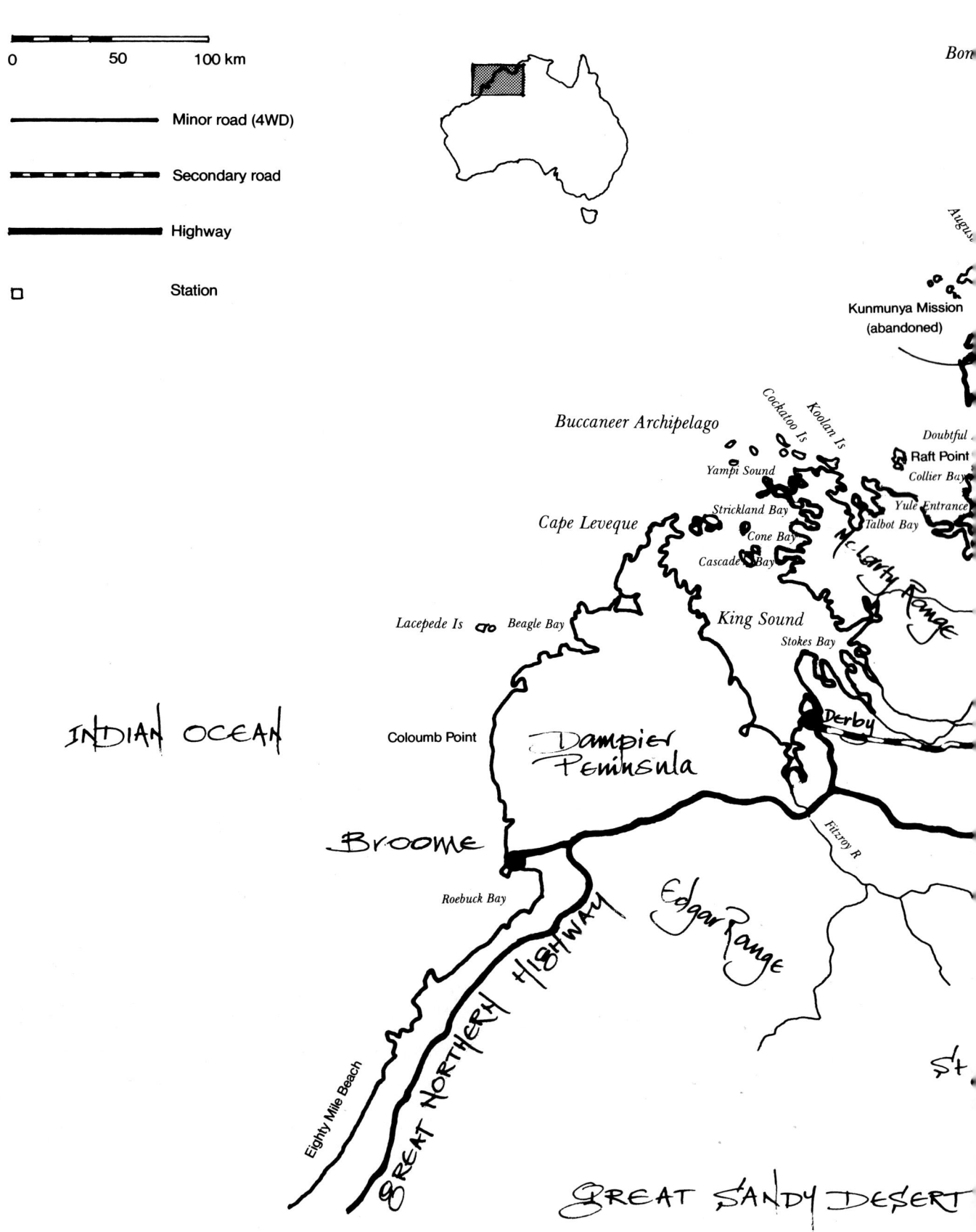

0   50   100 km

——————— Minor road (4WD)

━·━·━·━·━ Secondary road

━━━━━━━ Highway

□   Station

Bon

Augu

Kunmunya Mission
(abandoned)

Buccaneer Archipelago

Cockatoo Is

Koolan Is

Doubtful

Raft Point

Yampi Sound

Collier Bay

Strickland Bay

Yule Entrance

Talbot Bay

Cone Bay

Mc Larty Range

Cascade Bay

Cape Leveque

King Sound

Lacepede Is   *Beagle Bay*

Stokes Bay

Derby

INDIAN OCEAN

Dampier Peninsula

Coloumb Point

Fitzroy R

Broome

Roebuck Bay

Edgar Range

Eighty Mile Beach

GREAT NORTHERN HIGHWAY

St

GREAT SANDY DESERT

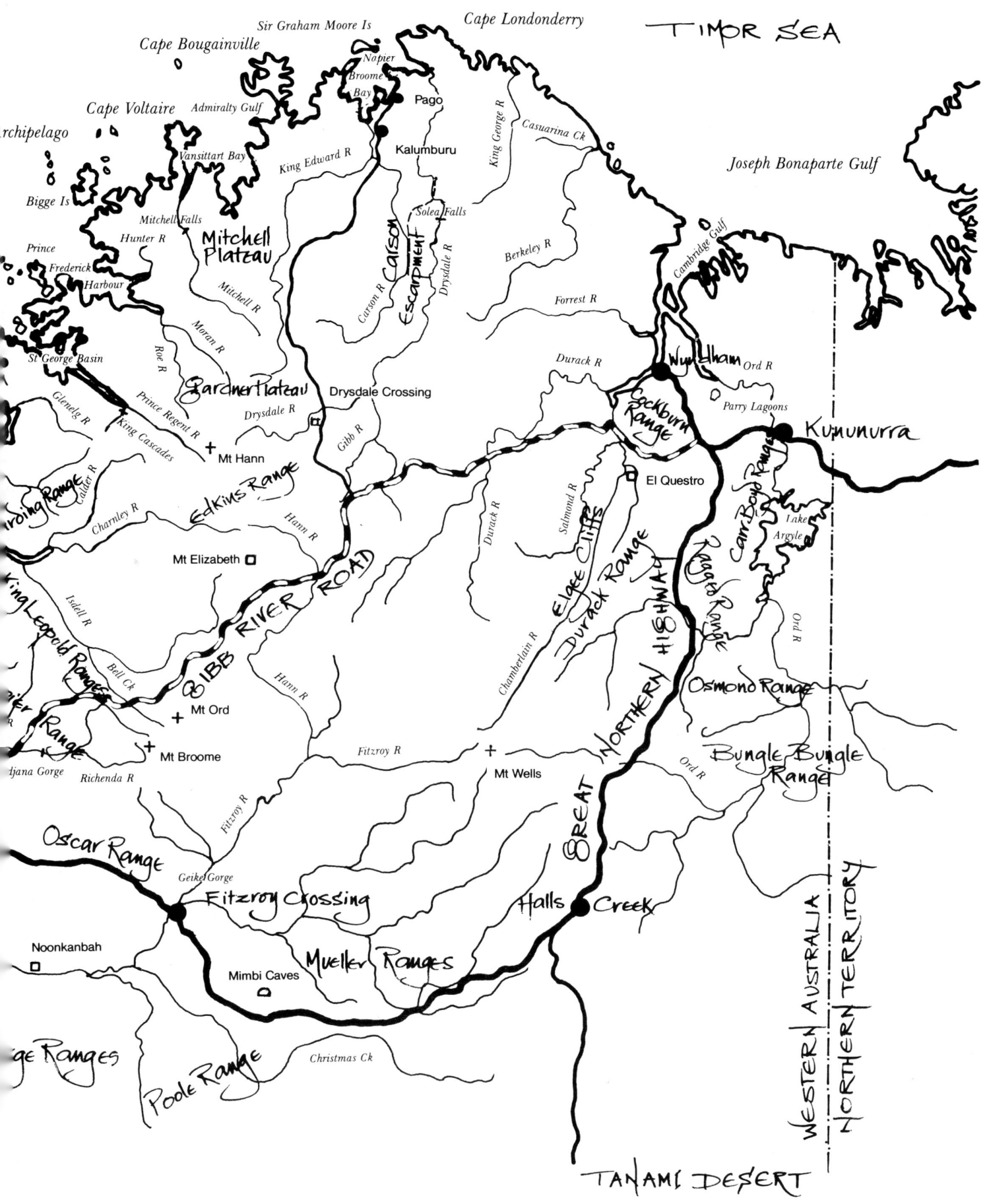

129°

TIMOR SEA

Sir Graham Moore Is
Cape Londonderry
Cape Bougainville
Napier
Broome Bay
Pago
Cape Voltaire
Admiralty Gulf
Kalumburu
Joseph Bonaparte Gulf
Archipelago
Vansittart Bay
King Edward R
Casuarina Ck
King George R
Bigge Is
Mitchell Falls
Mitchell
Plateau
Solea Falls
Prince
Hunter R
Mitchell R
Berkeley R
Cambridge Gulf
Frederick
Harbour
Carson Escarpment
Carson R
Drysdale R
Forrest R
Moran R
St George Basin
Gardner Plateau
Drysdale Crossing
Durack R
Wyndham
Ord R
Glenelg R
Roe R
Drysdale R
Sockburn Range
Parry Lagoons
Kununurra
King Cascades
Prince Regent R
Gibb R
Calder R
+ Mt Hann
Edkins Range
Hann R
El Questro
Salmond R
Carr Boyd Range
rding Range
Charnley R
Durack R
Lake Argyle
Mt Elizabeth
GIBB RIVER ROAD
Chamberlain R
Elgee Cliffs
Durack Range
GREAT NORTHERN HIGHWAY
Ragged Range
Isdell R
Ord R
King Leopold Ranges
Bell Ck
Hann R
Osmond Range
+ Mt Ord
+ Mt Broome
Fitzroy R
+ Mt Wells
Ord R
Bungle Bungle Range
Range
djana Gorge
Richenda R
Fitzroy R
Oscar Range
Geikie Gorge
Fitzroy Crossing
Halls Creek
Noonkanbah
Mueller Ranges
Mimbi Caves
WESTERN AUSTRALIA
NORTHERN TERRITORY
ge Ranges
Poole Range
Christmas Ck
TANAMI DESERT

129°

the Kimberley, they have again come from the sea: fishermen, traders, European explorers, pastoralists, missionaries and finally tourists, cast on this inimical shore.

A face behind the name

The title Kimberley, like so many epithets of the European colonial era, gives no clue as to the nature of the place. As with countless names from an expansionist age, it is simply a tag of long forgotten political indulgence.[2] However, in contemporary thought, the sense of the word Kimberley has gradually undergone a shift in meaning in the collective mind. Once synonymous with the great days of Australian pastoral prosperity and the challenges, hardships and romance of a pioneering frontier, the name is today increasingly linked with visions of remoteness, a wilderness untrammelled, and diverse natural beauty.

Enormous forces have militated against the taming of the Kimberley, allowing much of it to exist still as a vast tract of wild country. To say that this has occurred as the result of any single factor — remoteness and isolation from major populations, climate, terrain or geological structure — would be to deny the potency of the whole in shaping the nature of the place.

Administratively, the Kimberley is part of Western Australia: the State's far flung tropical region, north of latitude 19 degrees. Often cited as being larger than Victoria and Tasmania together, the region's combined local government boundaries encompass an area of 422 803 square kilometres.[3] However, these boundaries stretch far to the south of the Kimberley's logical geographical extent. The Kimberley, as defined by its major physical limits, covers a somewhat smaller area of approximately 300 000 square kilometres or 12 per cent of Western Australia. The singularity of the name, Kimberley, belies a considerable diversity of landforms, climate and natural systems that prevail across the region.[4]

Rivers and ranges

Physically, the Kimberley is quite unlike the rest of Western Australia. Its landscapes and climate are much more akin to those of the Northern Territory's Top End. The forms of Kimberley are echoed in the dramatic bluffs of the neighbouring Victoria River District and the stony escarpments and outliers that stretch on into Arnhem Land.

As we look at the map, the north-west corner of the continent appears almost like an island, an island embroidered with rivers. Much of what is regarded as the Kimberley is bounded in the south and east by the drainage catchments of its two greatest rivers, the Fitzroy and the Ord. Each is like the braided strands of an enormous moat, encircling and defining. To the north and west of the river basins sweeping curves of enfolded ranges arch in an enormous half circle from coast to coast. The King Leopold, Durack, Carr Boyd and Ragged ranges are some in a chain of folded bluffs and ramparts that extend over 600 kilometres in a near unbroken sweep. Here are the highest points in the Kimberley: Mt Ord (937 metres) in the King Leopold Ranges and Mt Wells (983 metres) at the southern end of the Durack Range, the highest point in the region. Captured within this arc of ranges, a maze of rivers drains radially to the Timor Sea, cutting its way through a monumental elevated plateau known as the Kimberley Basin.

Far from being flat or even, this central plateau has been intermittently eroded by heavy tropical rains for as long as 50 million years. The sharply dissected landscape that dominates the Kimberley today is the result. Like an immense, gently curving dome, the Kimberley Plateau steadily rises to a high point in the north-west near Mt Hann, 500 metres higher than the plains of the Fitzroy. From this hub flows all the plateau's drainage. Out of the original Kimberley Basin, deep river gorges and wide alluvial valleys have been honed.

To the south and south-east, where rainfall becomes a matter of chance rather than seasonal certainty, deserts take hold. The sweep of desert extends to the coast. It reaches the

Above: Mt Broome (913 metres), King Leopold Ranges.
Right: Unnamed tributary of the Isdell River. Rivers and
small streams alike have cut deep fissures through the
Kimberley Plateau.

Left, top: Crumbling sandstone cliffs at Cape Leveque, Dampier Peninsula.
Left: Cone Bay, just one bay of hundreds in a maze of island-studded inlets along the Kimberley coast.
Above: A hundred million years of erosion have sculpted the 'tiger-striped towers' of the Bungle Bungle Range, Purnululu National Park.
Right: Mangroves, King Sound.

Indian Ocean at the Eighty Mile Beach, south of Roebuck Bay, effectively isolating the Kimberley from the remainder of Western Australia. The Great Sandy Desert, an ocean of sand, disappears over parched horizons to the south, and further east the Tanami Desert reaches towards the heart of the continent itself. A labyrinthine mangrove-fringed coast, several thousand kilometres of treacherous tides, reefs and countless islands, bounds the tropic blue arc of the north and north-west.

On the western edge of the Kimberley, outside the swath of rivers and ranges, the Dampier Peninsula, a mostly flat and unrelieved extension of the Great Sandy Desert, pushes north. A complex mosaic of scattered vegetation covering vast sand plains, the peninsula forms the seaward enclosure to King Sound. Ripped by giant tides, this constantly turbid, shallow waterway is more than 100 kilometres long and 50 kilometres across at its broadest point. In addition to a string of minor rivers, King Sound takes the muddy flow of the Fitzroy and its tributaries, which stretch east almost to the Northern Territory border.

It is the rivers of the north, as much as the terrain through which they flow, that are at the heart of the Kimberley's character. All Kimberley Rivers are seasonal; they flow only during the summer wet season or in the months immediately following. Even the largest, the Fitzroy, Ord and Drysdale, dwindle to long, intermittent stretches of still water in the dry months. But whilst the rivers may wane, they are not ephemeral like the waters of the desert. There is always water in the Kimberley.

Australia's largest river system, the 5270 kilometre Murray–Darling, drains most of south-eastern Australia: a huge area of one million square kilometres. Yet with a remarkably small annual discharge of 22 cubic kilometres, it accounts for only six per cent of the continent's annual run off. Compared to the numerous rivers of the north, the Murray–Darling seems somehow puny. The Timor Sea catchment system — of which the Kimberley rivers form nearly half — discharges an incredible 75 cubic kilometres each year, or 21 per cent of the total run off for all of Australia.[5] This is more than three times that of the Murray–Darling, yet the entire catchment area draining to the Timor Sea is only about 700 000 square kilometres. Fifty per cent of Australia's total water resources are confined to the tropics north of 20 degrees, less than one-third of the continent's total area.

Australia's northern rivers are powerful as well as numerous. Running at peak flow, the larger Kimberley rivers rank amongst the most potent in the world. The maximum flow rate of the Ord River for instance, relative to the area it drains, is nearly eight times that of the Mississippi and almost one third as much again as that of the Amazon![6] Bald statistics perhaps, but testament to the immense amounts of water that can fall on such limited catchments.

The rivers of the north are all quite short. The 880 kilometre Victoria River in the Northern Territory is the longest. Amongst the Kimberley rivers, the Fitzroy–Hann system stretches 650 kilometres across the southern and central Kimberley. It drains much of the southern slopes of the plateau and the desert margins beyond onto a floodplain stretching from Fitzroy Crossing to King Sound. The Ord, rising near Mt Wells, flows east then north for 500 kilometres to the broad tidal flats and mangroves of Cambridge Gulf. The gulf also marks the end of the Chamberlain, which for most of its course flows on an unswerving path beneath one of the Kimberley's geographical phenomena: the 125 kilometres long Elgee Cliffs.

The rivers of the north-west Kimberley make a short and eager dash from the heights of the plateau to the coast. For much of their length, the Mitchell, Moran, Roe, Hunter, Prince Regent, Sale, Charnley and Isdell surge through steep-sided gorges in their helter-skelter charge for the sea. With more time and distance to travel, the King Edward, Drysdale, King George and Berkeley wander across the plateau, assuming guises varying from deep clefts in bedrock to broad sandy reaches, before they spill into the Timor Sea off the north coast.

In between these and other significant rivers, a filigree of lesser streams, creeks, lagoons and billabongs covers all but the driest parts of the Kimberley. Most are empty in the dry months, but some are spring-fed and therefore flow year round.

The presence of permanent water in its rivers and streams is truly the mark of the Kimberley. The heavy tropical rains, that in the passage of geological time, fashioned much of the Kimberley landscape, continue to sustain it. Filling its waterways, they provide a surge of life in marked contrast to the fierce aridity that grips much of Western Australia's expanse. The pastoralist and explorer Frank Hann fell to the allure of the Kimberley waterways in 1898, noting the striking contrast:

> This is the most astonishing country for rivers, creeks and lagoons. They intersect the whole country, and would be an immense boon to the more arid and rainless tracts eastward towards South Australia and Queensland...
>
> It was a perfect revelation to me, and certainly will be to others, especially in the eastern colonies, who believe West Australia to consist mainly of sandy deserts, tireless spinifex plains and salt swamps and lakes.[7]

Over the centuries, European explorers looking from the seaward side formed a very different impression of the Kimberley's bounty.

Great expectations

Nearly 300 years before the diesel throb of a luxury catamaran echoed off the sea-gorge walls of the north-west coast, exploration of a different kind was planned:

> This large and hitherto almost unknown Tract of Land is situated so very advantageously in the richest Climates of the World, the Torrid and Temperate Zones; having in it especially all the Advantages of the Torrid Zone, as being known to reach from the Equator itself (within a Degree) to the Tropick of Capricorn, and beyond it, that in coasting round it which I design'd by this Voyage, if possible: I could not but hope to meet with some fruitful Lands, Continent or Islands, or both, productive of any of the rich Fruits, Drugs, or Spices (perhaps Minerals also, &c.) that are in other Parts of the Torrid Zone, under equal Parallels of Latitude; at least a Soil and Air capable of such, upon transplanting them hither, and Cultivation.[8]

So wrote that maligned English buccaneer, scientific explorer and travel writer William Dampier in his *Voyage to New Holland in the Year 1699*. Dampier had first sighted the north-west coast of Australia (or New Holland as it was then known) 11 years earlier, whilst sailing aboard the privateer *Cygnet*, and the record of his adventures, *A New Voyage Round the World*[9] had sparked enormous interest in literary and scientific circles in England as the Age of Enlightenment began. Despite a negative impression formed from his first voyage, Dampier was curious to know more of the strange southern shores. His expectations remained undiminished. He led a second expedition in 1699, this time under official patronage. But his extravagant hopes for great discoveries were soon utterly dashed. He wrote of the north-west coast near Cygnet Bay on 5 September 1699:

> ... the Land I had seen as yet, was not very inviting, being but barren towards the Sea, and affording me neither fresh Water, nor any great Store of other Refreshments, nor so much as a fit Place for careening; yet I stood out to Sea again with Thoughts of coasting still along Shore to the North Eastward.

Only three days later Dampier decided to quit and retire to Timor. He eventually returned to England after exploring the New Guinea coast and the Indonesian archipelago, having failed for a second time to see any sign of the riches imagined to be hidden beyond that alien Australian coast. Dampier was not alone in his response to the ancient continent, such a new reality in the European mind. Disappointment, bordering on hostility, became the prevailing mood of the journals and reports from the first Europeans to fix their gaze on the tropical coastline of Australia.

Yet from the earliest rumours of the existence of a mysterious southern land, illusions had been cast of a place rich with gold and fortune. Fanciful expectations belied the reality of a seemingly forlorn and unyielding land.

Galaxy Swamp, a small permanent waterhole near the Drysdale River. The open waters of the swamp are carpeted by the waterlily Nymphaea gigantea.

Terra Australis

A great southern continent had persistently appeared on fanciful maps since ancient times. In the thirteenth century, Arab traders told Marco Polo of a land rich with timber, fruits and spices. What was described could have been any part of south-east Asia but references in Marco Polo's writings fuelled speculation for the following 300 years of a bountiful land in the south. The reports of Marco Polo and other travellers, venturing as far as Java, continued to strengthen belief in the existence of the southern land, Terra Australis.

It is impossible to say who followed the Aboriginal inhabitants in making a footfall on the Australian continent. The Chinese were trading with south-east Asia by the fifteenth century and the explorer Cheng Ho is thought to have reached Timor during that century. The Chinese were skilled and adventurous seafarers and quite possibly voyaged further south, either by accident or design. Similarly, Arab traders were operating in the region from about the same time and could easily have been blown onto Australia's north-west coast. However, no account survives of any such early contact.

The Portuguese were probably the first Europeans to make landfall in the region, having colonised the island of Timor nearby to the north at the beginning of the sixteenth century. Their great navigators, Bartolomeu Dias and Vasco da Gama, pioneered a route around Africa at the end of the fifteenth century. Within a short time, the Portuguese were the first European maritime power to enter and dominate the spice trade with Asia. Almost nothing is known of Portuguese encounters with the South Indies, or 'India Meridional' as they called the Australian continent. All that remains are a few intriguing references on contemporary charts.

One of the most tantalising pieces of evidence appears on an important chart known as the Dauphin Map. Produced in 1536 from undetermined sources, it shows a huge landmass named 'Jave La Grande' in considerable detail. This detail is more convincing than would seem likely for a work of fantasy or speculation. Correcting for navigational errors of longitude and map-makers' licence, the landmass bears an extremely good resemblance to the Australian continent. On the north-west coast, a large inlet is shown in the correct position for it to be a recognisable representation of King Sound.

If the Portuguese did land on Australian shores, it is possible they were unimpressed by what they found and did not bother to publicise their discoveries. They could also have been deliberately secretive. The sixteenth-century world was boldly divided into two notional hemispheres of control, one Spanish, the other Portuguese. The Australian continent at that time lay partly in the Spanish half. To produce the map, the Portuguese would have by necessity trespassed in their rival's realm![10]

By the end of the sixteenth century, the Dutch had supplanted the Portuguese and the Spanish as Europe's pre-eminent maritime nation, taking over as the colonial and trading power in the East. Keen to secure this position and increase their commercial advantage, the Dutch sought ways to speed the passage from Europe. Early in the seventeenth century, they began sailing east from southern Africa rather than immediately heading north-east towards India. Their ships made a quick passage in the strong and consistent stream of westerly winds encountered at high latitudes, before eventually veering to the north and their objective of the East Indies. Following this course, it was inevitable that the Dutch vessels would overrun their easterly heading and encounter the west coast of Australia. Dirk Hartog was the first. Sailing aboard the *Eendracht*, Hartog landed on an island off Shark Bay in 1616. Many more followed, skirting the coast on their journey north. Others were lost, wrecked on a barren and hostile shore. The west coast became an unwelcome but familiar sight to the Dutch.

Deliberate exploration inevitably followed. In 1644, Abel Tasman made the earliest known Dutch investigation of the north-west coast. With three ships, he mapped the Australian coastline from Cape York to the Abrolhos Islands. His journal of the voyage has been lost and any detailed impressions or information about landings are unknown. But Tasman's chart has survived, marking the position of a number of large off-shore islands flanking the north-west coast.

Neither Tasman nor Dampier 50 years later, provided any real stimulus to European curiosity and so the coast and hinterland remained as they had for aeons, whilst to the

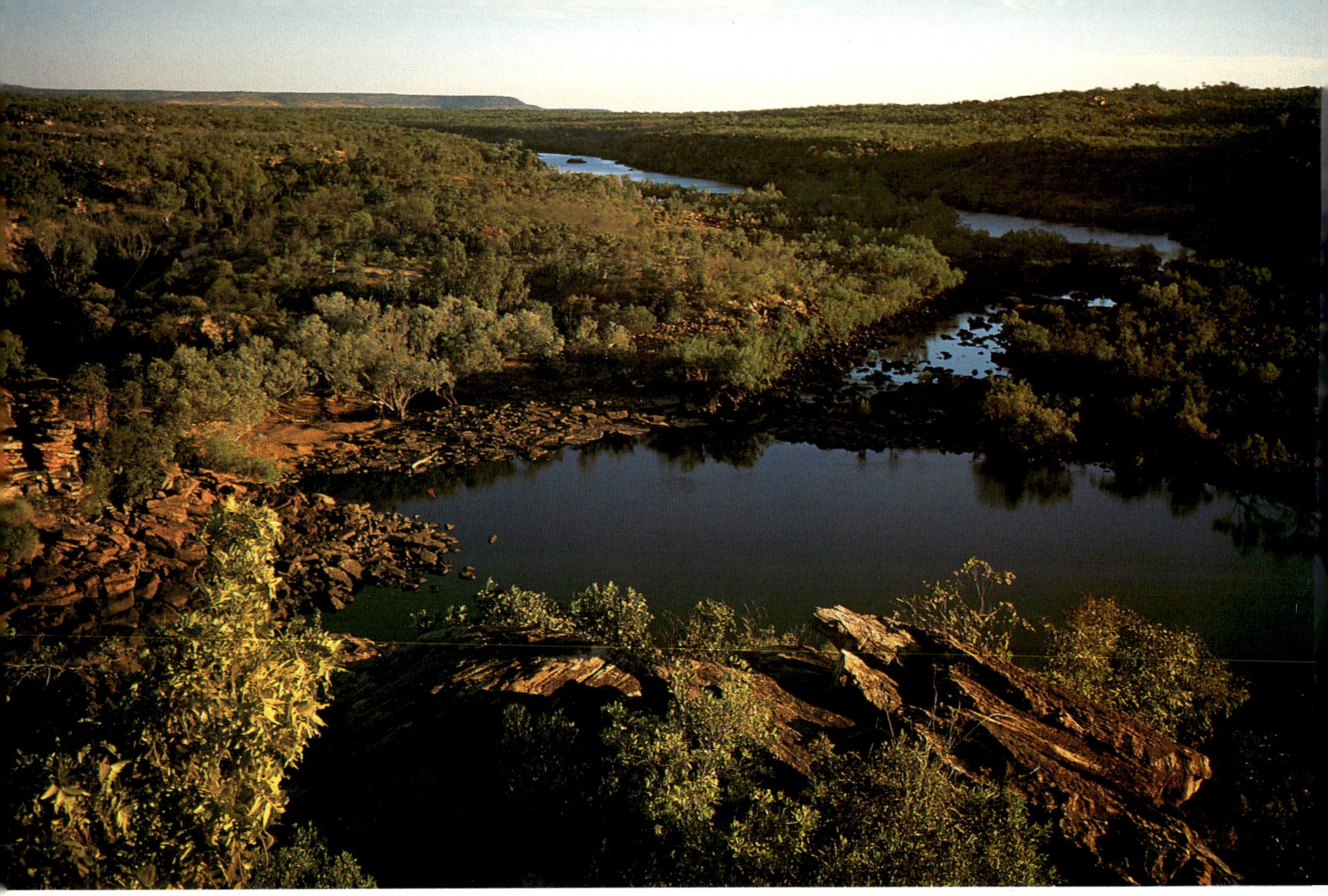

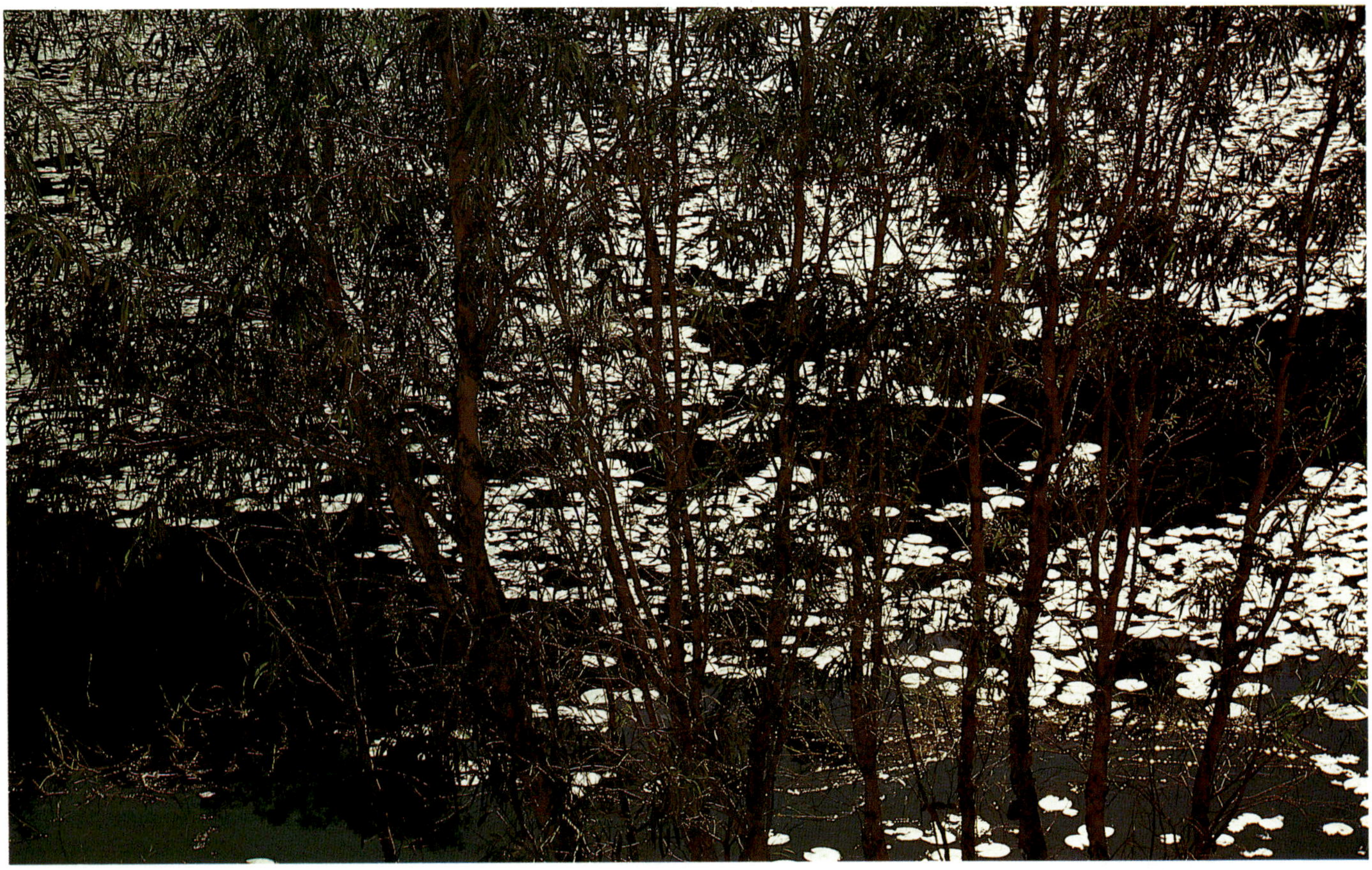

immediate north mighty empires grew and prospered in the archipelagos of the spice trade.

More than 100 years went by until the French sailed rapidly past at the beginning of the nineteenth century. They did nothing but litter the coast with Gallic names and it was not until nearly 120 years after Dampier, that the region attracted any detailed attention. Finally, almost 200 years after Dampier's aspirations were thwarted, the European grasp began to squeeze material wealth from the north-west of Australia.

And so the Kimberley finally yielded the rewards hoped for by Dampier and his successors. It yielded them for a time in great bounty. But the toll on the land was high and on its Aboriginal inhabitants, calamitous — a familiar price, exacted as part of colonial expansion and development throughout Australia.

Yet despite the toll, much at least of the Kimberley landscape today remains as it was when Dampier formed his unflattering opinions. Altering only as it always has, the Kimberley's timetable for change is still essentially that of its own natural systems.

1. The total population of the Kimberley in the 1986 Census was 22 033 (i.e. 1.5 per cent of the total population of Western Australia). Of these, 9 469 were Aborigines (i.e. 25.1 per cent of the State's Aboriginal population). Quoted in Western Australia, Department of Regional Development and the North West and Department of Planning and Urban Development, *Kimberley Region Plan Study Report*, Perth, 1990, p.18.
2. The region was named in 1870 for John Wodehouse, 1st Earl of Kimberley, statesman and Colonial Secretary of the day. Kimberley in South Africa was also named in his honour. Coincidentally both the African and Australian Kimberley have come to be the world's most important diamond-producing areas.
3. *Kimberley Region Plan Study Report*.
4. The Kimberley is often referred to in the plural. The title 'Kimberleys' perhaps reflects the attitude of early development, when isolation within the region itself was almost complete and the east and west were seen as very distinct sub-regions.
5. K.A. Bishop and M.A. Forbes, 'The freshwater fishes of Northern Australia', *Monsoonal Australia*, eds C.D. Haynes, M.G. Ridpath and M.A.J. Williams, A.A. Balkema, Rotterdam, 1991, pp. 80–81.
6. Australian Water Resources Council, *Review of Australia's Water Resources*, Australian Government Publishing Service, Canberra, 1976. Relative discharge is a measure of the volume of water discharged by a river each second in each area of catchment. It is measured in cubic metres per second per square kilometre.
7. Frank Hann, 'Exploration in Western Australia', *Proceedings of the Royal Society of Queensland*, vol. 16, 1900, p. 20 and p. 24.
8. William Dampier, *A Voyage to New Holland in the Year 1699*, vol. 2, London, 1709.
9. Published in London in 1697.
10. For an excellent discussion of the Portuguese and Australia see K.G. McIntyre, *The Secret Discovery of Australia: Portuguese Venturers 200 Years Before Captain Cook*, Souvenir Press, Medindie, S.A., 1977.

Left, top: Evening approaches. The Drysdale River in dry-season mood.
Left: Billabong, Drysdale River.

2

Plateau and range:
Kimberley geology

Depths of time

We climb down into a narrowing cleft of grey stone in Lennard Gorge. The water at the base of the gorge is lurid green with algae. It is possible to walk around the initial pools but thereafter the walls close in. There is only one way forward and we have come prepared. With airbeds inflated we slither under a net of orbspinners' webs and into the cool water.

It is an other-worldly place. At times barely a body-width apart, the walls rear up from the water and ascend through sharp overhangs and orange blocks. Sunlight glancing the rocks at the gorge rim and a strip of cobalt sky are the only reminders of the bleached terrain on top. We paddle past water-streaked walls, lying face-forward on our airbeds. Then the gorge widens and we join the resident water goanna on a broad shelf of stone. Time to bask and wonder.

The Lennard River traverses a landscape that is ancient beyond belief. On paper a geological history of 1 800 million years is just infinity in another guise. The learned texts and charts seem only to make this span of time more confounding. One answer is to immerse yourself in the landscape and give the imagination a long leash. And in the Kimberley there are few better places to fathom antiquity than in the depths of a gorge.

Down a boulder jam and back into the water. The chasm drops further and sweeps right past water-hewn grottos that arch over our heads. We glide around the bend and into a long reach of dark, jade green water.Here the walls stand over a hundred metres high. Tottering ribs of rock intrude into the gorge, framing a tangle of vines and ferns that are fed by a trickling spring. On the left a giant ramp rises to a sky now sheeted with cloud. As we approach there's movement on the slabs. A rock wallaby takes flight, weaving up the steep rock with improbable ease.

We have been swallowed by the gorge. Here we gaze upwards at stone scoured by water over many thousands of years. The simplest explanation for the Lennard River's baffling line through the King Leopold Ranges is the vast time period it has had to carve its path. From gentle beginnings draining down from the central Kimberley Basin the river has steadily kept on incising the underlying rock. From our airbeds we may not be looking at 1800 million years but the gorge has imparted an indelible impression of time.

At the end of the main canyon thunderclouds gather overhead. It feels as though we have been in the gorge all day but it's not even lunchtime. We decide to make camp anyway and choose a plot of safe, high ground.

The lie of the land

In the Kimberley, geology is everywhere on show. The region has, arguably, the greatest congregation of unmasked plateau and range country on the continent. For all its rejuvenating power the summer monsoon sustains only a sparse vegetation cover. Even during the wet season the hard facets of the landscape remain exposed, etched against cloud-laden skies.

The great bulk of the region is occupied by the Kimberley Plateau. This expanse of elevated benches and scarps is formed on the immense succession of flat-lying sandstone, shale and volcanic rock of the Kimberley Basin. Covering some 160 000 square kilometres, the central plateau is the dominant topographic feature of the Kimberley. It gives the region its signature forms: the plains and parapet clifflines, the slender gorges, the mesas and the cuestas. It is a landscape of rim and range, a realm of spatial silence.

On a geological map of the region, the Kimberley Basin is bounded by welts of metamorphic and igneous rocks. The band that arcs up to the north-west is the King Leopold Mobile Zone, while the belt that trends north-north-east is the Halls Creek Mobile Zone. Together they appear as a crucible in which the basin sits. These areas boast the oldest rocks in the Kimberley and the kind of complex and protracted history of folding and faulting — the 'mobility' — that geologists can spend a career unravelling.

Opposite: Alasdair McGregor, 'Late in the dry, Bell Creek' (gouache on board, 40 x 33 cm).

29

Geological Time Scale

Era	Period and features	Millions of years ago
Caionozoic	*Quaternary* Early human life. Ice ages generate widespread changes in plants and animals.	2
	Tertiary Rainforest conditions slowly give way to a drier climate. Mammals adapt and diversity.	65
Mesozoic	*Cretaceous* Widespread seas abound. On land the first mammals and flowering plants arrive.	135
	Jurassic Age of conifer forests and dinosaurs.	195
	Triassic Australia's first reptiles appear. Large ferns and palms become established.	225
Palaeozoic	*Permian* Vegetation diversifies. Large amphibians inhabit water margins.	280
	Carboniferous Gondwana moves south. Temperate climate gives way to glacial conditions.	345
	Devonian Plants advance on land. Fish widespread in seas and freshwater. First amphibians.	395
	Silurian First signs of plantlife on land. Primitive fish and corals develop.	435
	Ordovician More complex shelled animals become widespread.	500
	Cambrian Marine life diversifies with sponges, jellyfish, brachiopods and trilobites.	570
Proterozoic	*Pre-Cambrian* Primitive multicelled creatures develop in shallow seas.	2000
Archaeozoic	Formation of Earth. First continents and oceans take shape.	4500

Within the major geological divisions lie some of the best preserved and most conspicuous Pre-Cambrian landscapes in the world. So much of what makes the Kimberley distinctive and discrete from the rest of the continent has to do with geology. The fractured coastline, the limestone ridges, the rivers, the crumpled ranges and daunting escarpments: all are products of an ancestry, unique in Australia.

But the significance of geology transcends an explanation of the land's appearance. It is a key influence in the character and distribution of the region's plant and animal life. It directed the course of early white exploration and the subsequent pattern of settlement and pastoral activity. It has provided the region with potent prosperity, notably in the form of diamonds and to a lesser extent iron ore. But most telling of all is its role in the lives of the people who first inhabited this landscape.

For Aborigines the geology of the Kimberley is not a set of scientific concepts or a mere aesthetic spectacle. To tribal groups scattered across the region the stone structures, the broad overhangs and mushroom-shaped rocks, the terraces and enclosed ceilings have been central to their very existence and culture. Fashioned by the elements, such formations provided refuge from heat, storms and the wet months. For untold generations the rocks of the Kimberley offered sanctuary and a site for artistic and spiritual expression. And so the stone country was invested with a numinous power that echoes against the revelations of geological science like the thunder that accompanies a lightning flash.

*Opposite: Lennard River Gorge and resident Mertens' Water Monitor (*Varanus mertensi*).*

Above: Evening light on the mesas of the Poole Range at the fringe of the Great Sandy Desert. Left: Cuesta formations on the Pitt Range, south of Lake Argyle.

2 000 000 000 years of evolution

The Kimberley has its origins in the early Proterozoic era more than 2 000 million years ago. In this period geosynclinal sediments known as the Halls Creek Group were laid down and tightly folded over the entire region. These rocks underwent further intense folding and metamorphism concentrated along the two mobile zones. They were also intruded by various igneous rocks, including granite masses.

All this activity, spanning a period of some 150 million years, resulted in a complex interrelationship of rock types and structures. The Halls Creek Mobile Zone continued to be tectonically active beyond this time. The deformation and subsequent erosion of its rock formations provided a major source of sediment to the surrounding basins.

Around 1 850 million years ago, during a period of more subdued activity, widespread sedimentation took place in shallow inland seas. Evidence suggests that these deposits were swept down from the north-west. This is consistent with the widely accepted theory that India and chunks of Asia were yoked to Western Australia at that time. It was in this prolonged phase of deposition that the sedimentary rocks of the Kimberley Basin were laid down, most notably those of the Kimberley Group, which make up the bulk of the basin's five kilometre thickness.

The consolidation of these sediments around 1 800 million years ago was accompanied by a period of volcanism in which the flood basalts of the Carson Volcanics were extruded in great volumes, both on land and beneath the seas. The rock sequence was also intruded by widespread sills of Hart Dolerite. Up to three kilometres thick, these sills underlie virtually the entire Kimberley Basin and form one of the most extensive bodies of dolerite in the world.

From the time of its formation the Kimberley Basin has remained remarkably stable with only mild deformation in response to movements within the two adjacent mobile zones. Erosion continued across the basin with minimal interruption, creating the landforms that dominate the central Kimberley today.

Around 750 million and 670 million years ago the region was in the grip of two severe glacial epochs. The striking evidence for this is contained in some of the world's best preserved Pre-Cambrian glacial pavements, located in the eastern Kimberley. Ice sheets covered most of the region and glaciers freighted masses of rock debris into the shallow seas.

As the ice sheet melted so the rock debris dropped into the sediments on the sea floor, forming distinctive tillite: sedimentary rock interspersed with other rock types, like a chocolate bar studded with nuts. In the case of the Moonlight Valley Glaciation in the eastern Kimberley this deposition is thought to have taken place from a floating ice sheet, whereas it is thought that with the younger Egan Glaciation the ice sheet was grounded in shallow waters, leading to a greater mix of deposited rock types. Evidence of glaciation is also found in tillites near the Charnley and Lennard Rivers in the western Kimberley. [1]

In the Devonian era the continent, in response to plate tectonic mechanisms, had probably moved away from the polar region to warmer latitudes leading to a period of inter-glacial warming 370 million years ago. During this time all but the eastern margin of the Kimberley was fringed by a warm tropical sea. These rich waters were populated by calcareous algae and primitive limestone-building organisms known as stromatoporoids, which constructed an ancient barrier reef up to a thousand kilometres long that virtually ringed the Kimberley's Devonian mainland.

The reef structures developed close to the surface and as the sea floor gradually sank, the reefs grew, over several million years, to a thickness of more than 2 000 metres. The reef platforms often enclosed shallow lagoons with a floor of lime sand or mud. These deposits preserved one of the world's richest fossil records of early marine life, including corals, brachiopods, nautiloids, sponges, primitive fish and crustaceans. [2]

The relics of these reefs stand exposed today as sharply protruding limestone ridges, such as the Napier, Lawford and Oscar ranges that straddle the Lennard Shelf at the northern edge of the Canning Basin. A smaller reef complex is found north of Kununurra in outcrops of the Ningbing Limestone.

The Devonian age also saw the accumulation of sediments washed from the ranges of

Top: Limestone country with Boabs and Kapok Bushes, Oscar Range.
Above: Limestone gothic, Mimbi Caves.

the east Kimberley into the Hardman Basin south-east of Kununurra. This massive deposit compacted, forming a friable sandstone which was later eroded to create the spectacular domes and pinnacles of the Bungle Bungle Range. The curious shapes of these formations are explained by a weathering pattern that dissolved the quartz, bonding the sandstone together. Streams carved chasms in the rock to form the distinctive rounded pillars and ridges, while the fragile interlocking structure of the remaining stone developed a thin, protective silica skin. The colours of this outer skin are banded by orange silica and dark lichens.

By the end of the Mesozoic era 65 million years ago much of the sedimentation had been completed in the region and the Bonaparte, Ord and Canning basins were well established. In the period that followed, the landmass experienced great climatic fluctuations and sustained erosion and weathering. Yet for all these changes, over such an ineffable timescale, the dominant features of the region have remained intact. Like so much of this worn continent, the Kimberley shows its age.

Relics of a Gondwana shore

From the town of Derby the Gibb River Road strikes east across the plains of the May and Meda rivers. The country is flat and the woodland becomes more sparse as we leave the influence of the coast. Were it not for the bulbous figures of the Boabs (*Adansonia gregorii*) this 130 kilometre stretch of straight road would rank as one of the more tedious drives in the Kimberley.

It is the individuality of Boabs that attracts attention. Each has its own quirky profile and cradle of limbs that gesture skyward. A few bear bushy nests. Others have burst into leaf after early October rains. They stand against a sky that, to the north, is marbled grey and black with stormcloud.

Just when the scene begins to pall another dark apparition sprawls across the horizon. It could be mistaken for cloud but the outline is razor sharp. For a good many travellers this glimpse of the Napier Range is their first encounter with the conspicuous geology of the Kimberley.

The view can be deceptive. With its fluted towers and jagged ridges the range mimics the features of much grander mountain chains. At first it appears to be both taller and more distant than it really is. Up close the range is seen to rise little more than a hundred metres. Although diminutive, the sculptured detail of the shadowy grey limestone is eye-catching. The ramparts straddle the withered landscape like fortress walls. In the words of artist John Wolseley, 'They move like some ghost dragon across the savanna plains, where in Devonian times they stood as living reefs above the ancient sea floor of Gondwana.'[3]

To the east this fortress is breached by the Lennard River. Having cut its tortuous path through the King Leopold Ranges the river makes a dramatic exit to the plains through the sheer walls it has carved to form Windjana Gorge.

We arrive at dusk, and apart from three Freshwater Crocodiles, we have the gorge to ourselves. The river is at its lowest ebb. While we collect water from the sole remaining pool the sky becomes streaked with flapping shapes. For nearly 20 minutes fruit bats, in their thousands, pour out of the gorge. The air is thick with their squeaks and pungent smell. Some fly a straight course while others swoop and bank, at times swishing the surface of the muddy pool. Buttresses at the western end of the gorge stand against an orange sky flecked with the exodus of black wings. We drink our tea as the gorge walls cast gothic shadows over the river sand. Insects fizz around us. Our tea has an acrid taste which is presumably part bat, part crocodile and part 350 million year old limestone.

Remnants of the Devonian reef form a frontage to the south-western Kimberley, broken only by the passage of rivers like the Lennard and the Fitzroy. The soluble nature of limestone has here resulted in weathering, typical of karst landscapes. On top of the reef exposed rock has been dissolved by intense tropical rains to create a pock-marked pavement of depressions and raised fins. It is also in the nature of karst landscapes to form sinks, conical depressions in the limestone, which allow water to penetrate the rock and the weathering process to proceed from below. At the eastern end of these relic reefs groundwater has steadily dissolved the rock to fashion a seven kilometre network of subterranean passages known as the Mimbi Caves.

The surface terrain in this area gives little indication of the labyrinthine tunnels that lurk underground. The exposed outcrops stand less than two storeys above the spinifex plain. We set off across the pavement to inspect the caverns. The serrated blades of rock cut into the soles of our shoes and the black rock radiates a stunning heat. The potential consequences of a fall make us doubly careful with our footwork.

In nooks between the rock pillars, figs and vines cluster where they find shelter and can tap the moisture underground. We too thread a way into the depths through a narrow cleft. The beams of our torchlights pick out powdery silt billowing up from the floor. Parallel corridors lead to the main chamber and an elongated pool encircled by striking flowstones and formations. The air in this grotto is refrigerant. According to our pocket thermometer the temperature is close to 15 degrees Celsius cooler than outside.

The percolating solution responsible for these caves is concentrated along areas of weakness in the rock such as joints and bedding planes. As joints often occur in rectilinear patterns the process usually results in an interlocking grid of passageways.

A side tunnel leads to a huge exit cavern and the outside world. The sudden exposure to heat and light is dizzying. We stumble along the gravel creek-bed into a maze-like group of chasms. Here erosion has created a network of clefts with sheer walls open to the sky.

Walking through these rock canyons must be the nearest equivalent in nature to travelling city streets. We stroll past junctions, dead-ends and back alleys. Direct sun rarely reaches the depths of this limestone metropolis. Where light does penetrate, there is occasionally a solitary tree marking the middle of an intersection. Breezes, alternately cool and warm, brush through the deserted streets. Taking care not to be stranded by the fading daylight we retrace our steps. On the way out we are stopped in our tracks by the sight of a sleek black cat gazing at us from the shadows. The encounter befits the urban illusion, yet this feral presence instantly dissolves the sense of place and arrested time.

Over the threshold

The gaunt limestone ridges form a narrow strip, barely 20 kilometres wide, on the doorstep of the Kimberley.

Beyond lie the rounded Lamboo Hills, a jumbled belt of boulder-strewn country developed on granites and associated igneous and metamorphic rocks. Collectively known as the Lamboo Complex these rocks were the product of the region's second episode of metamorphism. This period of intense activity occurred after the formation of the Halls Creek Group but prior to the establishment of the Kimberley Basin.

The area features low ridges, often with smooth crests of granite that emerge on the horizon like huge reptilian tails. It is a lean, sparsely vegetated landscape with spinifex hills separated by narrow sandy flats where minimal surface water remains during the dry season. Elsewhere the granite is exposed in shingled spurs with large slabs of stone and shattered flakes.

The Lamboo Hills occupy a broad belt extending in an arc from the Yampi Peninsula on the west coast to near the Bow River south of Kununurra. Closer to the main plateau, the hills gradually give way to a more rugged terrain of hogbacks and cuestas, interspersed with open valleys usually formed on dolerite.

This more accentuated topography is in turn a prelude to the imposing ridges of the King Leopold and Durack ranges. These stand abruptly at the very margins of the Kimberley Plateau and include the region's highest peaks and some of its most celebrated vistas.

The ranges are intensely folded and faulted. This uplift has exposed the underlying rocks of the plateau, most visibly the resistant King Leopold Sandstone which stands in defiant cliffs and scarps along the ranges, interspersed with darker dolerite and arkose. High, domed peaks include Mt Broome (913 metres) and Mt Ord (937 metres) at the headwaters of

Top: Knife-edged weathered flutes and turrets cap a subterranean network of caverns and passages, Mimbi Caves.
Above: Limestone weathering, Mimbi Caves.
Right: Subterranean chapel, Mimbi Caves.

the King Leopold Ranges. To the east, marking the catchment boundary of the Ord, Chamberlain and Margaret rivers, stand the summits of Mt Wells (983 metres) and Mt King (970 metres) in the Durack Range.

Despite their expansive size and extent, these ranges do not constitute an impenetrable barrier. They are cleaved by the incisive gorges of rivers such as the Fitzroy, Margaret and Lennard which have their origins on the Kimberley Plateau.

The heart of the plateau

From a sandstone crest above Fred's Springs on Mt Elizabeth Station the view at every point of the compass is of undulating woodland. The trees are mainly eucalypts — Bloodwoods, Salmon Gums and Woollybutts — interspersed with the occasional Cypress Pine. In places ridges of orange rock emerge from the vegetation cover. At this elevation the country appears sweeping, verdant and almost subdued.

The only interruption to this extensive plateau is a group of square profiled summits on the northern horizon. In the argot of geologists these landmarks are monadnocks: formations that remain after erosion has stripped away the original land surface. In this instance they stand as tall blocks of King Leopold Sandstone above weathered sills of Hart Dolerite. The highest summit, Mt Hann (779 metres), is so distinctive it is used by international air traffic as a navigational reference point.

The uplifted terrain incorporating Mt Hann also marks the starting point for the principal rivers of the north-west Kimberley. At the foot of the mountain are the creeks which gather to become the legendary Prince Regent River. The ranges immediately to the north form the catchment of the Roe and Moran rivers, and display a stretch of landscape worthy of the encomium, 'wilderness'. Further north are the headwaters of the King Edward and Mitchell rivers. To the east the Kimberley's third largest river, the Drysdale, begins its meandering passage to the Timor Sea. From the Caroline Ranges to the south run the Hann River and the tributaries that join the Charnley River.

The spread of country around Mt Hann forms an elevated dome within the main Kimberley Plateau. This may be west of the plateau's precise geographic centre but it qualifies as a prime source, a heartland. Although the area has experienced local uplift, the rivers that have their origin around Mt Hann belie the underlying stability of the plateau. In most instances they are deeply incised into bedrock. Some fall in line with the constraints of fault and joint fractures, while others have slowly superimposed themselves upon the landmass, flowing down dipping slopes. In both cases the prevailing impression is of a gently dipping, deeply weathered surface, a landscape of Pre-Cambrian bedrock and ancient forms.

From the air the capacious extent of the Kimberley Plateau becomes apparent. At around 4 000 feet the overview of the terrain bears out the nature of the region as described by geologists. Just as science has the knack of summarising great rafts of time, so an aerial perspective helps to condense the physical features of the immense landscape. From this altitude the plains, outcrops and gorges, the embroidered detail, are perceived to belong to a much larger structure, an immense expanse of flat-lying rock.

Aloft over stone country

Approaching the headwaters of the Prince Regent River the sky is mantled with grey cloud. Our aircraft banks and we complete an orbit over Mt Russ, Mt Fyfe and Mt Agnes, with Mt Hann standing tall in the middle of this circuit. The country is convoluted with gorges. Creeks snake between promontories of high ground bounded by hundred metre high cliff-lines. To the south a rain shower is drenching Mt Jameson. On this February morning the scene has a sombre, almost wintery look but the air blasting in through the space where the door should be is hot and humid.

We drop 500 feet and track along the creeks that feed the Prince Regent. Beyond the

Top: Granite formations, Richenda River.
Above: The greening of sandstone. Wet-season growth near Mt Hann.

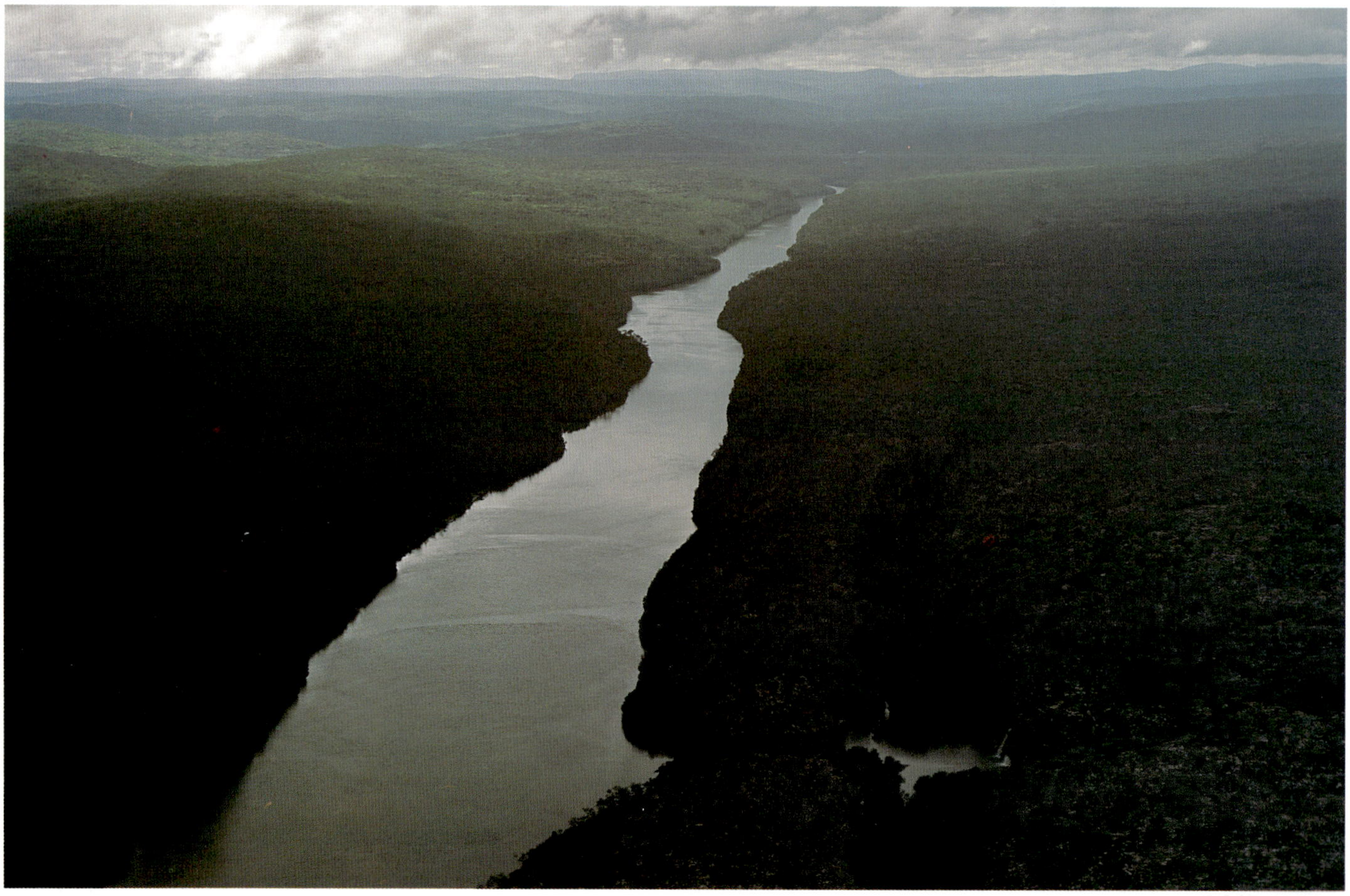

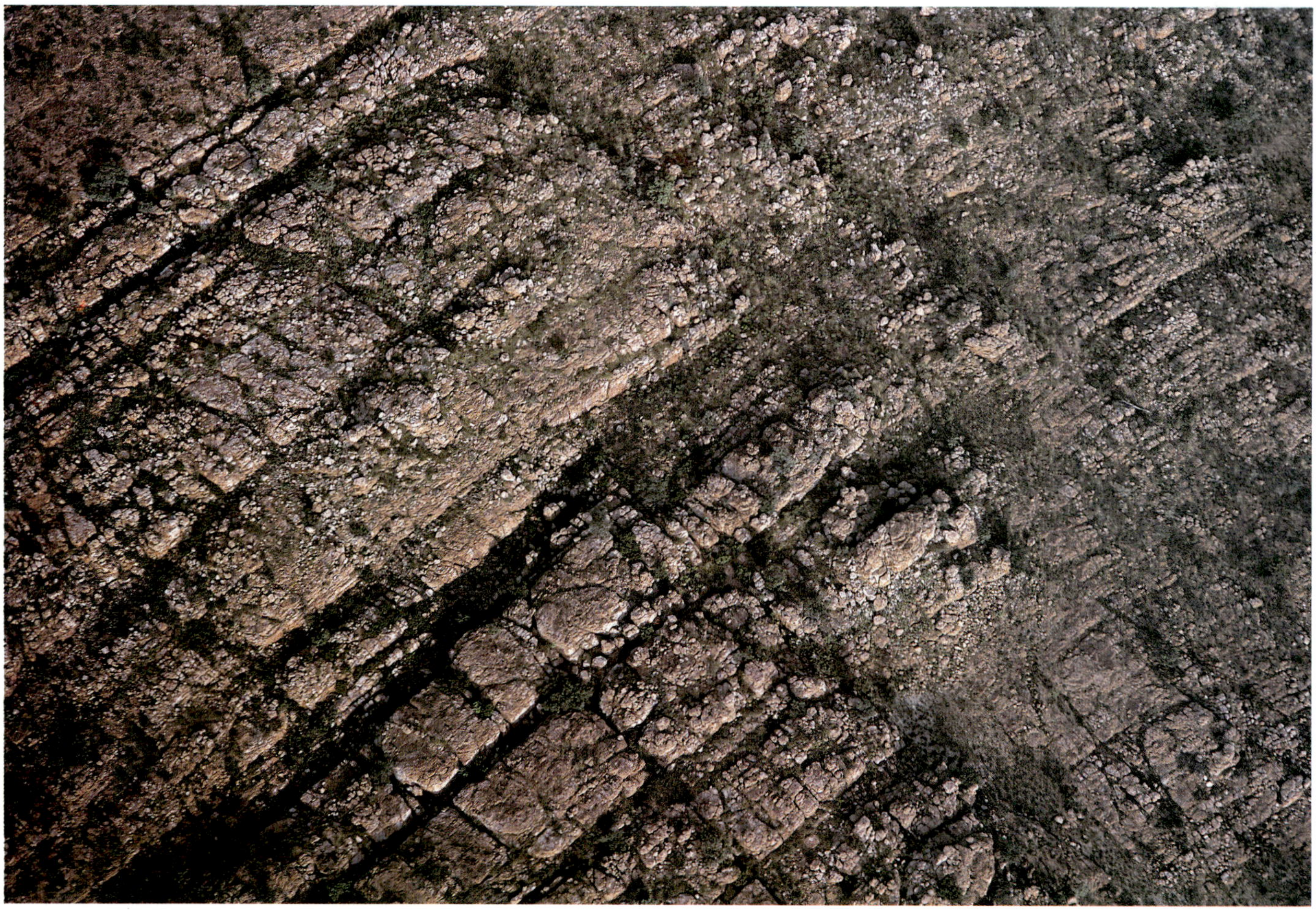

gorge country the river soon straightens and disappears beneath the cloud in an unswerving line to the horizon. As we follow its course the compass is steady on 310 degrees. The river drains down a master joint system, the Prince Regent Lineament, which extends for some 240 kilometres.

This fracture in the sandstone is intersected by other joints which meet the river at right angles. The main river sits in a shallow trough and traverses a flat, grey-green landscape. The vegetation cover appears sparse and scrubby. Growth is luxuriant only along the river's edge and by the terraces and falls where side creeks enter the main river.

We drop low over the famed King Cascades, which appear dwarfed by the surrounding terrain. A meagre wet season of minor showers in lieu of major downpours has produced only a modest flow over the tiers of stone. We turn north and fly along a straight tributary towards the headwaters of the Roe and Moran rivers. The cloudcover is broken and the emerging sunlight transforms the creek systems into ribbons of silver.

From their beginnings in the uplands around Mt Hann, the Roe and Moran rivers thread across what on topographical maps is called the Gardner Plateau. In geological terms this domain includes two physiographic subprovinces: the Prince Regent Plateau and the Gibb Hills.

The Roe River follows, in part, the boundary between these subprovinces. To the west extends the rugged, highly jointed King Leopold Sandstone. To the east lies a more subdued surface of rounded hills and low cuestas characteristic of the Gibb Hills that are formed on Carson Volcanics. Their presence alongside the Roe River marks the southern extremity of a formation that extends north across the Mitchell Plateau for 140 kilometres to the coast at Port Warrender.

From the air the transition from a sandstone to a basalt surface is marked by a noticeable change in vegetation. On the latter the grass cover is more lush and the trees are taller and more substantial. After skirting the Carson Volcanics the Roe River is joined by the Moran River then it veers westward through sandstone terrain for the final stretch to the sea.

We track its path, swooping across the alluvial flats and the press of mangroves to Prince Frederick Harbour. After the plateau's muted earth colours the milky, turquoise waters of the harbour are dazzling. We drop low over islands and steep headlands shrouded in rainforest. A dense cover cloaks the scree slopes that rise to pinnacles and ramparts of sandstone on the flanks of the Hunter River. The sight of all this tests our capacity for wonder, and our pilot needs no urging to linger.

He banks the plane in a broad loop that whirls us around Mt Anderdon and the gorge of the Hunter and its tributaries. Below lies a sanctum as remote as any part of the Kimberley. In this meeting place of plateau, river and sea, crocodiles haunt the tidal creeks and the vine thickets pulse with the calls of rarely sighted birds. In all likelihood the enfolding forest also serves as a refuge for living things as yet unseen and unnamed. By the providence of nature there are favourable rains and a cordon of cliff to fend off fires. From our orbit, or for that matter any other viewpoint, it is impossible to deny that the rivers, the forest, the rock, the creatures are one.

Climbing to 5 000 feet we turn and head north-east. Crossing over into the catchment of the Mitchell River the country opens out to the horizon. After an all-night storm the river is running high and wide, spilling into its overflow channels. At the Mitchell Falls the silty brown water fills the width of the gorge and crashes down the sweep of rock terraces. The pavements and trickling pools, where seven months earlier we had scrambled and swum, are now engulfed by floodwaters.

The falls are incised in jointed sandstone on the boundary of the Mitchell Plateau. Here the annual rainfall can exceed 1 600 millimetres. Delivered in violent wet-season storms this rainfall has not only carved striking sandstone formations, it has also had a profound effect on the Carson Volcanics that form the high plateau.

Prolonged leaching of this porous basalt surface has left a mantle up to five metres thick of bauxitic laterite, covering an area of nearly 400 square kilometres. With its concentrated

Left, top: The unswerving course of the Prince Regent River, a geological phenomenon.
Left: The incised and fractured forms of sandstone in the north Kimberley.

41

residue of aluminium oxide this deposit has inevitably attracted interest for its commercial potential. Since the deposit's discovery in 1965 the bulk of the plateau has been set aside for possible mining.

From the air our attention is not on bauxitic laterite but the splendour of the plateau's palm forest, another consequence of the locally abundant rains. We skim low over the forest with its company of eucalypts and palms forming a veil of green over the dark basaltic rock and rust-coloured gravels. Around the airstrip the forest is criss-crossed by mining-survey tracks. The temptation is to regard this grid of scars as a gross disfigurement of the plateau. However the awkward truth is that in this instance we owe our view of the terrain to an aircraft engineered from the residue of bauxitic laterite.

The plateau drops away, down through terraces and steep screes to the estuary of the Lawley River. Across this lush gulf lies familiar sandstone terrain. This area is still branded as part of the Prince Regent Plateau subprovince even though we are now hundreds of kilometres further north, over the King Edward River. The tag may seem confusing but the nature of the land below bears out its claim.

Our flight path follows a discernible band of lineaments and joints trending north-east in the King Leopold Sandstone. These fracture lines appear as deep creases in the rock, adding to the weathered visage of the plateau. Dissected pavements stand above the surrounding woodland as islands of stone. Their surface is deeply cut, forming groups of pinnacles and mushroom-shaped blocks girt by moats of vegetation.

This crevassed stone country dominates the coastal hinterland and northern reaches of the Kimberley. From the air it appears as a flat, bewildering expanse. You can see it all and yet you can experience none of the stone's sculptured detail, none of the entwining vegetation, none of the artistry.

We begin our descent to the airstrip at Kalumburu, Western Australia's northern-most settlement. The basalt plains are flush with new grass. On the landing approach we look east across the Drysdale River to the cliffs of the Carson Escarpment, the bastion of another subprovince, another stone horizon.

On the escarpment

The Carson Escarpment is one of the great landforms of the region. Marking the break between a belt of rolling Gibb Hills and the Warton Sandstone of the Karunjie Plateau, this vast run of cliffline stretches 200 kilometres north, from the heart of the Kimberley to the coast at Cape Londonderry.

No other geological boundary in the region is more clearly defined. Late in the day, when the angled sunlight floods onto the escarpment, the ramparts glow brilliant orange and terracotta. To make camp on its rim as we did on a hot June afternoon is to witness Pre-Cambrian geology at its most luminous.

The quartz-rich Warton Sandstone of the escarpment was deposited after the vulcanism that gave rise to the Carson Volcanics. In the sequence of rocks that comprise the Kimberley Group, the former is only about half the thickness of the King Leopold Sandstone. However in its jointing and weathering the Warton Sandstone is no less arresting to the eye.

From our camp below the lip of the escarpment we scramble to the crest. A dry wind combs through the grass and rattles the palm fans overhead. A hundred metres inland from the escarpment stand tilted slabs of rock. Behind these rise two monumental formations, undercut on all sides so they appear on the skyline like the hulls of yachts perched on stone keels. We pick our way through the boulder scree into the shadows of the outcrops. The ledges under the overhangs are burnished smooth. In some of the pockets and crevices there are freshly weathered flakes of rock and a dusting of fine, white sand patterned with animals' tracks. Along the underside of the overhang a black algal line marks where streaming stormwater finally falls free from the rock. Framed within this line is a ceiling decorated with

Previous page: The Carson Escarpment looking north along the Drysdale River.

For nearly 50 kilometres the dramatic cliffs and scree slopes of the Cockburn Range dominate the surrounding plains.

Monumental scree slopes flanking the dramatic gorge walls of the Cockburn Range speak of a landscape restless through untold years.

painted figures of small marsupials, cryptic shapes and unmistakable human forms.

The corridor between the two prominent outcrops is choked with tendrils and rock figs. We fight our way into the thicket, threading through spider webs and green-ant nests to climb to the flat summit. With the sun and the wind on our backs we look out across the spreading plateau. In the foreground is an archipelago of stone islands in a sea of vines and spinifex. Beyond lies more of the same country, more bare bedrock eroded by the scouring wind and rain.

In the Kimberley such views are repeated seemingly at every turn. To observe geology on this scale is to face the paradox of a landscape that claims a longevity almost beyond belief, yet everywhere shows signs of relentless decay. Its history can be posited by isotopic dates and detailed in stone formations, shaped by the winds of aeons. But to the human eye the antiquity of the land is most evident in the plateau's oceanic spaces. The country can be imagined to be as old as it is vast.

Basin and range

In the east the Karunjie Plateau finally gives way to the alluvial flats of Cambridge Gulf, the great tidal estuary of the Forrest, Durack, Pentecost and Ord rivers. This is the edge of the Bonaparte Gulf Basin, one of the three Phanerozoic Basins that border the Kimberley. At the head of Cambridge Gulf the Pre-Cambrian rocks of the Kimberley Basin make a spectacular encore appearance in the sandstone ramparts of the Cockburn Range.

Here the term 'range' is something of a misnomer. The Cockburn cliffs are not part of a single ridgeline, nor do they front a row of peaks. Instead, they encircle two linked plateaux, flanked by long slopes of scree and shale. These isolated mesa-shaped islands stand 600 metres above the surrounding lowlands, with the top half of this elevation exposed in walls of sandstone. From any aspect the plateaux are emphatic structures but their western rim is the most imposing, with great prows of rock overlooking the plains of the Pentecost River.

The sandstone and shale of the Cockburn Range are members of the Bastion Group. These sedimentary rocks date from the last phase of deposition associated with the development of the Kimberley Basin. The rock's horizontal bedding gives the plateaux their flat-topped appearance while the gradual decay of its clifflines has produced massive aprons of talus with abundant examples of ripple rock, suggesting that the original sediments were deposited as part of an intertidal mud flat. Viewed up close the walls are highly fractured. Tottering pillars and shattered overhangs loom above the screes where hardy Boabs and Kurrajongs have taken root. In sheltered gorges rainforest pockets are sustained by water migrating down from the high ground. Even here, under the gaze of the chiselled plateau walls, life flourishes.

The country to the south-east of the Cockburn Range marks the junction of two geological provinces: the Halls Creek Mobile Zone and the Ord Basin. This area encompasses some of the most diverse and fanciful topography in the region. It is also traversed by what was once the mightiest of all Kimberley rivers, the Ord.

The upper reaches of the Halls Creek Mobile Zone are dominated by the Carr Boyd Ranges. This area of intense folding and faulting has created landforms in sharp contrast to the Cockburn Range. The quartz sandstones, siltstones and shales of the Carr Boyd Group were deposited during a period marked by repeated changes in sea level and tectonic activity. This is evinced in spectacular ranges with jagged faultline escarpments and sheer sandstone bluffs on hogback formations. The area is deeply dissected by drainage gullies and the Ord River has carved a sinuous path through the heart of the ranges to create the Carlton Gorge.

To the east, the Carr Boyd Ranges are flanked by the formidable Ragged Range. This fortress of hulking stone pillars and abrupt walls has been weathered from a much younger red conglomerate sandstone. Westward, the range rises suddenly from undulating basalt hills forming a skyline of sharp stone. The eastern flanks of the range are ravaged by runoff streams which drain into the Ord Basin.

The Carr Boyd and Ragged ranges once overlooked extensive plains to the south. Now this stretch of the Ord Basin is inundated by the cerulean blue waters of Lake Argyle.

Top, left: 'Fossilised time' — the imprint of an ancient shoreline cast down from the walls of the Cockburn Range.
Top, right: The contorted forms of the Carr Boyd Ranges.
Above: The domes of the northern parts of the Bungle Bungle massif are reminiscent of Katatjuta (the Olgas) in Central Australia.
Right: The drama of natural process in the deep eroded chasms of the Bungle Bungle Range.

Completed in 1972, and Australia's largest artificial lake, Lake Argyle is the foundation of the ambitious Ord Irrigation Scheme. Covering nearly 1000 square kilometres, the lake forms a habitat for large populations of water birds. Its success in human terms has been more problematic.

The rocks of the Ord Basin include Cambrian volcanics, limestones and shales, and Devonian sandstones. Erosion of these rocks has created rich alluvial and black-soil plains. Out of this low-lying landscape emerges a remarkable collection of ranges and remnant formations.

To the south of Lake Argyle stands the Osmond Range, a broad plateau rising 400 metres above the surrounding plains. The bulk of the range consists of the Proterozoic Mt Parker Sandstone partly overlain by siltstone and Bungle Bungle Dolomite, a rich source of stromatolite fossils, the residual mounds of one of the world's most ancient life forms. The main plateau in the west is bounded by sheer cliffs and seamed with clefts formed by creeks along structural faults and joints. To the east the plateau breaks into ranges and cuestas that extend to the basalt plains of the Ord.

Less than 10 kilometres away, across the sandy flats to the south of the Osmond Range, lies the Bungle Bungle Range. This massif of Elder Sandstone was formed from deposits laid down in the ancient Devonian sea bed 350 million years ago. Covering some 45 000 hectares, the Bungle Bungle Range includes a central plateau surface which is bounded by a complex network of ridges and outliers. In the east and south the massif is clustered with an array of distinctive beehive towers.

From the air these congregations straddle the landscape in surreal display. Some domes stand alone, some are paired, while others are linked shoulder to shoulder. All wear vivid garlands of orange and black. Nowhere else in the Kimberley has the stamp of time created anything quite so extravagant to the eye. Within this labyrinth exists yet another world. The massif is deeply riven by gorges, some several kilometres long. Here the elements have hewn the sandstone and conglomerate into plunging ravines and scalloped chasms, creating an extraordinary refuge for a variety of ferns, vines and soaring *Livistona* Palms.

Like so much of the Kimberley's geology the domes of Purnululu can seem fanciful and enigmatic to the visitor. This landscape has nevertheless been embraced as part of human experience for at least 20 000 years. For Aboriginal people the bountiful Ord Basin, with its rivers and plains, its streams and gorges, has long been a natural focus. Everything in the country is connected to the patterns of seasonal life, the layers of tradition, the story telling and the ochre art. The rocks and ranges are bound up with a source of timeless knowledge and belonging.

1. D.B. Dow and I. Gemuts, *Geology of the Kimberley Region of Western Australia*, Geological Survey of Western Australia, 1969.
2. J.H. Thom, 'Kimberley Region', in *Geology of Western Australia*, Western Australian Geological Survey, 1975.
3. As quoted in J. Long, *Nomadism; John Wolseley; Twelve Years in Australia — Paintings and Drawings*, University Gallery, University of Melbourne, 1988.

Opposite: Alasdair McGregor, 'Palm grove, El Questro Station' (gouache on paper, 45 x 31 cm).

3

Tropical rhythms:
Climate and vegetation of the Kimberley

'The torrid and temperate'

William Dampier's description of Australia's north-west as being situated in the 'Torrid and Temperate Zones' is in part apt. For much of the year the region's climate could only be described as torrid. Located between latitudes 14 and 21 degrees south, the Kimberley lies very much in the tropical sway. High mean temperatures across the region and pronounced 'wet' and 'dry' seasons are characteristic of the climate. Each has a profound bearing on the nature of the place.

However, it is incorrect to assume that uniform conditions apply across the Kimberley's great geographic range. From the coast to the elevated plateau, from the ranges to the desert's edge, temperature, humidity and particularly rainfall vary markedly, and so contribute to the great diversity of the region.

Experiencing the Kimberley at differing times of the year gives a striking impression of climatic variability and its impact across the region. From November, close to the very driest time, in the isolated ranges on the edge of the Great Sandy Desert, to a wet-season February on the Mitchell Plateau nearly 450 kilometres to the north, the contrast could not have been made more apparent.

Daytime Kimberley temperatures are consistently high throughout the year and the diurnal range is small. They are most uniform in coastal regions and more extreme across the inland. Wyndham, at the head of the Cambridge Gulf, records the highest mean annual temperature of any recording station in Australia. It suffers an average daily maximum of 35.7 degrees Celsius for the year. Fitzroy Crossing in the southern interior swelters through November with an average maximum of 40.8 degrees Celsius. During the wet season, the extreme November and December temperatures are modified by widespread cloud cover. As the dry season takes over, they fall slightly. In June, July and August, elevation and distance from the coast even make sub-zero overnight temperatures and frosts possible on the Kimberley Plateau and the desert margins.

From August to December, the heat increases rapidly from the relative relief of 30 degree mid-year days. By December, daily temperatures in the southern Kimberley climb past 40 degrees Celsius with distressing regularity.

The St George Ranges, close to the fringe of the Great Sandy Desert, is a place of extremes. High maximum temperatures year round, and a rainfall usually restricted to sporadic summer thunderstorms, leave the landscape dry and watercourses scoured and empty for months on end.

A change of season

The rough hills and flat broad valleys of the St George Ranges have the exquisitely fragile yet somehow robust appearance of the desert. Spinifex hummocks cover all but the steepest parts in a thin and uniform straw-coloured blanket. Each hummock looks as dry and brittle as the fragile stony soils it protects with such a stubborn hold. Sparse eucalypts, lining washaways that have not been charged by water for at least eight months, stand firm under a searing sun as mid-day temperatures reach well into the forties. In the early afternoon, the meagrely vegetated red, flaky sandstone hills seem at times like the angry rim of an enormous furnace. We find partial relief by the side of a nameless dry creek where weathered overhangs offer narrow scraps of shade. The intense heat persuades us to spend most of the afternoon resting like rock-wallabies. This is Kimberley heat at its most ferocious.

But as the day slips away, the shimmering orange of sunburnt stone fades to the gentle mauves and muted ochres of evening. In the absolute clarity of a still and delicate night, the heat subsides to a soft enveloping warmth. It is close to the hottest part of the year, yet

Right, top: Early morning in the St George Ranges.
Right: The Mitchell Falls in wet-season mode.

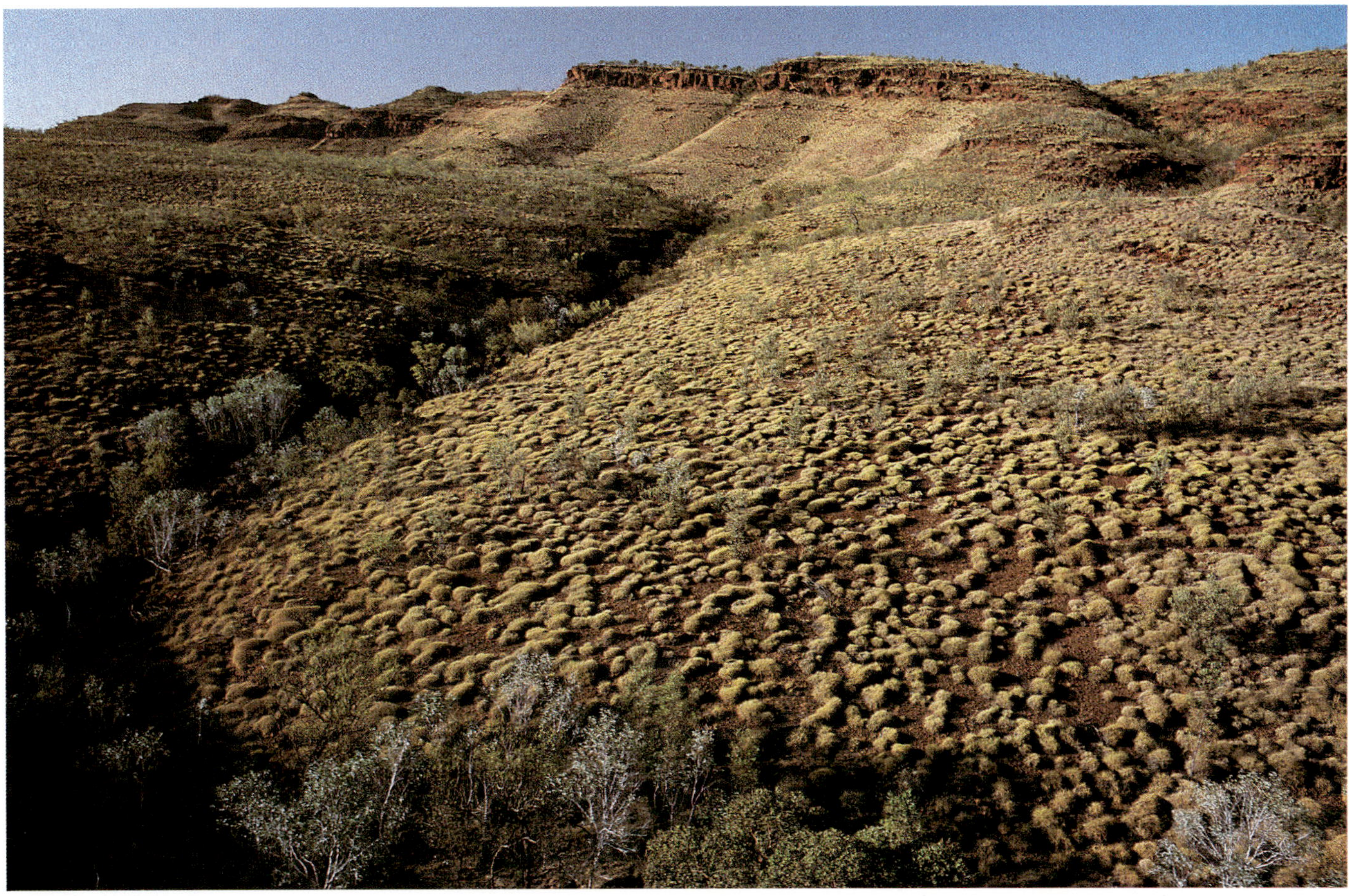

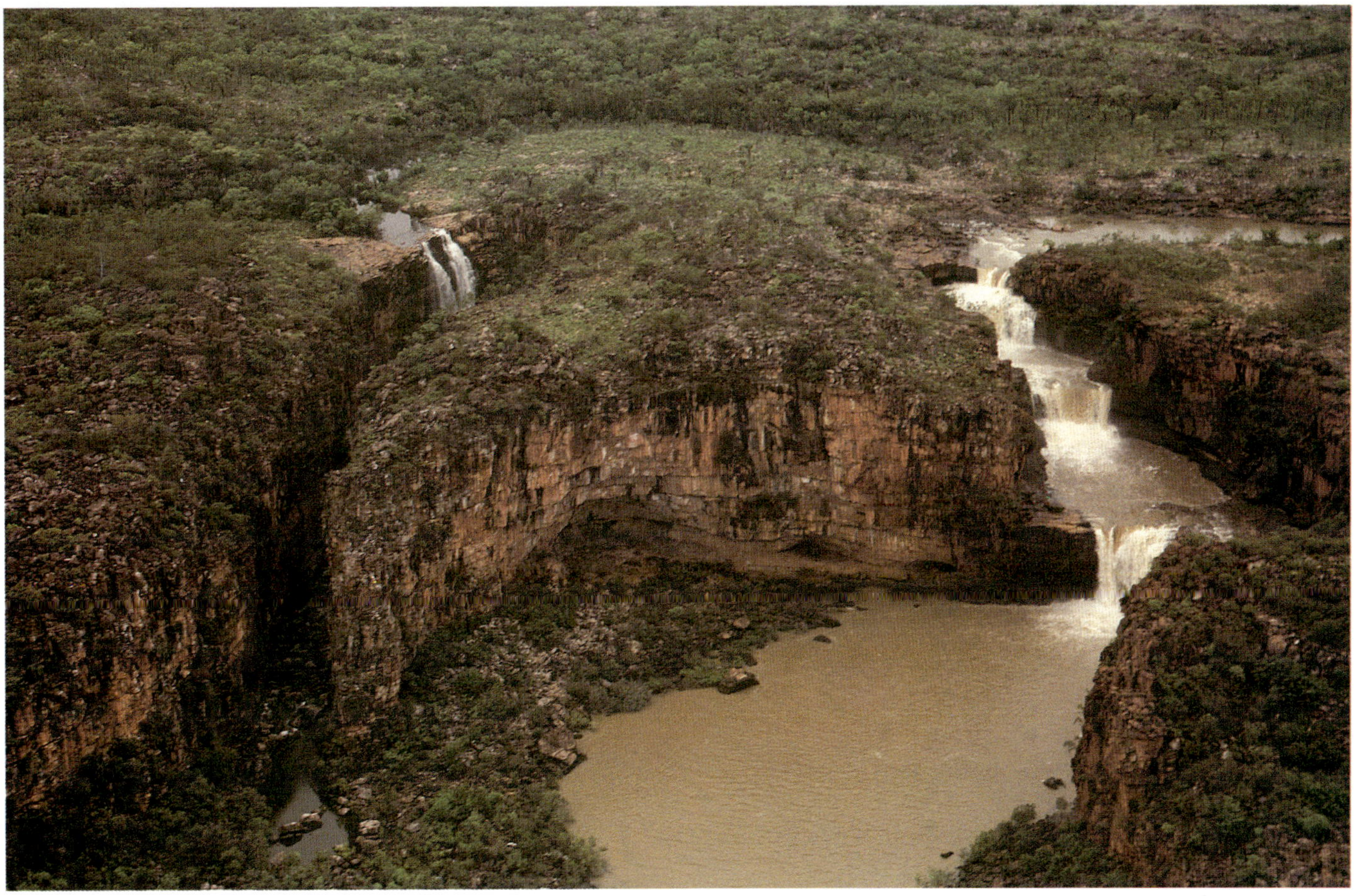

overnight the heat drains away. Towards morning the air feels refreshingly cool.

No such relief could be had closer to the coast, only three weeks before. As temperatures rapidly rise through October and November, humidity follows suit, eventually reaching its most extreme at the height of the wet season.[1] As could be expected, the Kimberley coast experiences far higher humidity than inland regions but the steamy, oppressive conditions of what is known everywhere in the north as the 'build up', reach a considerable distance from the coast.

An early November night brought no relief from the heat of an enervating Kimberley day in Windjana Gorge, just over 100 kilometres from the coast at Derby. The air beside the last remaining pools of the Lennard River hung heavy and still. Saturated with humidity and the vaguely fetid smell of a place impatient for renewal, it buzzed, fluttered and ticked with insect life. Sleep was elusive, as the river sand on which we lay steadily released its store of tropical heat from the day past. Tossing fitfully we noticed random stutters of distant lightning on the skyline. But the growl of thunder was absent. The lightning was too far off to be a threat to our already uncomfortable night. Rather than signalling an advancing storm, its pulse in the intensely humid air heralded something far more essential in the life of the Kimberley: the great annual shift in climate from dry to wet, part of the fundamental climatic pattern for most of tropical Australia.

The northern Kimberley and particularly the north-west is dominated by the effects of a tropical monsoon climate. Climatic patterns in this region are sharply divided between a prolonged dry period each year and a somewhat shorter but intense 'wet', typical of the wet–dry (or seasonal) tropical zone. This zone extends from the Kimberley, over the Top End of the Northern Territory, most of Cape York and the Great Dividing Range of North Queensland.[2]

'Elemental convulsions'

> … there came on a tremendous squall of wind, rain, thunder, and most vivid lightning. The peeling echoes of the thunder as they bounded from height to height, and from cliff to cliff, was awfully magnificent; whilst the rugged mountains which had just before looked golden in the bright light of the setting sun, were now shrouded in gloomy mists, and capped with dark clouds, from which issued incessant and dazzling flashes of lightning. During this grand and terrific elemental convulsion, our little boat was driven powerless before the blast.[3]

A common event for a January afternoon on the St George Basin at the mouth of the Prince Regent River! The description is by George Grey, leader of the first European party to explore the country in the vicinity of the Prince Regent in 1838. He attempted to negotiate the wettest part of the Kimberley at the wettest time of the year. Encountering torrential rains, violent thunderstorms and swollen creeks and rivers, Grey appears to have encountered a Kimberley wet season at close to full force.[4]

Practically all the year's rain in the Kimberley occurs between December and March. The greatest falls happen in the north-west, and encompass the scene of Grey's exploits, in an arc between Kalumburu and the Prince Regent River. Here, mean annual rainfall can exceed 1 400 millimetres. The north-west coast and hinterland lie in the course of prevailing summer winds that blow in from the Timor Sea and are directly in the path of developing tropical cyclones. The north-west receives the most reliable rains in the Kimberley. Even so, thunderstorm activity contributes a considerable proportion of the area's rainfall, making reliability a description reservedly applied.

Further inland and to the south, the wet is of shorter duration and is even less dependable. The monsoonal influence quickly diminishes. Rain usually falls as irregular thunderstorm deluges, rather than in widespread weather systems and cyclones. Halls Creek in the

*Right, top: Ghost Gums (*Eucalyptus papuana*) glow at last light below the St George Ranges.*
Right: February evening skies, northern Kimberley.

south-east records a mean annual rainfall of just 170 millimetres, only one-third of the maximum rain in the north.

Inland rains are confined to the wet season like those in the north but are considerably more erratic. At Halls Creek, total rain days for January, the wettest month of the year, have varied from two to twenty-two days since recording began in 1897.

The large-scale climatic forces that bring on the wet season in northern Australia are part of a general monsoonal weather pattern extending across tropical latitudes from Africa to the Pacific.

Maximum warming of the earth's surface and atmosphere generally occurs in the equatorial zone. Huge convection currents result, as warm drafts rise over the equator. These currents suck in air from polar latitudes, across the earth's surface towards the equator. At high altitudes, the warm air cools and descends as it circulates back towards the poles, completing the cycle. The rotation of the earth confines this circulation to tropical regions and causes the air flow to be directed obliquely. In the Southern Hemisphere this surface air movement becomes the south-east trade winds.

But these great circulating streams of air do not remain directly centred over the Equator. During the southern summer, the meteorological equator moves south and the strong vertical drafts affect the northern regions of Australia. Large volumes of moist air are drawn in from the north and north-west resulting in widespread rain and tropical cyclones.

In winter, the situation is reversed. Much of the Australian continent comes under the effect of descending streams of dry air. Prevailing winds reverse and the south-east trade winds blow over northern Australia towards Asia. Warm, dry weather results.

From April to November little or no rain falls in the Kimberley. August is the driest month of all. Parts of the Kimberley have never recorded rain at that time of year.

Cyclone coasts

During the wet season about 10 per cent of the world's tropical cyclones develop in the waters off Australia's north-west coast.[5] In a typical year, up to 10 cyclones may form in the arc between the Cocos Islands and Darwin at any time between November and April. They most frequently develop in January.

Cyclones start life as massive clusters of convective cloud which slowly separate from overall air movements. These clusters gradually gather together, forming into long bands of cloud spiralling in towards the developing eye. Pressure drops dramatically at the centre as gale-force winds develop. Cyclones at this stage of formation often veer towards the Kimberley coast, particularly in the early wet season.

As the cyclone matures it grows in size, both horizontally and vertically. Winds gather in intensity and extent. Torrential rain and flooding follows as the fully developed cyclone moves over the coastline. As it careers inland, the furious winds of the cyclone abate. A widespread rain depression usually persists in their wake.

Cyclones are very much chance events, albeit with a fair degree of frequency. Some years will bring forth several in the north-west region but by no means all wet seasons are beset by cyclones and torrential rains. As the result of a complex interaction between the strength and position of the tropical convection currents and distant meteorological phenomena, the wet may be spasmodic and poor. When warm waters replace cold in the eastern Pacific and convection occurs too far to the north, monsoonal rainfall will be diminished.

Poorer than average wet seasons occur at roughly two- to three-year intervals. The climate of northern Australia is not as uniformly seasonal as a superficial interpretation of statistics might show. In fact the variable time of the wet season's onset, its strength and duration, are all essential characteristics of the wet–dry tropical environment in Australia. Consequently, the climatic vagaries of the north have also had a profound effect on human activities in the region. In the pre-European Kimberley, poor rains put considerable stress on Aboriginal food reserves. A bad season for inland peoples often meant shifting to the coast, where the food resources were less affected by seasonal fluctuations. For the pastoral industry of more recent times, the wet season has been relied upon to bring on the growth of annual grasses. The failure of summer rains can mean despair for the remaining months of the year as rain outside the wet season is rare indeed. Such was our experience of a Kimberley wet.

From lean to green

It is late February and the feeling throughout is that the rains have to come soon. The last wet had been a big one in parts of the Kimberley. Cyclone Daphne caused massive flooding of the Fitzroy River and surrounds in February 1991. At the height of the floods the river was 30 kilometres wide at Fitzroy Crossing! But this year rainfall everywhere had so far been well below average.

Since the previous November, the whole region has been only teased by delinquent thunderstorms. Coursing erratically over the landscape, they bring a deluge to one escarpment and leave the next dry. Each gathers quickly, staging a menacing show of light and a grumble of thunder as winds bluster furiously from all directions. Heavy rain follows but generally lasts for less than a couple of hours. Sullen, overcast skies intermittently pierced by the searing heat of the tropical sun make for a steamy and oppressive aftermath. Whilst the rivers are not yet raging, the storms have washed from the landscape the desiccation of the dry season's lingering tail. Many areas are now bathed in a vivid but tenuous green.

The Mitchell Plateau records the highest rainfall of anywhere in Western Australia. With a yearly average exceeding 1 600 millimetres, the expectation of plentiful water in February seemed reasonable. Even in the dry days of the previous June on our last visit to the plateau many of the creeks had been flowing vigorously. From the air, the plateau and its imposing basalt ramparts plunging away to the Admiralty Gulf looks unfamiliarly lush and verdant. But the green mantle, the first flush of new growth in response to early rains, belies a meagre wet.

On the ground the reality is dry and unyielding. All surface water has drained away, soaked into the parched soil or transpired into an already near-saturated atmosphere. Camp Creek, an intermittent tributary of the Mitchell River, had been gently flowing in the previous dry season, even in its upper reaches. It should have been running fast but is instead reduced to a widely spaced string of sluggish pools. In this wettest part of the green Kimberley the vicissitudes of the wet season are readily apparent.

We have been on the plateau for a short time. In the dark-grey gloom of the late afternoon of our second day, the first signs of change appear. Faint lightning flickers on a distant horizon. Soon after, the muffled beat of thunder drumming on a far off escarpment presages a memorable night. We are about to realise our expectations of a Kimberley wet. As darkness quickly advances, the pulses become more intense. Random staccato bursts light the heavy drapery of cloud with a spectral glow. Jagged barbs of pure white arc between cloud heads. The thunder rapidly turns to a malevolent roar, reverberating across the flat terrain like the timpani from some demonic orchestra. Again and again it booms over the tree tops, rolling on to a sudden and violent string of crescendos.

Violent gusts whip through our campsite, towards the storm, then drop. The storm appears to be moving away. But in an instant, the wind backs and thunder and lightning roll on towards us. The first raindrops pelt down with stinging ferocity as the sky ignites in a strobing glare. The temperature plunges and rain spears down in torrents. Intimidating gusts jerk disdainfully at our tent-fly, at times hurling the full deluge over our increasingly sodden bodies. Immediately above, thunder rents the air whilst the rain continues unabated. It falls all night and most of the next morning, leaving the plateau completely awash!

But as quickly as it had gathered, the torrent subsides. At morning's end, the rain eases to less than a drizzle as a thin grey light is squeezed from beneath the sombre mists blanketing the plateau. A chorus of frogs greets the softness of the storm's demise and the gentle sounds of birdlife replace the final mumblings of thunder, now safely far off.

(We learn later that the storm on the Mitchell Plateau was associated with the outer edge of a tropical cyclone, active but stationary, some distance off the coast. Denied further rain from this cyclonic system, the plateau reverted to lying in wait for erratic thunderstorms and the increasingly remote chance of a fully developed cyclone crossing the Kimberley coast.)

Oceans of grass

Grass, great seas of it. From both the air and the ground, this is often one of the most striking impressions of the Kimberley: a thin underlay beneath a sparse scattering of trees, reaching to the horizon and beyond. The development of these savanna woodlands is a principal feature of the wet–dry tropics and is nowhere more evident than in the Kimberley. Tree crowns are thin, allowing ample light to reach an understorey of scattered small trees, shrubs, herbs and an almost total cover of grass.

The shapes of the dominant plant communities are in large measure a direct response to the pronounced wet and dry seasons of the region. Plants are required to contend alternately with the climate of the jungle and that of the desert.

Differing strategies are employed by plants to cope with the long drought periods, at the same time being ready to respond and compete for moisture and nutrients whenever optimal conditions prevail. Some plants remain in a growing condition throughout the year, seeking moisture from deep within the soil and so resist the drought. Most trees, shrubs and evergreen perennial grasses, including the spinifexes (*Triodia* species) are of this type. The eucalypts are most able to tap soil moisture at depth and are consequently the pre-eminent genus in the tree layer. Much of the northern Australian woodland is dominated by two species: Woollybutt (*Eucalyptus miniata*) and Stringybark (*E. tetrodonta*). The Woollybutt–Stringybark alliance, whilst prominent in the Kimberley, gives way in many areas to other dominant eucalypts such as Grey Box (*Eucalyptus tectifica*). In the tropical woodland, eucalypts form mixed communities but may also be found as single dominant species over large areas.

Other plants evade the drought. The tropical woodland supports a considerable number of deciduous trees and shrubs. They shed their leaves as the dry season advances, only to burst into new growth during the wet. Even some eucalypts have adopted this strategy in the north. Conspicuous deciduous species found in the Kimberley are the red-flowering Kurrajong (*Sterculia viscidula*) and the widespread Kapok Bush (*Cochlospermum fraseri*) which enlivens the sea of dry grass with its golden crop of flowers in the dry season. Drought-evading grasses such as Kangaroo Grass (*Themeda australis*) die back to a perennial tussock but grow vigorously when conditions permit. Like deciduous trees, some vines and creepers discard their aerial parts in the dry season. Leaves and stems die off, leaving tubers dormant beneath the ground, waiting for rain. The wet season in the Kimberley stone country is alive with scrambling, trailing and climbing plants that only announce their presence after the first rains of the season.

Then there are the species that are renewed annually from seed. These include herbs and grasses of all sizes. Widely distributed, Annual Sorghum or canegrass (*Sorghum* species) grows from seed each wet season in the medium to high rainfall parts of the Kimberley. It rapidly develops into dense tracts up to four metres high. Forcing a path through stands of canegrass can be a most unpleasant task, particularly in April and May when the flower heads of its lanky stems bristle with spear-like seed. The seeds dislodge with the slightest movement, showering the hapless intruder with hundreds of sharp, burrowing projectiles. Falling to earth, the seeds drill into the hard, dry ground where they wait to germinate at the onset of the wet season.

Ephemeral herbs such as Bush Everlastings or Mulla Mullas (*Gomphrena canescens*) sprout, develop, flower and disperse new seed in the course of each year. From February to late August they carpet sandy soils in the tropical woodland with masses of globular, papery, pink flowers.

*Left: Young Fan Palms (*Livistona eastonii*) after rain on the Mitchell Plateau.*

Top: The tropical woodland, King Leopold Ranges.
Above: The Kapok Bush (Cochlespermum fraseri) *against the grand vista of the Cockburn Range.*

60

Variations on a theme

The Kimberley has been divided into four broad natural regions or botanical districts: Dampier, Hall, Central Kimberley or Fitzgerald, and Gardner.[6] Throughout each, plant communities exhibit a range of common characteristics closely influenced by climate, topography, geology and soil type.

The Dampier Botanical District

The Dampier Botanical District in the south-west is bounded by the Great Sandy Desert on its southern edge. A vegetation change aligned with the Kimberley Basin's boundary at the foot of the King Leopold Ranges defines its limit in the north and east. Rainfall is low to moderate.

This part of the Kimberley is dominated by a remarkable plant association known as 'Pindan'. Found on low-lying sandy plains and alluvial flats, it is dominated by a tall shrub layer of acacias beneath a sparse tree layer. Not found outside the Kimberley, it covers more than 60 per cent of the district. Mature acacias form thickets that block out most other tree species and suppress the grass layer. When periodic fires completely clear the acacias, for several years the plains revert to a sparse savanna before the acacias once more regain their ascendancy. Common species are the Pindan or Seven Years Wattle (*Acacia eriopoda*), with Desert Walnut (*Owenia reticulata*) and Roughleaf Bloodwood (*Eucalyptus setosa*) in the tree layer.

On the floodplains of the Fitzroy and Lennard rivers, the conspicuous Boab appears. In the eastern corner of the district, termite mounds scatter amongst Ghost Gums (*Eucalyptus papuana*) and a sea of Bluegrass (*Dichanthium* species) and Ribbongrass (*Chrysopogon* species).

The Napier and Oscar ranges, extraordinary remnants of the Devonian reef, knife their way across the southern Kimberley. This limestone country is clad in plants that appear well adapted to a moonscape! Limestone Spinifex (*Triodia wiseana*), dominant amongst the grasses, forms brittle, spiky hummocks over the sharply eroded formations. Contorted Sandpaper Figs (*Ficus opposita*) and scattered Boabs and Kurrajongs cling to one of the most forbidding but impressive landscapes in the Kimberley.

Hall Botanical District

In the east Kimberley, the Hall Botanical District ranges from the dunefields and sandy margins of the desert, north across the plains and rough hills abutting the Kimberley foreland to the artificial shores of Lake Argyle.

Much of the district lies in the semi-arid zone. Consequently the vegetation is sparse, with spinifex hummock grasslands covering nearly all its extent (*Triodia* species).

On the edge of the desert, a series of ranges rises abruptly from the Fitzroy River's floodplain. The Poole, Shore and St George ranges are largely bare and rocky, supporting not much else but spinifex and a very thin scattering of stunted trees and shrubs: Variable-barked Bloodwood (*Eucalyptus dichromophloia*) and Roughleaf Bloodwood, acacias and grevilleas. On the flats surrounding the ranges, the gnarled and twisted form of Bauhinia (*Lysiphyllum cunninghamii*) bending low to the ground, contrasts the expansive white limbs of an occasional Ghost Gum.

The ridges and hills around Halls Creek are dotted with Snappy Gums (*Eucalyptus brevifolia*) over spinifex hummocks with some randomly bunched grasses gaining a foothold between.

Extensive, 'black soil' clay plains occur in the east Kimberley overlaying basalt. They are virtually treeless and are dominated by Mitchell Grass (*Astrebla* species).

North towards Lake Argyle, the rainfall is higher and the vegetation cover is consequently not as impoverished as on the desert fringe. Flanking the Ord River, the Bungle Bungle Range and the nearby Osmond Range support diverse plant communities. The red sand plains surrounding the Bungle Bungle massif are covered by woodlands of Silver-leaf Bloodwood (*Eucalyptus collina*) and Snappy Gum over spinifex and Wiregrass (*Eriachne* species). The spectacular *Grevillea wickhamii*, with its stiff blue-grey holly-shaped foliage and bright red, drooping flowers, is a feature of the plains. Secreted in the gorges of the Bungle Bungle Range are several plants only recently recorded for the first time in Western Australia. They include an as yet undescribed *Livistona* Palm.

Central Kimberley or Fitzgerald Botanical District

The Central Kimberley or Fitzgerald Botanical District extends from Cambridge Gulf, then south-west to the King Leopold Ranges and east across the Kimberley foreland. Together with the north Kimberley it comprises the highlands of the region.

This is spinifex country. Seventy per cent of the district's plant communities are dominated by the hardy, drought resistant Curly Spinifex (*Plectrachne pungens*), carpeting thin, sandstone-derived soils. A low savanna woodland sprawls over scattered mesas and hills. Much of the sandstone country within the district is home to the showy Scarlet Gum (*Eucalyptus phoenicia*) with its bright orange flowers and flaky rust-coloured bark. It is found in association with the gnarled, twisted form of *Eucalyptus ferruginea*. On ridge tops or away from the licking flames of grass fires, the sparsely scattered Northern Cypress Pine (*Callitris intratropica*) stands in distinctive relief from the surrounding eucalypts. Amongst the thinly dispersed shrub layer, grevilleas and acacias are common. The Fern-leaved Grevillea (*Grevillea pteridifolia*), with its enormous sprays of golden orange nectar-laden flowers, is a memorable sight of the central Kimberley. In the King Leopold and Durack ranges, Snappy Gums often occur as the dominant eucalypt and may be found in pure stands, particularly in drier areas. Just west of the King Leopold Ranges, in the Lennard Hills, a surprisingly diverse community is supported by meagre pockets of soil between bare outcrops of granite, particularly amongst the shrub layer and smaller trees. Found here are Kurrajong, Kapok Bush and the Billygoat Plum (*Terminalia ferdinandiana*). The unassuming Billygoat Plum was traditionally an important Aboriginal source of food and medicine. Its fruits have been found to be the richest known source of vitamin C.

Small areas of basalt in the central Kimberley have been eroded to form wide plains and low hills with a deeper soil cover than in sandstone country. Grey Box is dominant throughout much of the tree layer, and Curly Spinifex is replaced by a diverse range of short grasses.

Gardner Botanical District

The northern Kimberley's higher rainfall (over 700 millimetres annually) is reflected in the richness of its flora. Known as the Gardner Botanical District, its boundary corresponds to the southern limits of a tall grass savanna woodland and extends from Walcott Inlet to beyond Cambridge Gulf in the east. The district is a mosaic of gentle basalt hills and plains, and rugged sandstone country.

In the sandstone country the grass layer is dominated by canegrass on deep soils and the upper storey by Woollybutt and Stringybark. In rough stone country where soils are thin, the Variable-barked Bloodwood predominates. Common in the understorey and near watercourses is the Screw Pine (*Pandanus spiralis*), aptly named for its spiralling habit. A variety of small trees and shrubs scatter through the open forests and woodlands: *Terminalia*, *Grevillea* and *Acacia* species and the light-green foliaged Northern Kurrajong (*Brachychiton diversifolius*). The Turkey Bush (*Calytrix exstipulata*), with its mass of small pink flowers, is a familiar sight in the dry season understorey.

Rivers and streams are flanked by ribbons of forest, often dense and luxuriant. Avenues of *Terminalia platyphylla*, cadjeputs (*Melaleuca leucadendra* and *M. argentea*), *Ficus* species and towering River Red Gums (*Eucalyptus camaldulensis*) back fringing thickets of sharp-spined *Pandanus aquaticus*. The Freshwater Mangrove (*Barringtonia acutangula*) spreads over sandy embankments, trailing pendulous clusters of multi-stamened red flowers, low over the water.

The sandstone country towards the north coast becomes extremely rough and rocky. Topsoil is meagre and rainfall declines. Consequently the vegetation is often stunted and sparse. Fan Palms (*Livistona loriphylla*) sway on broken sandstone scarps amidst gnarled eucalypts such as the powdery, white barked *E. herbertiana*. A diverse but scattered array of small trees and shrubs including Emu Apple (*Owenia vernicosa*) and Elephant-ear Wattle (*Acacia dunnii*) ekes out an existence between heavily fissured and broken sandstone.

*Top left: Fields of Mulla Mullas or Bush Everlastings (*Gomphrena canescens*), Mitchell Plateau.*
*Bottom left: The flowers of the Fern-leaved Grevillea (*Grevillea pteridifolia*) drip with nectar, King Edward River.*
Top right: Capparis jacobsii *blooms in darkness, its rarely seen flowers drooping in the morning light. King Leopold Ranges.*
Bottom right: Grevillea wickhamii, *Purnululu National Park.*

Left, top: Sparse woodland dominated by Snappy Gums (Eucalyptus brevifolia) *in the King Leopold Ranges.*
Left: Elephant-ear Wattle (Acacia dunii) *on the Carson Escarpment, with Emu Apple* (Owenia vernicosa) *above the skyline. Drysdale River National Park.*
Above: Cadjeputs (Melaleuca leucadendra *and* M. argentea) *line tranquil reaches of the Drysdale River.*

Above: Rainforest margins, Mitchell Plateau.
Left: Pockets of rainforest survive in narrow gorges. Isdell River.

The basalt country of the north supports plant communities quite distinctive from its sandstone expanses. Running mainly in a north-south belt from the Gibb River Road to Kalumburu, the basalt-derived soils are covered with a savanna woodland of tall grass. Here the dominant eucalypts are Grey Box and the deciduous Large-leaf Cabbage Gum (*E. grandifolia*). A striking tree, the Large-leaf Cabbage Gum sports a stark white trunk and branches and large fleshy leaves. The gentle terrain of much of the north Kimberley basalt country has been utilised for cattle grazing, on a well-developed grass layer that often reaches two metres in height.

On the Mitchell Plateau where tropical rains are heaviest, extensive tall forests of Stringybark and Woollybutt are carried on red clay loam over hard basaltic laterite. The highly leached nature of the soil allows an association normally occurring on sandstone to grow over basalt. A distinctive feature of the Mitchell Plateau forests are Fan Palms (*Livistona eastonii*). Growing on spindly trunks up to 10 metres, they gather in almost pure stands on some parts of the plateau. Nowhere else in Western Australia are palms found in such profusion.

Fringing the steep flanks of the Mitchell Plateau is another intriguing plant community that until as recently as the 1960s was believed to be entirely absent from Western Australia — rainforest.

Ancient remnants

> ... steep rocky ridges of hills, furrowed with channels formed by the torrents that doubtless fall from their elevations during the season of rains, through interesting bushes which clothe the declivities with a luxuriant verdure. These thickets afforded me some variety of plants... [7]

This appears to be the first recorded observation of a rainforest environment in the Kimberley. It was made by Allan Cunningham, the famous botanist accompanying Lieutenant Phillip Parker King's surveys of the Kimberley coast between 1818 and 1822. Remarkably, apart from this and one or two other scant references, the existence of Kimberley rainforests was unknown to science until their 'discovery' in 1965 in the course of mineral exploration on the Mitchell Plateau. Their existence had previously been dismissed by two botanical surveys of the northern Kimberley in 1921 and 1954.

The Kimberley rainforests are like those in most of the wet–dry tropics of Australia. They are 'rainforests' in the broadest sense but are more accurately described as monsoonal vine forests and thickets. [8]

The monsoon forests encountered in the drier parts of tropical Queensland, the Northern Territory and Western Australia are far less imposing in appearance than the dense rainforests of the wet tropics and very restricted in extent. However, rather than negating their importance, their limited distribution and collective size reinforces their status as special communities. Kimberley rainforests are the most restricted of all.

They occur as small scattered pockets in the arc between Broome and Cape Londonderry and within 150 kilometres of the coast, in areas where annual rainfall exceeds 600 millimetres. The most notable concentrations occur on the Mitchell Plateau and the Bougainville Peninsula.

In the Kimberley as elsewhere across the north, the rainforests stand as an intriguing testament to the struggle between plants of distinctly different origins. The now dominant flora that has evolved in Australia is pitted against the descendants of the tropical plants that once clothed the ancient supercontinent of Gondwana and also against the recently arrived species from Asia (Indo–Malayan flora).

More than 120 million years ago, Gondwana began to break up into separate land-masses. Over the following 70 million years, Africa, India, South America, Antarctica and Australia all drifted apart. Then about 50 million years ago, Antarctica separated from Australia, leaving the northern continent free to drift towards Asia. Simultaneously, the world's climate grew increasingly cool and arid. As a result, tropical forests, which at their greatest extent covered nearly all of the formative Australian continent, dwindled to mere

Thickets of Pandanus acquaticus *form dense margins along the riverbank. River Red Gums (*Eucalyptus camaldulensis) *stand close behind, shrouded in the June early morning mists at Drysdale Crossing.*

Rainforest pool on Forest Creek, a tributary of the Drysdale River.

remnant communities. They were eventually confined to the north, an area with a warmer and wetter climate, thanks to the continent's continuing drift towards Asia.

As the tropical climate settled into its monsoonal pattern approximately 30 million years ago, the stress on the ancient surviving rainforests increased. In recent geological history upheavals in the world's climate resulted in still further decline. Times of intense glaciation worldwide resulted in long episodes of cool, dry weather over Australia. Rainforests retreated from all but the most favourable locations.

Additionally, periods of glaciation meant a decline in sea levels. At various times in the last two million years, narrow stretches of water from the Indonesian Archipelago separated the fused landmass of Australia and New Guinea. This allowed vigorous colonising species from the forests of Asia to gain easy access south. The old Gondwanan species, already in decline, were further threatened by these invaders from the north. But the old flora, though greatly reduced, never became totally extinct. Many rainforest species in the Australian tropics of today owe their ancestry to the ancient plants of Gondwana and not the forests of Asia.

The annual dry season droughts and long spells of increased aridity led to greater fire frequency. Rainforest species had not evolved to cope with fire. Whilst the forests declined, *Eucalyptus, Acacia, Grevillea* and other fire-tolerant, locally evolved genera prospered, opportunistically supplanting the sensitive rainforest species, pushing them back to patchy refuges afforded by rainfall, permanent water and topography. The arrival of the Aborigines and their propensity to use fire as a hunting tool possibly accelerated this process.

But whilst the wet–dry monsoonal climate and long periods of aridity did not suit many species of the permanently moist tropical rainforest, others adapted to it and survived. They took fragmentary shelter in the most favourable locations: at the base of clifflines and southerly aspects, in deep gorges and fissures in the heavily dissected plateaux, and close to any source of moisture. Here they evolved a range of strategies to deal with the stress of the sharply seasonal climate. Some species became deciduous, whilst others remained evergreen but developed small, leathery leaves.

Deciduous trees are a conspicuous feature of the monsoon forests scattered across northern Australia today, sprouting vigorous and often large leaves that are capable of a high rate of photosynthesis during the wet growing season. They shed their foliage in the dry as a response to continual drought conditions. Plant growth is assured and water loss minimised. Deciduous species often dominate the canopies of rainforests in the drier parts of northern Australia.

Kimberley monsoon forests occur as discrete patches ranging in size from thickets of a few plants to areas of about a hundred hectares, but few exceed 20 hectares. More than 1500 patches have so far been identified but their total area is less than 8000 hectares. Despite their diminutive scale and limited extent they are biologically rich and diverse.

More than 450 plant species have so far been identified in Kimberley monsoon forests. This is about 25 per cent of the entire region's flora. Similarly, the forests serve as bird havens, with colourful tropical species like the Torres Strait Pigeon (*Ducula bicolour*) feasting from abundant-fruiting trees. More than 140 species, nearly half of the birds found in the Kimberley, have so far been recorded in the region's forests. A significant number are totally dependent on these forest pockets for their survival in the region.

The fight for the forests

Clothed in luscious and vivid green canopies, patches of semi-deciduous monsoon forest lie snugly on the narrow scree slopes below the bluffs of the north-west coast. At the shore, they tail off into mangroves or are bordered by small white aprons of sand. In some locations well-developed forest covers quite large areas. At the mouth of the Hunter River a strip of rainforest runs in a near complete band along the base of the cliffline for several kilometres. Close by on Prince Frederick Harbour, away from the threat of fire, dense forest patches clad the folds of small islands. The presence of monsoon forests on off-shore islands, which often receive considerably less rainfall than the mainland, indicates that their size and distribution has more to do with the absence of fire than the availability of water.[9]

Above: Rainforests hug the shoreline beneath protective bluffs, Prince Frederick Harbour.
Right: Climbers and vines, prominent features of Kimberley rainforests, Mitchell Plateau.

Cycads (Cycas basaltica), *festooned with wet-season creepers, prosper amongst the boulder-strewn slopes of the Mitchell Plateau.*

On the Mitchell Plateau, monsoon forests are found in over 400 small patches, totalling more than 1 000 hectares. None exceeds more than about 20 hectares. The edges of the Mitchell Plateau fall away in precipitous benches of basalt, with steep talus slopes strewn below. Over the jumbled confusion of basalt boulders at the base of these cliffs, dense vine thickets invariably take hold. Looking along the wooded rim of the plateau, through extensive stands of Fan Palms, the vine thickets stand out in immediate contrast. Even within their diminutive, almost 'corner of the garden' size they give a sense of robustness and density appropriate to their position in the evolution of the tropical environment.

Kimberley monsoon forests can be one of the most frustrating and difficult environments to move through. Without a dense and lofty tree canopy preventing light from reaching the lower levels of the forest, the leaf-strewn ground supports an amazing jungle of vines, creepers and small shrubs, all opportunistically fighting for the light. But here there are no eucalypts, no grevilleas, no grasses and no fires. It is a different realm to the Kimberley outside.

The world beyond the forest shows many signs of the dominance of fire, the tether on its being. The trunks of numerous palms stand dense and black amongst the expanses of soft, recently sprouted grasses. An occasional grove of ancient Cycads (*Cycas basaltica*) watches sentry-like on the boulder-strewn hillside, their thick, defiant trunks similarly wreathed in charcoal and withered fronds.

With nonchalant indifference to our presence, a giant Brahman bull, shoulder deep in grass, continues to munch lazily on the abundant wet-season herbage along the margins of the forest. For a fleeting moment the scene is almost idyllic. But the bull and his ilk spell trouble for the conservation of monsoon forests in the Kimberley. Many of the more accessible patches are being trampled, allowing savanna grasses to invade and fire to eat insidiously at the forests.

Traditionally, the monsoon forests were important food storehouses for Aborigines. Their carefully managed burning practices sought to preserve the forests, not destroy them. Now, feral stock and random fires wander far into these remote parts of the Kimberley.

The tension between the rainforest and the savanna, a balance between two opposing biological forces, is itself now under threat from new agents of change. Perhaps the bull on the Mitchell Plateau, the intruder on the edge of the forest, symbolises a tension between the natural elements of the entire Kimberley and the outside world.

1. Kalumburu, close to the north coast, records a mean relative humidity in February at 9 a.m. of 74 per cent.
2. Only parts of the far north Queensland coast and immediate hinterland have a wet–tropical climate. Average annual rainfall in excess of 2 800 millimetres (double the highest Kimberley falls) ensures the existence of luxuriant wet–tropical forests, absent from the rest of the Australian tropics. Even so, more than 60 per cent of the rain falls between December and March as a result of the summer monsoon and tropical cyclone activity.
3. George Grey, *Journals of Two Expeditions of Discovery in North-West and Western Australia*, vol. 1, T & W Boone, London, 1841, p. 125.
4. It is interesting to note Grey's rainfall records for the months his party spent in the vicinity of the Prince Regent and Glenelg Rivers (op. cit., p. 250). They are consistent with the variability of rainfall during the wet season and the frequent dry spells that can intersperse periods of rain. Number of days in which rain fell, December 1837 to April 1838: December, six days; January, 19 days (1–19 January, 12 days; 19–28, four; 29–31, three); February, seven days; March, 12 days; 1–12 April, two days.
5. A tropical cyclone is a rotational low-pressure system of tropical origin in which mean winds measured over ten minutes reach 63 km/h or more. The effects may be widespread but the intense winds of a mature cyclone are concentrated in a radius of less than 100 km. Winds rotate around the central, calmer 'eye' (an area of intense low pressure) and may reach speeds of up to 200–250 km/h. The majority of mature north-west cyclones gust to 150–200 km/h.
6. J.S. Beard, *Vegetation Survey of Western Australia*, University of Western Australia Press, Perth, 1979.
7. From Cunningham's unpublished journals of 1818–22, quoted in Australian Heritage Commission, *The Rainforest Legacy*, AGPS, Canberra, 1987.
8. The term 'rainforest' is taken to include the evergreen forms found in the wet tropics and also the monsoon forests and vine thickets of the wet–dry tropics. The forests of the wet–dry tropics are deciduous in varying degrees and are often described as 'raingreen' (i.e., their canopy is only green during the wet growing season).
9. Patterns of vine-thicket occurrence on the Bougainville Peninsula also indicate this. Receiving about half the rainfall of the nearby Mitchell Plateau, the peninsula still manages to support numerous patches of vine forest like the plateau itself. The complex, dissected shape of the peninsula reduces the risk of the spread of wildfires in contrast to the open, sprawling terrain of the plateau. Since the cessation of regular Aboriginal use of the area, the extent of vine thicket has increased with a corresponding decrease in fire frequency. J.S. Beard and K.A. Clayton-Greene, 'The fire factor in vine thicket and woodland vegetation of the Admiralty Gulf region, north-west Kimberley, Western Australia' in *Proceedings of the Ecological Society of Australia*, vol. 13: *Ecology of the Wet–Dry Tropics*, eds M.G. Ridpath and L.K. Corbett, 1985, pp. 225–30.

4

Creatures of the North:
Adventures with Kimberley wildlife

Nights on the river

The low, jumbled cliffs on the eastern side of the river, still orange with the sun's fire, reflect like copper in the long pool ahead. Slivers of mauve, fading to pink then silver, dance and slide across this burnished surface in gentle pressure waves as the boulders downstream intrude. We decide to camp on rocks in the midst of the flow. On either side of what is to be our island home for the night, the Drysdale River slips quietly by, the mirrored sheen replaced by softly effervescing cascades gliding away towards darkness.

From atop the long rock bar, the jasper pinks of polished sandstone glow warm in the twilight. Great slabs of pavement, thrown together, then ground down by the fitful urgency of the river, tell of forces monumental. Yet in the midst of the river's occasionally turbulent path, plant life has managed a foothold; a few small Rock Figs (*Ficus platypoda*) have tenaciously worked their spreading roots into fissures in the water-worn stone, and where sand accumulates in the lee, scraggly, small cadjeputs find anchor.[1] Emphasising the extent of the flood-tide, debris from the previous wet season — sticks, dry grass and pandanus fronds — hang ragged in the cadjeputs, several metres off the ground.

Even in the middle of June, well into the dry season, the decision to camp on this enormous rock island seems somehow tinged with daring. There was of course absolutely no danger; rain (let alone a flood) is the nearest thing to impossible in the Kimberley at this time of year. But to sleep on rock pavements that six months before were submerged beneath the maelstrom is a tantalising thought that brings the power of the place ever closer.

Amidst the domestic chores of making camp, the last flush of the brief tropical twilight catches the length of the river valley in a pulse of colour. The day's final band of garrulous Little Corellas (*Cacatua sanguinea*) makes a rowdy pass low overhead, off to one of the many roosts strung out along the river. Its passing sees the day finally slip into night.

We linger over the best of bush meals. Watching our campfire's wavering light in shadow play with the water-scoured markings of our surrounds, we are at first unaware of the presence of a denizen of this rocky island. Long after last light, the pavements remain warm, slowly radiating the stored heat of the day. A python finds an ideal abode between the folds of a recently turned-out sleeping bag and the captured heat of the rock. When disturbed, our interloper beats a hasty retreat, leaving us with only a fleeting impression of mottled brown markings. Our snake was probably a Children's Python (*Liasis childreni*), a species found throughout the northern two-thirds of Australia in habitats as varied as coastal rainforests and the central deserts. A small snake reaching a maximum length of only 1.5 metres, it hunts by night, preying on small mammals, birds and reptiles.

Returning to the calm and tranquillity of our mid-stream evening, we stretch out on the gentle warmth of wide expanses of rock slab. Out on the water, reflected starlight has long since replaced the last glow of evening. But amongst the shimmer of silver, something moves. The resident crocodile has stirred! With a splash and a thwack the reflections shatter. Our camp, at the upstream end of such a long rock bar, is safe from the Estuarine or Saltwater Crocodile. It would be a tenacious 'saltie' indeed to have come this far up river. The local inhabitant is a Freshwater Crocodile (*Crocodylus johnstoni*).

The Freshwater Crocodile is often seen in the long, tranquil pools that linger in the major rivers, billabongs and lagoons of the Kimberley throughout the dry season. A timid creature, it is quick to dive from view when approached. It is not a dangerous predator of large mammals (unlike its much larger estuarine cousin) but if provoked will inflict significant wounds with its formidable teeth.

Reaching a maximum length of three metres in males and two metres in females, the Freshwater Crocodile is quite distinctive in appearance. Its olive-brown, motionless body and long, smooth and slender snout are common sights poised just at the water's surface.

Foraging mostly at night, it probes for crustaceans and swipes at fish with its fine, sharp teeth. Frogs and insects as well as small reptiles, birds and mammals are also eaten.

Nesting takes place in the late dry season around August and September. The female

Opposite: Alasdair McGregor, 'Mesa billabong, Drysdale River' (gouache on paper, 60 x 46 cm).

seeks out sandy stretches near permanent water. Here she scratches a shallow hole and lays a clutch of about 20 eggs. With temperatures rising towards the end of the dry, incubation is accelerated. The pattern of fluctuation in nest temperature and the duration of incubation within the eggs is thought to determine the sex of developing Freshwater Crocodiles. Eggs hatch at the start of the wet season, in November and December. Insect life — a major food of the young crocodiles — is abundant at this time, and with water everywhere the young hatchlings disperse easily.

However, mortality is high. Up to 96 per cent of eggs or young die in the first two years. Nests may be drowned by occasional sudden storms at the end of the dry season and there is also little parental care for the nest. The Sand Monitor or Gould's Goanna (*Varunus gouldii gouldii*) is known to be a heavy predator of the undefended eggs, and cannibalism of hatchlings by larger crocodiles is known to occur. If they survive past infancy, they may live for 60 years.

During the wet, the crocodiles follow the margins of the water as it spreads out over wide areas. But as the rivers and billabongs shrink during the dry season, populations return to stretches of permanent water where many individuals sometimes crowd into small pools.

Prominent in the nocturnal feast of our resident crocodile would have been the ubiquitous Sooty Grunter (*Hephaestus fuliginosus*). Sometimes known as Black Bream, it is common in the billabongs, creeks and rivers of the north. Part of an extremely rich aquatic fauna found in the Kimberley, the Sooty Grunter is one of 26 fish species recorded in the Drysdale River National Park, the highest species count of any river in the region. The Kimberley's fish fauna is quite distinctive, with 16 endemic species and one endemic genus found in the region.

Another common fish in the waterways of the Kimberley and northern Australia is the incredible Archerfish (*Toxotes chatareus*). Also found in South-east Asia and New Guinea, the Archerfish patrols near the surface of pools, close to the bank and the overhanging vegetation. From here it is poised to shoot down unsuspecting insects and spiders with a deftly aimed volley of water droplets.

Bowerbirds, Brolgas and Black Cockatoos

First light, and the low strands of cloud behind the rocky turrets of the ridgeline glow pink, then orange, just before the first sunburst sets the ordered confusion of stone on fire. Early mornings and evenings near water in the Kimberley are punctuated with the song and clamour of birdlife. The environs of the Drysdale River are no exception. So far 129 species have been recorded in the area encompassed by the National Park. The Drysdale lies at the transition between the wetter north-west Kimberley and the semi-arid eastern Kimberley. Birds found in the west such as the Emerald Dove (*Chalcophaps indica*) and the Shining Flycatcher (*Myiagra alecto*) are not found further east than the Drysdale; similarly, species favouring semi-arid conditions such as the Gouldian Finch (*Erythrura gouldiae*) are not known further west.[2]

The Kimberley itself is home to 241 of the more than 700 bird species found in Australia. Many are common to other parts of the north and the continent in general. Of the Kimberley species, 13 are shared just with the Top End and only one, the Black Grasswren (*Amytornis housei*) is endemic to the region. It is only found amongst the rough spinifex gullies of the north-west. Some birds, such as the Purple-crowned Fairy-wren (*Malurus coronatus*), exist in the Kimberley as a distinct race, differing from the same species in other regions in details of plumage.

The presence of abundant birdlife is the vital spark of life along the river and its adjacent rock terraces and gullies. The constant soft and repetitive underscoring of all Kimberley sounds, morning and evening, is the note of the Peaceful Dove (*Geopelia striata placida*).

Opposite: Cadjeputs and Rock Figs (Ficus platypoda*) find a tenacious hold amidst the rock bars of the Drysdale River. The scoured and water-worn sandstone speaks of countless wet seasons when each year the exposed pavements are subjected to the floodtide.*

Wheeling flocks of twenty or more spectacular Red-tailed Black Cockatoos (*Calyptorhynchus magnificus*) swoop across the floodplain woodland and down over the river, alighting in a rowdy commotion amongst the fringing cadjeputs. After drinking at the water's edge they take off with the flash of a flame-red tail and a great cacophony of metallic cries.[3] Flying low amongst the trees, the flock heads for the open woodland. Here it will feed as a group on the seeds of the Woollybutt and the Swamp Bloodwood (*Eucalyptus ptychocarpa*).

Meanwhile, Blue-winged Kookaburras (*Dacelo leachlii leachii*) sit high in the riverside forest, calling back and forth across the water. A lonely, high-pitched, crow-like cackle, their call seems quite at odds with the famous voice of the closely related Laughing Kookaburra.

Breaking camp early, we boulder hop from our rock-island camp to the nearest bank and set off to explore the hidden worlds amongst the gullies and rough stone country flanking the river. Looking downstream, drifts of cream-coloured sand swing round the outside curves of the river in long, open banks. By the water's edge, lines of river detritus mark the daily drop in level like scum rings on the side of a bath. Come October, long stretches of the river will be dry.

Punctuating the open expanses of river bank, casually arranged sand gardens of flowering shrubs cluster about weathered pink and grey boulders. Amongst the bare slabs protruding from the sand drifts, the ubiquitous gummy spinifexes *Triodia pungens* and *Plectrachne pungens* form loose clumps, their long, stiff leaves glinting with sickly smelling, sticky resin in the early sun. The mass of yellow-orange, fine-stamened flowers of the Bridal Tree (*Xanthostemon paradoxis*) is a common and distinctive feature of the gardens and the rocky terraces behind. The Bridal Tree's broad, pliable leaves are a favoured nesting material of the Green Tree Ant (*Oecophylla smaragdina*). A biting annoyance to the unwary trying to force a passage through the undergrowth, Green Ants are found throughout the tropical north. When clambering through rocky and overgrown terrain, their industrious nests of cut leaves adhered with silk are invariably disturbed at the most awkward moments.

It had been a busy night. The sand is criss-crossed from refuge to water's edge with evidence of the hours past. The tracks, some indecipherable, others quite distinct, betray the activity of the riverbank under the mask of darkness. Dingoes, crocodiles, wallabies, snakes and any number of small marsupials and rodents had all come this way using the night as a shield: as forager, hunter or hunted. Distressingly, there also appears to be the evidence of that scourge of native animals, the feral cat. The largest and most distinct mammal tracks are probably those of the Agile or Sandy Wallaby (*Macropus agilus*). The most common wallaby in northern Australia and the lowlands of New Guinea, it is at home on the riverbank and nearby grasslands.

Moving away from these sandy expanses, up into the jumbled and ragged stone country that steps back from the river, we disturb several White-quilled Rock-Pigeons (*Petrophassa albipennis*) that were superbly camouflaged in mottled browns between the clefts and boulders. We are startled by the smack of their wings as they flee in explosive flight from under our feet. Winging low over their rocky domain, they take shelter in a rock crevice close by.

Further up the hill, secreted amongst the tangled vegetation and fanciful, rocky outcrops, lives one of the Kimberley's most curious and engaging inhabitants, the Great Bowerbird (*Chlamydera nuchalis*).[4] Clad in drab greys and browns, it is hard to believe that this dull-looking bird belongs to a family whose closest relatives are the Birds of Paradise from New Guinea and north Queensland. The Great Bowerbird does not sport the resplendent plumage of its rainforest relatives, the Satin and Regent Bowerbirds, and apart from being the largest member of the family, there is nothing about its appearance that earns it the name, 'great'. But first impressions can be misleading! It is the bird's behaviour rather than its appearance that is so astounding.

As we explore the vine thickets and dry, shaded alleys that run maze-like through the stone country by the river, the Great Bowerbird's presence is always sensed. Rustling and hopping through the straggling thickets and fruiting trees, they emit a variety of calls, most bordering on the lunatic. Descriptions of the bowerbird's peculiar vocal repertoire are difficult to muster. Their most common sound is a long and repetitive 'squelching' or wheezing rasp. This may be interspersed with a range of clicks and harsh notes that in turn is

*Top: Freshwater Crocodile (*Crocodylus johnstoni*), El Questro Station.*
*Above, left: Children's Python (*Liasis childreni*), Mimbi Caves.*
*Above, right: The Rainbow Bee-eater (*Merops ornatus*) burrows into sandy banks to nest, Napier Broome Bay.*
*Bottom, left: Green Tree Ants (*Oecophylla smaragdina*), a source of 'bush tucker'. Their abdomens have a sharp lemon taste. Walcott Inlet.*
Bottom right: Fallen melaleuca leaves and feathers, Drysdale Crossing.

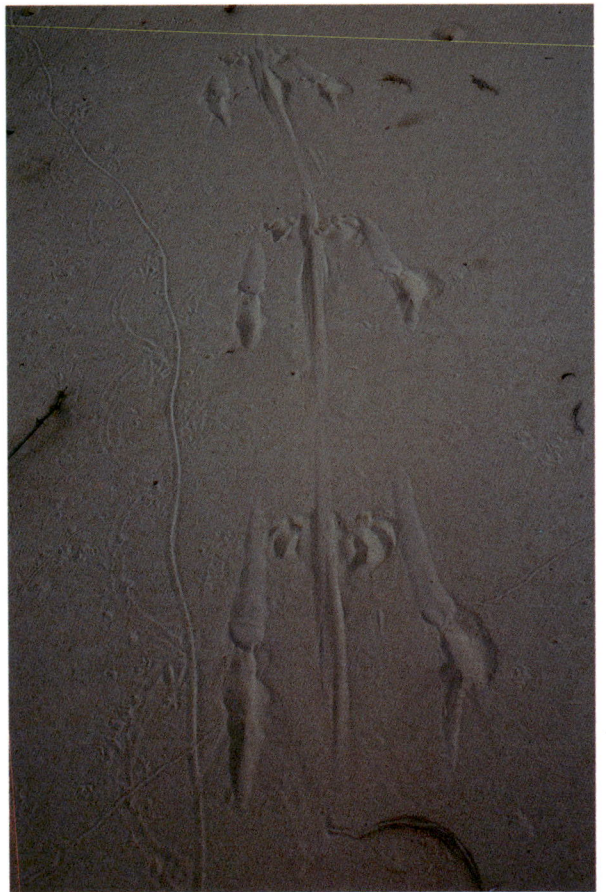

Top: Blue-winged Kookaburra (Dacelo leachii leachii), Ord River.
Left: Tracks of the Agile Wallaby (Macropus agilus), Drysdale River.
Right, above: Two bowers of the Great Bowerbird. The bower in the foreground appears to be abandoned, perhaps being robbed to build the one behind. Drysdale River.
Right, below: The male Great Bowerbird (Chlamydera nuchalis) chortles its expansive repertoire of sounds from vantage points in trees and bushes surrounding his bower. Drysdale River.

interrupted by a cascade of mimicry delivered with absolute bravura. They call constantly, the male advertising to the female and rivals alike his own presence and the location of his place of enchantment — the bower.

No less amazing than this cacophony of song are the architectural endeavours of the male. John Gould, the renowned English ornithologist and artist, wrote in the 1840s of his observations of the bowerbird's building efforts:

> These extraordinary playing places have been the source of much speculation, and by some persons have been considered to be made by the aborigines as cradles for their children, but it is now known that they are places of resort for both sexes of these birds at that season of the year when nature prompts them to reproduce their kind... These highly decorated halls of assembly must therefore be regarded as the most wonderful instances of bird-architecture yet discovered. [5]

In common with nearly all species of this family, the male Great Bowerbird constructs an elaborate race of sticks, twigs and strands of grass. In small openings amongst the leaf litter, he scratches a runway or avenue, the floor of which he lines with a carefully arranged mat of fine sticks. The walls of the runway, the male bird's 'bower', are about 45 centimetres high, one metre long, and set 20 centimetres apart. They are generally arranged in a north–south orientation and often arch right over, touching at the top, making the structure almost like a fully roofed corridor. The industrious male, not content with the bare walls and floor of his edifice, then sets about painting and decorating.

Taking a wad of vegetable matter in his beak, the bowerbird 'paints' the walls of his bower with a mixture of plant juices and saliva. As a finishing touch, a staggering quantity of found objects are collected and displayed in piles at either end of the bower and in the centre of the runway. He ranges far and wide, up to a kilometre from the bower, seizing prized objects and returning to add them to his burgeoning display. Bleached snail shells and animal bones, pieces of white or grey stone, quartz crystals, white flowers, lumps of charcoal and wallaby dung are all piled on the bird's display ground. Objects are often sorted into categories. At one bower not far from a once inhabited rock shelter we even found a few small stone artefacts and worked flakes.

The male's bower and its collection of prized objects are both lure and backdrop to his courtship display. Once a female is within range, he will cavort excitedly, displaying outstretched wings and the only bright colour on his body, a normally hidden lilac patch on the nape of the neck. He will seize an object from his collection and prance about with it held high in his beak or make an excited volley of calls. Mating invariably ensues, taking place within the bower itself. Male bowerbirds are promiscuous and will copulate with any number of females. The nest is separate from the bower and after courtship and mating the male plays no further part in the cycle of life, leaving incubation and the rearing of chicks and fledglings entirely to the female.

Our days by the river are marked by fleeting moments of great excitement, often precipitated by the sudden and almost unexpected appearance of some form of resident wildlife. Invariably, the best opportunities for observing these local inhabitants are on the river itself. We travel in an inflatable boat wherever water levels and terrain allow, and so quietly slip into their world. We see the gorgeous Rainbow Bee-eater (*Merops ornatus*) in brilliant darting flight, seizing insects on the wing, and the Rufous or Nankeen Night Heron (*Nycticorax caledonicus*) quietly sheltering by day in the tangle of pandanus fringing the river. At dusk and at dawn the heron will fly out, in search of aquatic life and insects or the nests of other birds to plunder.

Enter *Emydura australis*, a species of Side-necked Turtle. One of three freshwater turtles found in the Kimberley, it is a common but fleeting sight as it dives to safety in the large pools of the Drysdale River. As a welcome source of food for Aboriginal people, the behaviour of this very timid animal may in part have been shaped by persistent hunting across countless generations.[6]

Kimberley rivers in their dry-season mood show a number of faces. Long, wide and languid stretches of still water often end unpredictably. They suddenly give way to sand bars and braided streams that flow through great mazes and alleys of pandanus, the haunt of enormous, orb-weaving spiders. Deep-green, shaded canals and shallow strands of tepid water the colour of pale straw, all disappear abruptly into intractable sandbars. Holding back the sand, casual groups of cadjeputs lean downstream, bent by the seasonal yoke of floodwaters from months and years past. Interspersed amongst the cadjeputs and fringing pandanus, graceful, white-trunked River Red Gums, some up to 20 metres tall, dance and sway in gentle reflection along open stretches of the river. The most widespread eucalypt in Australia, River Red Gums are equally at home standing feet-immersed in the floodways of the Murray River, or fringing the rivers and billabongs of the tropics.

This is the stage of the Brolga (*Grus rubicundus*). A common enough bird throughout the waterways of the north, it is nevertheless an elusive sight at close quarters. Brolgas, in pairs or small groups, purposefully stride the sandbars and river margins at a stately pace but take to the air in nervous retreat immediately an alien presence is detected. Sliding down river, we occasionally see them lightly striding across the sand, making for open space. Their near silent flight — on broad, up-swept wings and with long legs and neck fully extended — is, like all their movements, imbued with grace.

But it is the dance of the Brolga that is perhaps the most perfect embodiment of that grace. Dances take place between the monogamous pairs at all times of the year, not just in the wet season when they breed, and are possibly as much concerned with pair bonding as with courtship. In an elegantly choreographed display, the opposing Brolgas bow and bob, their giant grey and black wings effortlessly poised, intermittently quivering. Springing on reed-like legs, they bound backwards and trumpet, necks extended high in the air.

If the Great Bowerbird is the outrageous philanderer, the Brolga by comparison appears to be a model of rectitude. In the course of the year, Brolgas may range over large distances in search of food but return each season to the same areas of swampy ground to breed, probably mating with the one partner for life.

Lagoon life

Sharing the aquatic stage with the Brolga, Australia's only member of the stork family, the Jabiru or Black-necked Stork (*Xenorhynchus asiaticus*) can occasionally be seen strutting with imperious bearing through the shallow reaches of Kimberley rivers. These imposing black and white birds, sporting slender, bright-red legs, are however more at home around the wetland margins of lakes, swamps and intertidal mangroves.

Wetlands in the Kimberley are limited in extent. There is no vast network of seasonally inundated or permanent swamps as exists on the coastal plains around the margins of Arnhem Land. However, the richness and diversity of the freshwater habitats in the region are perhaps intensified by the relative scarcity of those habitats. Permanent lagoons and swamps in the Kimberley serve as important dry-season refuges for many local species.

The Ord River snakes nearly 80 kilometres across extensive alluvial plains before reaching the East Arm of Cambridge Gulf and the Timor Sea. Drainage across the flats is slow and ill-defined. Numerous wet-season channels, creeks and the overflow of the Ord itself, end in freshwater swamps. Waterbirds gather in their thousands to feed and breed at Parry Lagoons, south-east of Wyndham. As the surrounding terrain desiccates, the waters of the lagoons continue to support dense fringing communities of cadjeputs, pandanus, River Red Gums, Ghost Gums, Coolabahs (*Eucalyptus microtheca*) and scattered groves of Boabs.

The Boab is very much a symbol of the Kimberley. Widespread throughout the region and the neighbouring basins of the Victoria and Fitzmaurice rivers, the distinctive Boab is nonetheless restricted to a very specific range of habitats. It is a tree of the drier parts of the Kimberley: on sandstone hillsides and sandy plains or amongst the sharp limestone ridges of the Napier and Oscar ranges. It stands isolated or in small, family-like copses beside creeks, drainage lines and lagoons of the semi-arid west and east Kimberley. It was first described by Phillip Parker King in 1820:

> ... a tree... had for some time puzzled us from its immense size and peculiar appearance ... the gouty habit of the stem, which was soft and spongy, gave it an appearance of disease: but as all the specimens from the youngest plant to the full-grown tree, possessed the same deformed appearance, it was evidently the peculiarity of its habit.[7]

Top: The Olive Python (Liasis olivaceus) *is widespread in the Kimberley. Its habitats vary from rainforest to rocky hills and woodland. Yampi Peninsula.*
Above, left: Wide-ranging over much of northern, eastern and southern Australia, the Sulphur-crested Cockatoo (Cacatua galerita) *is usually encountered in the Kimberley along river margins or anywhere close to water. Drysdale River.*
Above, right: Emydura australis, *a species of Side-necked Turtle, Drysdale River.*
Right: Nests of the Fairy Martin (Cecropis ariel), *Mimbi Caves.*

83

Top: The Parry Lagoons near Wyndham provide vital feeding and breeding grounds for enormous numbers of waterbirds. Much of the Kimberley lacks significant permanent water outside the major rivers.

Left: Native bees pollinate the beautiful waterlily Nymphaea violacea, *common throughout freshwater billabongs, swamps and streams of northern Australia. Drysdale River.*

*Right: A juvenile Comb-crested Jacana (*Irediparra gallinacea*) deftly balances on lily-pads using its extremely long toes. Widespread in the rest of the north, the Jacana is a declared rare species in Western Australia, being restricted to the waterways of the east Kimberley. Packsaddle Swamps near Kununurra.*

All aspects of the character of this strange deciduous tree seem somehow touched with the bizarre. Its writhing, wasted branches, bare for much of the year, sport large, fragrant, creamy flowers just before the wet season. These are followed by a crop of large, pendulous fruits covered in a velvety fuzz. Encased within the hard, brittle shell of the Boab fruit is a storehouse of seeds and an edible mealy pulp (both once important Aboriginal foods). A possible relic from Gondwana, its closest relatives are today found in Africa and Madagascar.

Out on the lagoon lies a carpet of waterplants. The delicate pink flowers of the waterlily *Nymphaea violacea* stand just above the water surface reflecting lazily in the tranquil shallows. Small flotillas of Pacific Black Ducks (*Anas superciliosa*) and Wandering Whistling-Ducks (*Dendrocygna arcuata*) cruise amongst the lilies. At the beginning of the dry season, duck numbers are low; but as seasonal waterways disappear, their population on the lagoons grows to nearly 20 000. Similarly, large, noisy gaggles of Magpie Geese (*Anseranus semipalmata*) gather to breed, building floating nest platforms on swampy ground as the wet season advances.

The diversity of species using Parry Lagoons is impressive. A total of 27 000 waterbirds from amongst 54 species were recorded during a dry-season survey in 1986. Ibises, herons, pelicans, Brolgas, Jabirus, egrets and spoonbills all eagerly congregate to fish and forage in the warm, shallow waters so richly blessed with aquatic life. In good seasons, the wetlands fill to capacity and the area becomes a major breeding ground for waterbirds.

Migratory visitors to Australia, like the Wood Sandpiper (*Tringa glareola*), use scattered wetlands as stopovers on their long journeys. They leave their breeding grounds in the marshy tundra of Siberia each September, flying south to spend the southern summer at favoured refuges such as Parry Lagoons.

Last refuge

The Kimberley is home to about 70 species of native mammals. The largest group, the bats, number at least 28. More bats are still likely to be found and described. Many Kimberley mammals are common to the rest of the north and the continent as a whole. Naturally there are strong links with Arnhem Land, reflecting similarities of habitat. Several species of rats, bats and the rare Rock Ringtail Possum (*Pseudocheirus dahli*) do not occur outside these two regions.

The richest concentration of mammals in all families occurs in the heavily dissected, high-rainfall country in the north-west. No other similarly sized area in Western Australia is so richly endowed. On the Mitchell Plateau, 39 species have been recorded, and equivalent concentrations also occur in the Prince Regent Nature Reserve. The north-west is home to all three mammals endemic to the Kimberley: the Scaly-tailed Possum (*Wyulda squamicaudata*); an insect-eating bat, the Yellow-lipped Eptesicus (*Eptesicus douglasi*); and the Warabi (*Petrogale burbidgei*), a species of rock wallaby.

By comparison, in the Drysdale River National Park, with its higher proportion of open grassland and woodland, only 28 mammals were recorded in a 1975 survey. This park is home to large and widespread populations of grass-dwelling mice, well adapted to the drier environment: Western Chestnut Native-mouse (*Pseudomys nanus*), the Delicate or Little Native-mouse (*Pseudomys delicatulus*), and *Pseudomys laborifex*.

A substantial wilderness, the north-west Kimberley is a rare example in mainland Australia of a region traversing a range of habitats in which the mammal fauna is thought to remain intact. Because of its remoteness and mostly unaltered state, it is likely that no localised extinctions have occurred. In the Kimberley, the north-west is the last refuge of the Golden Bandicoot (*Isoodon auratus*). Widely distributed throughout northern and central Australia until the 1930s, the Golden Bandicoot has failed to survive the advent of the pastoral industry and has suffered a drastic decline. The Golden-backed Tree-rat (*Mesembriomys macrurus*) has similarly retreated to the north-west and is now presumed extinct from the drier parts of its range in the southern and eastern Kimberley. This reduction in range is thought to be due to pastoralism.

In the southern Kimberley, the species of the tropics give way to those of the desert. Some areas (such as the Edgar Range, on the edge of the Great Sandy Desert, south-east of Broome) are home to both. They are like scattered islands, vital for wildlife refuge and survival. The Sandy Inland Mouse (*Pseudomys hermannsburgensis*) is found in the Edgar Range, at the northern extremity of its distribution; and the Bilby or Dalgyte (*Macrotis lagotis*), once widespread across arid and semi-arid Australia, has retreated here to one of its last strongholds. A population of the Kimberley race of the Black-footed Rock-wallaby (*Petrogale lateralis*) is endemic to the Edgar Range.

Champions of the gorge

Night closes fast in the tropics. The last rose-glow from a late dry-season day fastens a sparse skyline black against the aura. Boabs, the trees that seem more animate than botanical, pose with outstretched and upturned arms on the high horizon above our camp. We have stopped for the night at a long pool. The pool is fed by a series of delicate waterfalls on Bell Creek, a tributary of the Isdell River in the western Kimberley.

Against the stillness of the ridge above, something moves. It twitches again, then another shape appears: two silhouettes against a deepening sky. Short-eared Rock-wallabies (*Petrogale brachyotis*), out foraging in the twilight. Champions of the gorge, rock-face and cliff, they are the most abundant and widespread rock-wallaby in the Kimberley. Flighty gymnastics usually deny the viewer an adequate glimpse of these superb animals.

Living in small family groups, Short-eared Rock-wallabies never venture from a defined territory of rocks, shelter and associated pasture. Similar in behaviour to many species of rock-wallaby, they are secretive by day, preferring to graze in the early morning, evening and at night. One of four rock-wallabies found in the Kimberley, like the smaller Nabarlek or Little Rock-wallaby (*Peradorcas concinna*) they are also found in Arnhem Land.

Closely resembling the Nabarlek, but restricted to the rugged King Leopold sandstone country of the Mitchell Plateau and a few islands in the Bonaparte Archipelago, is the smallest of all rock-wallabies, the endemic Warabi. With a body length averaging just 32 centimetres, this shy and largely nocturnal animal was not discovered until 1978 and only photographed for the first time in 1985; such is the remoteness of the north-west Kimberley.

The landscape of the Kimberley is so often given its relief and profile in the descent of gorges, rather than the high horizon of soaring ranges. Bell Creek to the south-east of Walcott Inlet spends most of its life ambling across a gentle, gradually narrowing, grassy valley between the King Leopold and Isdell ranges. As it reaches the north-western end of the valley, it abruptly cuts into an imposing gorge, then cascades nearly 15 kilometres to join the similarly cleft Isdell River in its run to the turbid waters of Walcott Inlet. Sparsely vegetated stony hills extend in all directions from the rim of the gorges, spreading into a complex network of broken, thin-soiled country. Struggling to reach more than 10 metres in height, Woollybutt, Grey Box and Bloodwoods scatter across a skyline punctuated by the occasional, bulbous Boab or the shapely and distinctively foliaged Emu Apple. A scraggly assortment of shrubs — acacias, grevilleas and figs — take hold amidst the angular scree and the dry, tenacious grass cover dominated by hummocks of Curly Spinifex. The brilliant yellow flowers of the lanky stemmed Kapok Bush dot the understorey.

This rough terrain above the gorges is the habitat of the Euro, or Hill Kangaroo (*Macropus robustus*). A generally solitary animal, the Euro, in several quite distinct guises, is master of the hills throughout much of Australia. Solidly built with a coarse coat, the Euro's colour varies from dark grey to reddish brown in at least four sub-species. The individuals we encounter in the Kimberley are generally a rusty dark grey. When surprised, they bound with great power and agility towards refuge amongst the rocky slopes.

Opposite: A Boab (Adansonia gregorii) clings to the steep sides of an unnamed rocky ravine on El Questro Station. Well adapted to the seasonal droughts of the dry season, the Boab stores requisite moisture in the fibrous pith of its swollen trunk and branches.
Overleaf: Bell Creek, a tributary of the Isdell River.

Sheltering by day in the shade of rock overhangs, Euros graze in the evening on spinifex and other grasses. Well adapted to arid conditions, they can survive on meagre pickings and are able to range considerable distances from water. Across northern Australia, the Euro is sometimes seen sharing its ground with the Antelopean Kangaroo (*Macropus antilopinus*), an inhabitant of the tropical woodlands that occasionally ventures into the hills.

Our days by Bell Creek are spent camped on a water-scoured rock terrace beneath a yawning bluff of weathered sandstone. Water-streaked in grey and black on orange, the angular blocks of this great wall rise upwards and outwards in irregular steps. In near-permanent shade at the base of the wall, a luxuriant colony of ferns prospers under the constant trickle of water seepage.

It is here that we seek relief from the ferocity of early November afternoons. Many of the local inhabitants do likewise, remaining at rest, cloistered in shade during the heat of the day. So much of Kimberley wildlife is secretive and in addition nocturnal, hidden to the casual daytime observer.

A widespread creature of the night is the Northern Quoll (*Dasyurus hallucatus*), found across the north in broken rocky country from the Pilbara to north-eastern Queensland. This small, grey-brown, white-spotted animal hunts by darkness in search of reptiles, insects, fruits, and small mammals, such the Common Rock-rat (*Zyzomys argurus*). It is a brazen scavenger around human habitation, as we find out when our supply of muesli disappears during the course of one night. The morning reveals a trail of the stuff wandering across the rock pavement and into the boulders above our camp.

As an opportunist, the quoll may be better able to battle disturbances to its environment than many animals of a similar size.[8] Many such creatures of the Australian night have sadly slipped quietly away to the brink of extinction or beyond, in barely the space of living memory.

Feral herds

Feral animals, the intrusive latecomers to Australia's mammal populations, are a menace in the Kimberley, just as they are across the continent. Cats, horses, donkeys and cattle are found throughout the region. Rabbits, foxes and goats are fortunately absent from most areas, only being encountered on the arid margins in the south. Pigs are occasionally seen but are not as numerous in the Kimberley as in the wetter Arnhem Land environment.

Cattle-grazing in the region has nearly always been conducted as a free-range endeavour, without the aid of fencing. Consequently, wild cattle now roam unmolested in some of the roughest country imaginable. They can be encountered in the most surprising places. From deep in the canyons of the Cockburn Range, to luxuriant rainforest margins on the Mitchell Plateau, feral cattle are unfortunately everywhere. Mustering in such inaccessible terrain is costly and even with the aid of helicopters is often impractical, so the beasts run free. They congregate singularly or in small groups along watercourses, swamps and adjacent grassland. Their trampling and localised grazing can have a severe effect on plant communities. Along the banks of Forest Creek, near the Drysdale River, we witnessed a unique closed-forest community being degraded by cattle; we saw them rubbing against larger trees, and browsing on and trampling the sparse understorey. Feral cattle can also be a threat to Aboriginal rock-art sites, where sheltering beasts use rock walls as scratching posts, rubbing and abrading the painted surfaces.

The donkey, now the major feral pest in the Kimberley, was first used as a pack animal during the Halls Creek goldrush late last century. It is an animal of the perennial tussock grasslands and as such competes directly with cattle for feed. Feral donkeys can gather in large herds of several hundred. The quiet stillness of nights spent anywhere in the grasslands of the Kimberley is often disrupted by the distant, raucous braying of jack donkeys, a harsh note appropriate to the damage done by these beguiling but destructive creatures. Their intense grazing, trampling and domination of water holes leads to considerable pasture loss and erosion. Each year they are shot in their thousands with little effect on total numbers.

The impact of introduced animals, both pastoral and feral, on the native fauna of the

Top left:Young Boab (Adansonia gregorii), *Isdell River.*
Top right: A Euro (Macropus robustus), *ever alert during its afternoon foraging above Bell Creek.*
Left: The Nabarlek (Peradorcas concinna) *was thought to be the smallest of all wallabies until the discovery in 1978 of the Warabi. Casuarina Creek.*
Right: With branches generally bare during the dry season, the Boab bursts into leaf at the start of the rains. Its gourd-like woody fruits may be up to 25 centimetres long and 20 centimetres in diameter.

*The Mertens' Water Monitor (*Varanus mertensi*) is common near pools and lagoons in the Kimberley. It is often seen basking on logs or rocks, easing into the water when disturbed. Solea Falls, Drysdale River.*

Kimberley is not fully known. There are of course the obvious effects of predation by cats on reptiles, amphibians, small mammals and birds. Destruction of riverside habitats by cattle has led to a drastic decline in the distribution of the Purple-crowned Fairy-wren; and the White-browed Robin (*Poecilodryas superciliosa*) has similarly all but vanished from its former common haunts on the Ord and Fitzroy rivers.

However, a more subtle and insidious environmental change throughout the semi-arid and arid parts of Australia, including the Kimberley, has had a profound effect on the survival of a disturbing number of native mammals.

Since the arrival of Europeans and their animals, great demands have been placed on the productive capacity of the Australian continent. In the drier regions, the native fauna is keenly adapted to one of the most marginal environments on earth. The introduction of competing mammals and particularly herbivores has resulted in a critical depletion of the available food for smaller native animals. Stretched to the limits of survival, the grasp of the most affected species on the ecological life-raft has always been tenuous. In many ways the shift of resources away from the native fauna resembles an increase in aridity, which has meant a decrease in the carrying capacity of the environment. Hence the declines and extinctions have been worst in the arid and semi-arid regions.

Research has shown that mammals within a critical weight range have been most besieged. In Western Australia, animals varying from 35 to 4 200 grams have declined in numbers and distribution or have been driven to extinction.[9] Smaller mammals are not so demanding on productivity, and larger species are generally more mobile and able to forage widely. In the Kimberley, species within this weight range, such as the Golden Bandicoot and Brush-tailed Phascogale (*Phascogale tapoatafa*), have disappeared from the arid and semi-arid parts of the region.

Altered fire regimes may also be implicated in species decline. Patchy mosaic-like firing practised by the Aborigines has been replaced by less frequent but more extensive seasonal blazes which have probably restricted localised food supply and refuge for some species.

The wettest parts of the north and north-west Kimberley now seem to be one of the last mainland refuges for a number of species. The area does not support large numbers of introduced animals, and the fragmented, rocky terrain provides ample shelter from fire and predators. The high rainfall ensures adequate productivity. Decline in some species may be happening, however, on the drier margins of the north-west. Observations by Aboriginal elders of the Mowanjum Community suggest that this is starting to occur in parts of their country receiving annual rainfalls around 900 to 1 000 millimetres.[10] This means that the area bounded by Walcott Inlet, Mt Elizabeth and the Drysdale River — less than a quarter of the Kimberley, and a tiny proportion of the State — is the only part of Western Australia so far to escape the impoverishment of its natural environment. A potent reason among many for a concerted conservation effort!

1. In northern Australia, cadjeput applies to members of the *Melaleuca* genus, of which more than 20 species are found in the Kimberley. Cadjeputs are also found in Asia. The name derives from the Dutch *kajoepoetih*, which in turn derives from the Malay *kayu* (wood) + *putih* (white). A number of spellings may be encountered, including cadjeput, cadjebut, cajuput and cajeput.
2. Flocks of Gouldian Finches have unfortunately dwindled across the bird's range in the last 20 years. Once numbering in their thousands, they are now rarely seen in groups of more than a hundred. Changes in the fire regime and the introduction of parasites from domestic aviary populations have been cited as reasons for the decline.
3. Only the male Red-tailed Black-Cockatoo possesses a solid red tail. The female is duller, with a spotted and barred yellow pattern over its body and a yellow orange-barred tail.
4. Adult Great Bowerbirds average nearly 35 centimetres in length.
5. J. Gould, *The Birds of Australia*, London, 1848. Gould was probably the first to use the name Bowerbird to describe this family of birds.
6. The other species encountered in the Kimberley are the Northern Snake-necked Turtle (*Chelodina rugosa*) and the Northern Snapping Turtle (*Elseya dentata*).
7. P.P. King, *Narrative of a Survey of the Intertropical and Western Coasts of Australia*, vol. 1, John Murray, London, 1827, pp. 423–24.
8. The Northern Quoll is thought to have declined in the East and West Kimberley but is still very common in the Northern Kimberley and across northern Australia in general. A. A. Burbidge and N.L. McKenzie, 'Patterns in the modern decline of Western Australia's vertebrate fauna: Causes and conservation implications', *Biological Conservation*, vol. 50, 1989.
9. Ibid.
10. Ibid.

5

Distant lives, distant times: Aboriginal life in the Kimberley before the Europeans

Narrow straits

It is a day like any other. But imagine that 50 000 years still have to pass before Europeans edge along the north-west coast of the Australian continent in their flimsy ships. The shore that they will dream of is for now far from this coast, lying hard against a ragged inland escarpment.

Massive ice sheets cover the world's temperate regions as the planet is gripped by cold. Mean annual temperatures plunge by up to 10 degrees Celsius. Glacial activity is at its greatest in the Northern Hemisphere, with ice accumulating in some locations to depths of two thousand metres and more. As this mantle of ice advances, enormous quantities of water become entrapped, causing sea levels to fall by more than 100 metres from their previous high levels. Coastlines run after the ever-falling tide line as the smallest islands and continents alike take on new and enlarged forms.

In the shallow seas to the north and the north-west of Australia, the retreat of the coast-line is considerable. When sea levels reach their lowest, New Guinea and Tasmania are joined to the Australian mainland in one continuous landmass. In the low-lying north, the Gulf of Carpentaria forms what is possibly the world's largest brackish swamp. Along the north-west, the precipitous bluffs and ramparts that will form much of the future Kimberley shore are part of an almost continuous escarpment set behind the Sahul Shelf, a vast coastal plain that stretches away towards Asia for several hundred kilometres. The coastline is less than 90 kilometres from Timor.

Sundaland, the ancient landmass of continental Asia, incorporates Borneo and Sumatra and reaches as far east as Java. The island chains of the Indonesian Archipelago are linked by land bridges or at most are only separated by short stretches of water. Each is considerably narrower than the straits that will greet the Europeans centuries hence. At no stage is the land bridge complete, but with the extent of open ocean drastically narrowed by falling seas, the prevailing geography is at its most propitious for the first immigrants to make the sea-crossing to 'Greater Australia'.

First immigrants?

As startling as it may seem the continent could conceivably have already welcomed visitors and permanent occupants during previous episodes of favourable geography. Similar declines in sea level had prevailed in the past. Glacial extremes occurred 60 000 and 100 000 years previously, with lesser fluctuations at even earlier times. It is quite conceivable that Australia saw its first human occupants during one of these phases. The genus *Homo* had already been foraging in the savannas of tropical Sundaland as far east as Java for almost two million years. In the course of such an enormous passage of time, countless circumstances must have arisen to precipitate either chance encounters or deliberate forays over the horizon. However, the as yet unanswered question remains: did such early coastal dwellers develop sufficient skills to be able to build suitable water craft for such an uncertain journey?

As intriguing and plausible the possibility of such early occupation of the continent may be, no conclusive evidence has yet been found to support human occupation as far back as 100 000 years before our own time. For the present, the assumption should be made that the first inhabitants arrived sometime near a period of maximum glaciation, approximately 50 000 years ago.[1]

The motives that compelled the progenitors of Australia's original inhabitants to leave supposedly established patterns of existence and venture to shores beyond their known world must unfortunately always remain as issues of conjecture. Some are certain to have arrived accidentally, without any influence over their own fate, hapless castaways swept up by storm, current and tide. Yet others may have been willing participants in one of the very earliest sequences of maritime migration anywhere in the world, responding to the loss of hunting and gathering lands as the ice sheets thawed.

Opposite: Alasdair McGregor, 'To the Isdell' (gouache on paper, 45 x 31 cm).

Bolts of fire

Sea levels rise and fall in the space of years as ice sheets advance and retreat. Land areas expand and populations shift as the seas drop. After newly emerged living space is colonised, the glacial tide turns and the waters return. The colonists are confronted by the rapid and inexorable loss of recently-won ground. Nomadic groups, returning to lowland areas in the course of seasonal movements, find their territory further diminished as each year passes. Dislocation and social stress result. Population pressures mount as economic territory is drowned. Land essential for hunting and gathering is lost, the cause unknown, the outcome distressing and irreversible. This may be the impetus for a besieged population to turn its gaze seaward.

The dry season is nearing its end. Angry thunderstorms roll across the withered tropical savanna without releasing a drop. The prehistoric earth remains arid as much of the world's water is trapped in ice. Fires flare, torched by lightning that cracks to the ground. Billowing plumes of smoke rise high into the sky as the fires rage and die, not yet quenched by the monsoon. They are a signal, a presence from beyond the southern horizon. In time, they may coax the first emigrants to embark upon a perilous one-way journey.

Three routes seem most plausible as possible pathways for the earliest venturers to Australia. From Kalimantan they could move east to Sulawesi and on to north-western New Guinea via a string of narrowly separated islands. Alternatively, they could move from Java to Bali, Lombok, Flores and finally Timor before continuing west or striking south towards the Kimberley. Perhaps all routes are favoured at varying times. But of all the possibilities it is the latter, with a final leg from Timor to the Sahul coast of the Kimberley, that presents the least degree of danger. At times of lowest sea level, it involves only one major sea crossing, the last 80 to 100 kilometres to the northern Australian shore.

Despite the relative narrowness of this last gap, it looms as a major impediment to colonisation. Very few mammal species from the richly endowed ecosystems of Asia have successfully crossed the watery divide. Only mice, rats and bats have so far made the crossing to the continent of the marsupials. Why should humans have any greater success? To them, such a journey on the most rudimentary of water craft must be a daunting prospect indeed. The craft that are used for the crossing are almost as ephemeral as the waves on which they ride. If they are made of bamboo, as is likely, they are strictly one-way craft. They will find that the new shores ahead are not home to such a supply of suitable boat-building materials.

A journey, perhaps prompted by the chase for a plume of smoke on the horizon, must evoke fears as monumental as those that will be felt by European mariners thousands of years later. As the Europeans in turn set out to find the 'new world' over more distant horizons, their terror will be a belief that sailing too far means plunging off the edge of the world itself.

The ancient Kimberley coast lying in wait for the first colonists does not differ greatly from the tropical savanna that will greet the Europeans in northern Australia. The major Kimberley rivers spill out across the flat plain of the Sahul, joining forces before reaching the sea. The Fitzroy, Isdell, Prince Regent and Charnley flow together to the north-west and the Drysdale, King Edward and Mitchell systems join in the north. Further east, the Durack, Pentecost and Ord merge with the Victoria and Fitzmaurice rivers from the Northern Territory. Despite the prevailing arid conditions, the major rivers ensure an adequate supply of permanent water over large parts of the Sahul.

Life on the edge of the Sahul probably follows the patterns of the intensively marine-based existence followed to the north. People who have successfully negotiated the perils of the open sea are well placed to harvest the Sahul shore. As more immigrants arrive and native-born populations increase, communal groups spread out in either direction along the coast. It is probable that the continent is rapidly populated. The new inhabitants scatter around the coastal fringes, perhaps within as little time as 2 000 years. After 10 000 years they have reached the southern coastal margins.[2]

Left: The alien shores of north-west Australia have changed little in appearance since the first immigrants landed some 50 000 or more years ago. Strickland Bay.

Ancient life

So far, only the broadest approximations can be made of the patterns by which the Australian continent was populated. Detailed evidence of occupation movements in the Kimberley is still not available and any record of the very first Kimberley residents has been lying beneath the Timor Sea for many thousands of years.

Just as the occupants of the islands to the north were disrupted by fluctuations in sea level, so the newly arrived generations were disturbed in the Kimberley. As sea levels shifted, severe stress was inflicted on the ecosystems of the coast. Shorelines moved by tens of metres each year and ephemeral supplies of fresh water vanished. In time, some groups gradually abandoned the coast and adapted to a totally land-based life.

The early Kimberley inhabitants were aided in their struggle with the new environment by the discovery of many familiar edible plants, previously associated with their northern origins. The hunting and exploitation of the strange Australian fauna must have required some learning, but by means of the major river valleys and their rich aquatic resources, a rapid and secure occupation of the hinterland was achieved.

The earliest occupation sites so far discovered in the Kimberley are relatively young when compared to those in the south, a paradox perhaps explained by the total obliteration by the sea of those early beginnings. Excavations of a rock shelter on Koolan Island in the Buccaneer Archipelago, by archaeologist Sue O'Connor from the University of Western Australia, have revealed occupation dating back in excess of 27 000 years. So far, this is the oldest archaeological site yet found in the region. Whilst not yet proven, it is quite possible that the shelter was in use 40 000 years ago. Being an off-shore site, albeit in very close proximity to the mainland, its age has added significance in extending proof of the very early occupation of the Kimberley coast.[3]

Examination of the material excavated from the Koolan Island shelter revealed that the occupants enjoyed a rich and diverse marine diet, augmented at various stages with terrestrial and freshwater fauna. Shifts in the composition of the diet point to changes in the surrounding environment as the climate changed and sea levels fluctuated.

In the eastern Kimberley, archaeologist Charles Dortch of the Western Australian Museum excavated a site known as Miriwun.[4] Located in the valley of the Ord River, it was inundated by the construction of Lake Argyle. His investigations revealed that the site was occupied in the period between 18 000 years ago and the advent of Europeans. The Miriwun occupants left a record of a bountiful life that fully exploited the resources of the riverine environment. Their diet included a range of marsupials, rodents, lizards and snakes as well as a rich aquatic fare of turtles, fish, crocodiles and molluscs. Magpie geese were an important food source. Large quantities of their egg shells amongst the deposit indicate wet-season concentrations at the shelter, when groups gathered to exploit the breeding birds.

The Kimberley, successfully occupied, provided all the necessities of life with a fair degree of seasonal certainty. Admittedly these necessities were not always readily won but the prevailing environment was sufficiently easy to allow a culture and technology of considerable sophistication to develop. Rather than a matter of mere survival, much of life remained for the exploration of mythology, ritual, art and meaning.

Australia in pre-European times, unlike New Guinea and Asia, was never the setting for agriculture involving the intensive planting of crops or husbanding of animals. Most of the indigenous plants and animals found throughout the continent would not have been suitable. Australian Aborigines, perhaps by deliberate decision, stuck to the life of the hunter–gatherer and as a result their traditional life, particularly in the Kimberley and the rest of the north, was very much influenced and constrained by the cycle of the seasons. In northern Australia, Aborigines identified and responded to a complex sequence of seasonal change, not just the 'wet' and the 'dry' recognised by Europeans. The people of Kalumburu in the northern Kimberley, for instance, recognised seven distinct seasons.[5]

Right, top: Fluctuating sea levels washing long-vanished islands and shorelines sealed the fate of the unknown first colonists. Fletcher Islands, Collier Bay.
Right: The many rivers of the Kimberley eased a path for permanent occupation of the region. The Roe River as it enters Prince Frederick Harbour.

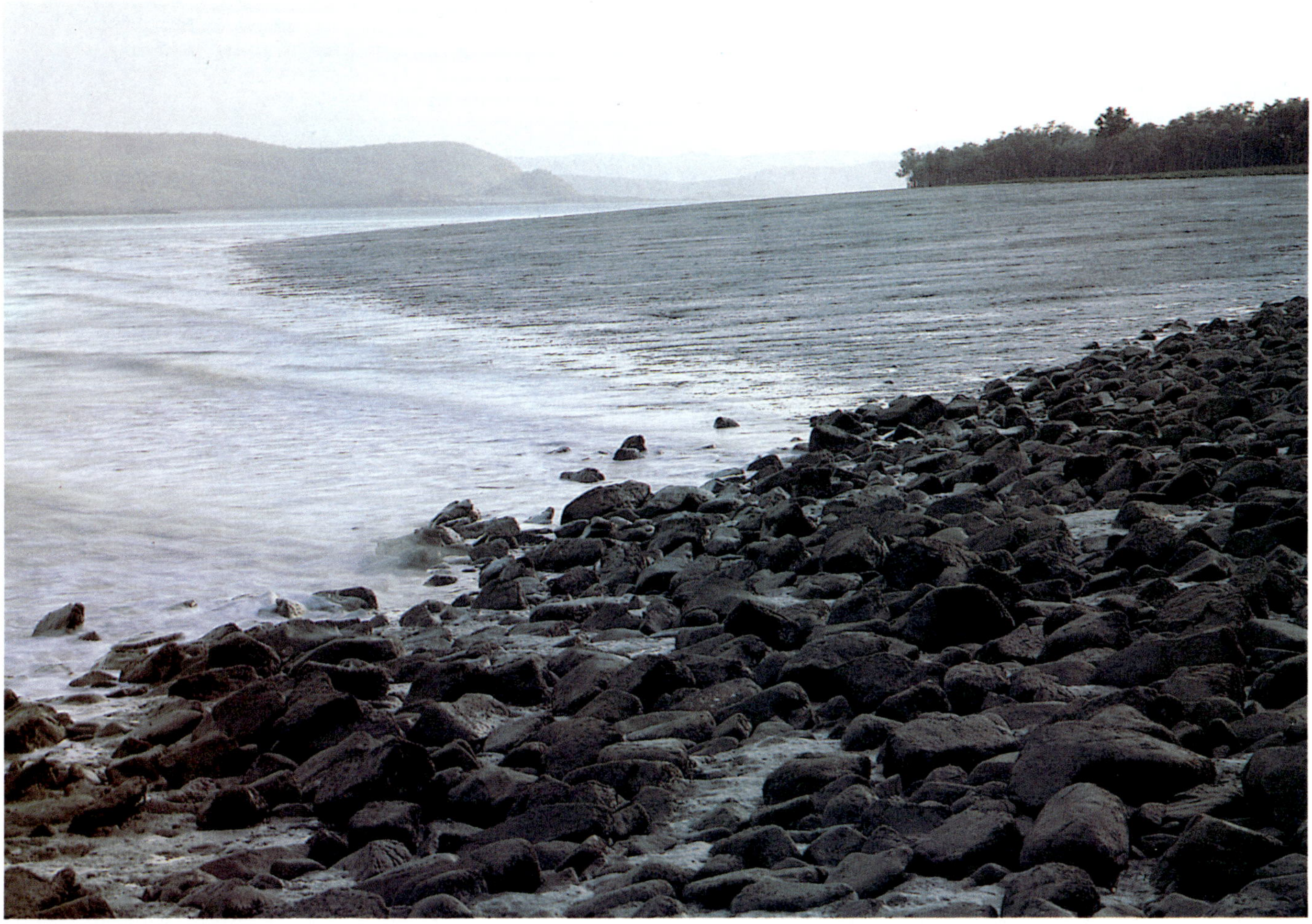

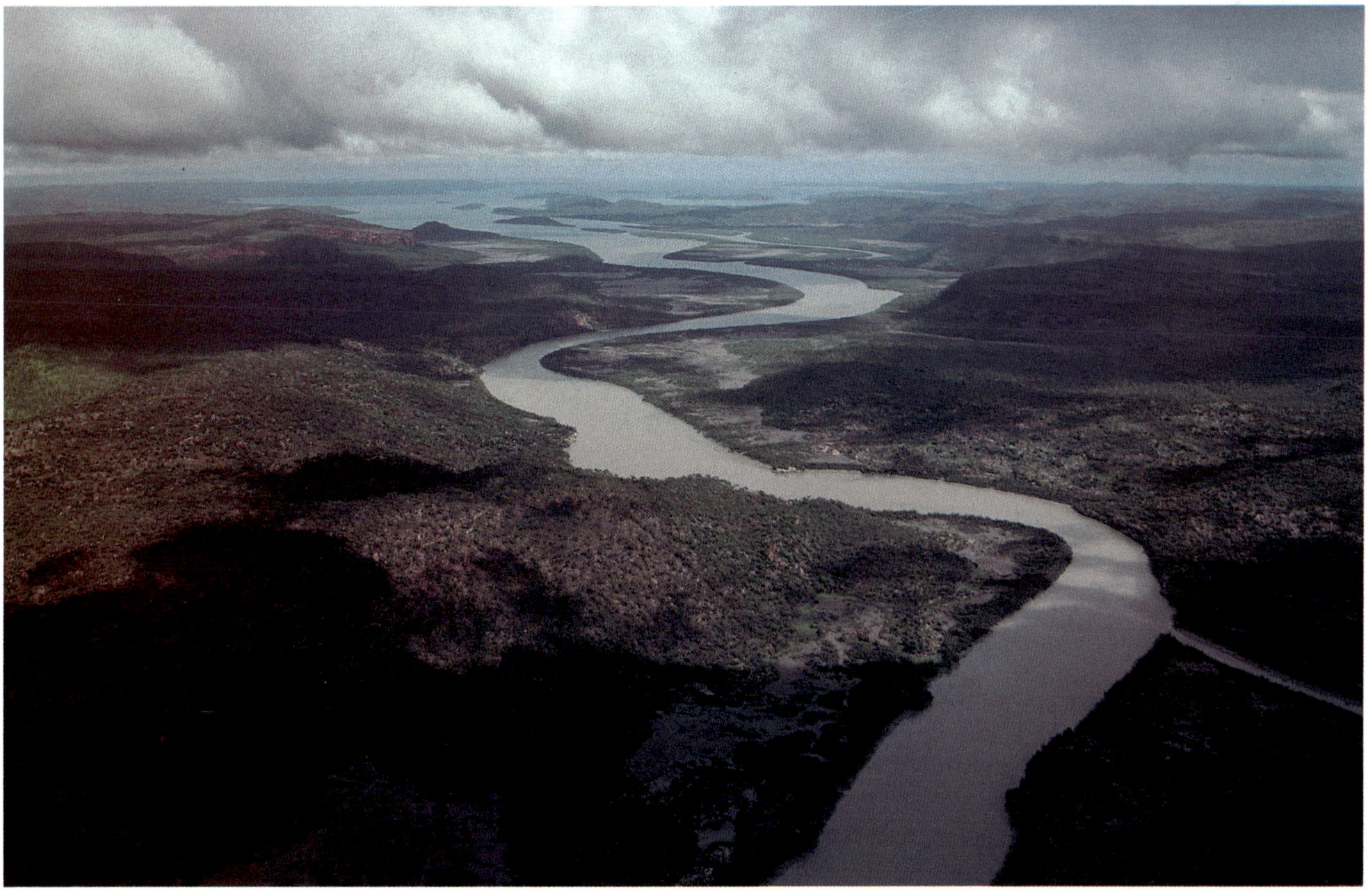

Left: Cumulus clouds gather behind the distinctive Northern Cypress (Callitris intratropica) as the Wandjinas bring on the rains.

Top: Rock art of great power and impact is found throughout the Kimberley — the heritage of a people who lived far beyond the level of mere survival. Panda-Goornya, Drysdale River.

Above: The rivers flood as the wet season takes hold. Mitchell Falls in early February.

Following the seasons

From late October to early December saturating humidity builds as temperatures soar to their annual extremes. Dry storms encircle the afternoon horizon as violent wind gusts fling dust and debris high into the air. The night sky is spiked by random pulses from the distant arc of dozens of lightning strikes. Fires flare and the atmosphere thickens with smoke. As gushing waterfalls dwindle to a trickle, then finally spill their last, the remains of the seasonal billabongs turn to mud, then dry out and crack.

Moving in from the north west, the billowing white masses of the first clouds of the monsoon appear. The cloud spirits, the omnipotent Wandjinas, bringers of plenty as well as destruction, hurl lightning, then torrential rain down on the land. Rivers surge and flood as the earth turns green. The rains continue unabated, inundating the landscape and forcing the people to vacate their riverside camps. They move to higher ground, seeking refuge under rock overhangs or beneath the cover of paperbark shelters. In areas such as the Mitchell Plateau and the Montgomery Islands stone-walled structures with paperbark or spinifex roofing are built as protection from the frequent downpours.[6]

John Lort Stokes, while exploring the west Kimberley coast in 1838 aboard HMS *Beagle*, found substantial five metre high structures on Bathurst Island that he assumed were wet-season shelters:

> … here we found several native habitations of a totally different and very superior description to any we had hitherto seen in any part of Australia; they bore a marked resemblance to those I had seen on the S.E. coast of Tierra del Fuego … Stout poles from 14 to 16 feet high formed the frame to these snug huts — for so indeed they deserve to be termed — these were brought together conically at the roof; a stout thatching of dried grass completely excluded both wind and rain, and seemed to bespeak the existence of a climate at times much more severe than a latitude of 16° 6' south would lead one to anticipate.[7]

George Grey also described Aboriginal huts, this time in the vicinity of the Prince Regent River: 'Their huts of which I only saw those on the sea coast, are constructed in an oval form, of the boughs of trees, and are roofed with dry reeds. The diameter of one which I measured, was about fourteen feet at the base.'[8]

January and February, the time of greatest rains, are poor months for food collection. The waterlogged ground restricts mobility. Hunting, the main source of food at this time, is impossible in heavy rain. Gathering of plant foods is similarly restricted, and the supply of root crops is meagre, due to the immaturity of the new season's growth. Fires prove difficult to keep alight and living conditions can be cold and uncomfortable. General health declines as wounds refuse to heal and rheumatism grips after wet nights on sodden ground.

Along the coast conditions are generally better. Food stocks hold out with little change in the availability of marine resources throughout the year. The rains mean that the rich but normally dry off-shore islands and their surrounding reefs can be visited. An ample supply of fresh water is assured. Some groups move from the hinterland to join their coastal relatives during the poorest and wettest months. Coastal and island peoples generally lead a more sedentary life than their inland neighbours. They move short distances to more comfortable campsites, often to avoid plagues of sandflies and mosquitoes that infest sandy areas and mangroves during the wet.

By April the rains have eased to an occasional storm and the valleys are reoccupied. 'Everything is ripening' say the people of Kalumburu. It is a time to exploit the root crops that are fast maturing in areas of sandy, well-drained soils. This is a task performed by women. As the country dries they are able to work closer and closer to the crops of the alluvial plains, creeks and river banks.

The Reverend J.R.B. Love, an early observer of Kimberley Aborigines, spent time amongst the Wororra people of the north-west and recorded much of their daily life in great detail. He describes the activities of Wororra women:

> They leave camp early each morning, each carrying her 'ungum' (a shallow canoe-shaped bark dish) and 'wondoon' (digging stick). They return usually in mid-afternoon, when the wives go to their respective husbands and cook and share the food gathered …
>
> The finest of the roots is a kind of yam known as 'karja'. This is in season in March and

is the root of a climbing vine. The root is about the size of a man's arm. It is soft and milky when raw, but when baked in the ashes it becomes floury like a potato, and is excellent eating ... Some of the roots are very woody, some very hot to the taste, and the most attractive looking of all (a brown potato-like root, shaped like a Brazil nut) is very bitter.

The women will frequently make a several days' expedition away from the main camp, gathering and cooking roots as they go. Finally they return to camp with several days' supply, when all lie idle till the food is consumed.[9]

The grass is fired to ease access and to press the hunt. The men only hunt large game or spear fish, turtles and Dugongs on the coast. Love describes the hunt of the Wororra people:

A number of men, all that may be in one camp at the time, will surround a hill, set fire to the grass round its base, and wait for the kangaroos to fly from the fires along the gullies, where, at likely places, are posted men armed with spears and spear-throwers. In these fire hunts the kangaroo is speared on the run. A party of twenty men will get as many as half a dozen kangaroos in a day's burning of one hill.

The fire drive may also be communal, with women and children herding kangaroos, euros and wallabies towards the waiting finality of the men's spears. All other food is gathered by women, the men being preoccupied with matters of myth, ritual and ceremony. Love remarked:

Wororra women set out cheerfully, with no breakfast, to find what food the day's hunting may bring forth. Not till they have found something to eat, dug it out of the ground, caught it with the dogs, or chopped it from a hollow tree, will they break their fast; and, on three days out of four, the men will not eat till their wives return in the evening with the day's collection.

Despite the picture that Love paints, the men's contribution to the communal fare is at times critical. When general food stocks are low, their quarry from the hunt may be the only

Omei Purgo, the champion spear thrower in action.' Drysdale River Mission, Pago, c.1920.

barrier against hunger. Besides root crops, the women collect a wide variety of fruits and with the aid of Dingoes, hunt for small game and anything larger they can catch. They also gather native honey, a prized delicacy.

In the months from May to August, temperatures drop to pleasant levels and on the Kimberley Plateau the nights are cold. Food is relatively plentiful and there is time for communal gatherings, trade, marriage and ceremony. Swift-flowing rivers shrink to a string of torpid pools as clear warm days follow each other with absolute predicability. Plant poisons are added to the pools to kill fish. In the Kalumburu region as many as six fish poisons are used, some being effective in both fresh and salt water. The warm shallow waters of the continuing dry months are littered with a variety of waterlilies. Prominent among them is the magnificent *Nymphaea gigantica* with its large blue-mauve flowers strewn across idyllic billabongs. Women gather the tubers and edible stems of these and other lilies. The tubers are roasted or in some cases baked, then pounded to flour from which cakes are then made and cooked in the ashes.

Through September and into October the grip of the dry tightens. Populations contract to the very edges of permanent water. As the heat builds, foraging becomes harder. Tubers are increasingly difficult to locate in places already tilled. Fires have now scorched large areas, destroying foliage and any clues of the root crops beneath the ground. Those that are found are often shrivelled and of diminished value.

In the distance, the rumble of muted thunder rolls over the November landscape as the men sing for the rains, supplicating the Wandjinas, the bringers of storms, to send the great clouds in from the sea, to renew life and rejuvenate the people.

Population and plenty

Despite the diversity and richness of Kimberley food stocks and the undoubted ability of the people to eke out an existence, shortages did occur. In bad seasons when the rains were late or poor, considerable stress could be placed on food resources. The Kimberley storehouse was not of unlimited capacity. The quality of the wet season could vary across the region as a whole, but generally hardships endured by one group would also be suffered by the next. Moving to another group's territory would not have been of any advantage unless it involved shifting to an ecologically different location. And then there was the constraint of distinctly defined territorial boundaries to be negotiated.

The pre-European Aboriginal population of the Kimberley is estimated to have been about 10 000 and was divided into about 30 'tribes'.[10] Each tribe occupied an area of continuous territory and spoke its own language. There were between 20 and 50 languages traditionally spoken in the Kimberley in at least six interrelated language families, of uncertain relationship one to another. Each language family linked several connected tribes.[11]

Patterns of familial, clan and tribal association in the pre-European Kimberley were as astoundingly complex as in any Aboriginal society. This complexity was reflected in the large number of tribes for a relatively small area and the diversity of social organisation and kinship patterns found across the region. Within the tribe, small bands formed the basic functioning unit of everyday life. The size of a band of people and the territory they occupied was closely related to the ability of the territory itself to sustain them. In fertile areas of northern Australia, bands averaged 25 to 50 people with smaller numbers in dry zones. The extent of territories varied according to the geography and relative abundance of resources within that area. The more fertile the area, the less nomadic were its inhabitants. The Bardi people of the Dampier Peninsula for instance, were content to lead an almost sedentary life reliant on the harvest of abundant marine resources occurring within their territory. In the Kalumburu region, territories known as 'gras' were upwards of 65 000 hectares and represented the normal foraging range of the band.[12]

Bands formed the economic basis of the society and were flexible in their membership but all contained a core of related clansmen who shared a responsibility for the clan's estate.

The Wororra and the neighbouring Ngarinyin people maintained a social organisation that had shared features with much of the Kimberley and many tribal groups outside the

Above: Magpie Geese (Anseranas semipalmata), an important Aboriginal foodsource across the wetlands of northern Australia. Right: The living environment, Drysdale River.

region. In this area as elsewhere, the custodianship of land was vested in the clans. Clan estates were usually clearly defined by geographical features such as ridges, creeks, rivers or shorelines. To ensure cordial relationships between neighbouring groups, clan links were cemented: in kinship, ritual and ceremony. Disputes did not occur over territory, as each clan acted as a trustee rather than an owner. Conquest was unknown.

Under extremely complex kinship rules that had the effect of maximising ties between the entire tribe, men always married outside their own clan. In addition, daughters were given in marriage by their fathers to clans other than those from which the men took their own wives. Ties through kinship were used to facilitate the formalised entry to another clan's territory. For instance, in the wet, a time of depleted resources for inland groups, visits to coastal areas meant a chance to share in the seasonally consistent marine resources with relatives from the same clan living on the coast. Entry to another clan estate had to be signalled and was not permitted whilst the men of the clan were absent.

A vital function of the clan system was the custodianship of mythology and belief. Each clan estate was home to spirit places where men 'dreamt the spirit' of the unborn child. In addition, the estate's central focus was on its Wandjina site where the great mythological heroes and associated animals and plants were depicted as clan totems. Each clan relied on the next to retouch the paintings at the other's site. This was meant to ensure the bounty of supply of a variety of species not necessary depicted in any one clan's paintings. The Wandjinas themselves performed acts of creation within each estate, changing the physical features of the surrounds in their movements across the landscape in the time of the Dreaming.

Transcending the division of the tribe into clans was its simultaneous division into two distinct halves known as moieties. Each clan belonged to one of the moieties and consequently identified with that moiety's unique array of totemic animals and mythological stories. For instance the two Wororra moieties each held to three pairs of animal heroes. On one side, the Arbulari moiety was connected with 'Arura', the Euro or Hill Kangaroo and on the other, the Arungari moiety associated with 'Wangalina', the Antelopean or Red Kangaroo. Clans of neighbouring tribes belonged to the same moieties, enabling inter-tribal relations to be forged in a complex exchange network. This network was called the 'wunan' in the west Kimberley and 'winan' in the east. Just as women, tradable goods, foodstuffs and ritual objects were exchanged between clans, so too were they distributed via the moiety system further afield. Pearl shell for instance, travelled from the coast to the desert, whilst boomerangs from the south ended up as ceremonial clapsticks in the north, far outside their utilitarian range. The exchange of women between moieties had the effect of creating long chains of familial contact and enabled formalised movement and interaction over large areas.

Marriage into the same moiety was strictly forbidden. A man's wife had to come from a clan of the opposing moiety. As if to formally reinforce the point, certain related members of the tribe belonging to the same moiety were not even allowed to look at each other or utter the other's name. In a series of taboos known as 'rumburrb' to the Wororra, a man shunned his mother-in-law, her brothers and sisters, and was banned from contact with his mother's brother's wife. The formalised spurning was reciprocated by the other party.

Through this and all the other complex kinship and spatial controls of clan and tribal interactions, movement was formalised, resources were spread and conflict was minimised. But in the confines of such a tight system, aberrations were bound to occur. Egregious behaviour did happen and social mores were flouted. Young men were denied wives whereas older men may have had several. Whilst part of the perpetuation of a social hierarchy, with the additional benefit of curbing population growth, the denial of women to young men led to inevitable tensions. In frustration and resentment they were naturally inclined to steal the women of the older men. Retribution could be swift, unwavering and brutal. Women were themselves the frequent victims of brutality and sometimes murder.

To ensure that each group lived in as balanced and cohesive relationship as possible with its neighbours and within its own confines, population-control measures were adopted. The availability of food resources had some effect on population numbers, but active and passive measures were also adopted. Foeticide and infanticide were both widely practised

Top: Fire, a potent force for survival and environmental modification, Mitchell Plateau.
Above: After the first rains, the country comes alive with new growth. Mitchell Plateau.

when family numbers grew too large. In times of extreme food stress the old and infirm might be left to die.

Population control also occurred by attrition. Skirmishes between neighbouring tribes were a frequent event. They were not concerned with land, conquest or material possessions and were often incited by seemingly minor or obscure circumstances. For fear of being speared by a neighbour, tribal boundaries were carefully observed. Love made the following observations:

> When a man is killed by an enemy the slayer flees to a remote district of his own tribe to escape retributive justice. The fear of the Wororra is that he will be speared by a Ngarinyin when out hunting alone, and, in fact, in each recently reported case of death by violence … it was alleged that he was speared by a man of this tribe.

And so a fine but tenuous balance was struck between population and plenty as a complete system of survival and social organisation was interwoven with the land and its naturally occurring resources.

It is probable that agriculture, widely practised in Asia and New Guinea more than 5 000 years ago, was never countenanced as an option for subsistence in Australia. Yet the food resource of the two regions overlapped. A number of the plants that thrive under reliable rains in the gardens to the north also occur in Australia and were part of the Aboriginal diet. But in the markedly seasonal and rather unreliable summer monsoon climate of northern Australia, their agricultural potential would be much diminished. Additionally, most of the indigenous plants and animals found throughout the continent are inherently unsuitable for adaptation to the agrarian life.[13]

With the relative abundance and variety of naturally occurring foods in northern Australia, there was no incentive to increase production by increasing effort (agriculture involving a cost in time and exertion). Pressures on food resources could be more efficiently controlled by remaining mobile or regulating population numbers to suit the carrying capacity of the land. It cannot be determined with certainty that Aboriginal people persisted with the hunter–gatherer existence by choice but if they did, it seems to have been a decision backed by an innate collective logic and understanding of the land.

The corporeal and the spiritual

The assurance of survival, despite seasonal food shortages, is not the onerous and all-consuming task that a superficial observation might indicate. An appropriate degree of effort was expended on survival: for the women an average of about five hours each day, and for the men considerably less. Ample opportunity remained for attention to matters transcendental rather than the temporal. There was time for dance and time for song. Stories were told, recounted and developed — stories that were old, thousands of years past. The crucial times of life, initiation and death were attended by ceremony and ritual. Bodies were painted, incised with ritual scars and decorated with feathers and fur. Magic and the great themes of creation were given their place in ritual sites where spectacular paintings adorned rock walls and ceilings.

Just as the art, ritual and ceremony of the Kimberley evince a vibrant and complex society far from being preoccupied with mere survival, the material culture of pre-European Aborigines in the Kimberley shows considerable technological development and sophistication, well suited to the tasks of everyday life. Many of the items are unique to the region. Distinctive stone spear-heads (known as Kimberley points), jointed bamboo and hardwood spears, carefully made bark coolamons and buckets, and substantial double wooden rafts were all part of Kimberley technology.

Stokes described a raft found on an island in the Buccaneer Archipelago:

> It was formed of nine small poles pegged together, and measured ten feet in length by four in breadth; the greatest diameter of the largest pole was three inches. All the poles were of the palm tree, a wood so light, that one man could carry the whole affair with the greatest of ease.[14]

The potent Wandjinas, life force of the Kimberley. Munuro, King Edward River.

Dancing. Drysdale River Mission, Pago, c.1920.

In the region between King Sound and the Prince Regent River a craft known to the Wororra as the 'kahlua' was made from a pair of rafts like those described by Stokes. Two separate rafts were dragged into the water. One was placed over the other, lapping at the centre, with the tapering ends facing inwards. No attempt was made to lash the two halves together; their combined weight and buoyancy was relied upon to keep the craft together.

North of the Prince Regent River a dugout canoe was employed by coastal dwellers. A more mobile and speedy craft than the log rafts, it was introduced to the region at some time before the end of the eighteenth century by fishermen from Makassar in Sulawesi. Along the north coast the dugout canoe was used to travel considerably longer distances than was possible on log rafts. Voyages of nearly 40 kilometres were made across Admiralty Gulf from Cape Bougainville, via the Institut Islands to Cape Voltaire. Similar distances to the north of Cape Voltaire, Cassini Island and Long Reef were also frequently travelled.

The distinctive Kimberley points represent the acme of stone-tool technology in the region. They are amongst the finest implements made anywhere in Australia. Love described their manufacture in the hands of Wororra men:

> The Wororra man when travelling always keeps his eyes open for conveniently-sized bits of stone, which he will take and use in making spearheads at his leisure. A suitable piece is held in one hand, and with a stone held in the other hand it is roughly knocked into a shape approaching the finished design. After this first stage three special implements are used, a roughly pointed stick known as 'kurrinjulp', then the ulna of a kangaroo, and finally a small bone of a kangaroo. In the second and two succeeding stages of manufacture the spearhead is held obliquely and on edge upon a piece of paper-bark placed on a large stone. With the kurrinjulp, flakes are now broken away from the edges of the spearhead by pressure. As the spearhead begins to assume the desired shape the 'choormba' or ulna of kangaroo replaces the kurrinjulp, until the stone is worked into the final leaf shape, when the small kangaroo bone is used for chipping out the serrations along the edges of the spearhead, completing its manufacture … The entire process of making a spearhead takes about half an hour. Each spearhead can only be thrown once, as the point is broken very easily, consequently spearhead-making is the most constant employment of the men.[15]

Such finely worked implements were probably first manufactured in northern Australia somewhere between 4 500 and 3 000 years ago. They are very different in size and refinement from earlier implements found throughout the continent. The Dingo is also thought to have

110

Above: Elaborately adorned figures, evidence of an ancient people and a sophisticated culture. Bradshaw figures, Drysdale River.

Right: A living shelter used after European occupation of the Kimberley. Stone spear-heads have been replaced by steel. The baler shell was used to carry water. (In some parts of Australia the baler shell was also an important item of trade.) Drysdale River.

arrived in Australia at a similar time. A radical shift in technology and the simultaneous arrival of an Asian animal befriended by humans, suggests that these new items in the Australian 'stone tool-kit' may have been part of the baggage carried by a fresh wave of immigrants from the north.

After the arrival of Europeans, glass and ceramics obtained from the insulators of telegraph lines provided very desirable raw materials for the manufacture of Kimberley points. At their finest, Kimberley points became more than just weapons. They are true works of art and were valued for more than their utilitarian purpose. As items of trade, they were exchanged far outside the region. In the desert they were used as surgical implements in the ritual circumcision of young men.

Alien worlds

Across the millennia Aboriginal people of the Kimberley evolved a complex life and culture, totally integrated with the land and its resources. Across the continent, the people of other regions similarly developed, adapting to the necessities of their own surrounds in like manner. Australia moulded its first inhabitants, and they in turn, did much to change the nature of the place to suit their own ends. The evolution of the continent and its people occurred in virtual isolation. Except for the gradual and widely spaced infusion of further immigrants from the north, as and when the geography of the region permitted, Australia was left alone for almost all of its monumentally expansive history.

The first sustained contact with outsiders undoubtedly occurred with the voyages of the Makassans. By the end of the eighteenth century at the latest, they were making annual visits in the wet season to the northern Australian coast. From the Gulf of Carpenteria to the Kimberley, as far south as the Lacepede Islands, they came in search of trochus and pearl shells and bêche-de-mer (trepang or sea cucumber).

Visits by stray fishing boats may have been occurring for centuries but were now overwhelmed by organised expeditions. As many as 200 sailing prahus, each with a crew of 30 or 40 men, probably made the annual crossing to Arnhem Land and the Kimberley. The Makassans set up camps along the Kimberley coast, favouring off-shore islands or promontories for ease of defence. Here they processed the bêche-de-mer: boiling, smoking and drying this prized delicacy for export via their home ports to the markets of China. The coastal people were impressed by the Makassans' dugout canoes, which they coveted and inevitably stole. Aboriginal women in turn were no doubt abducted by the Makassans. Retribution from both sides followed and hostility amongst the Aborigines to the outsiders grew. The Makassans fortified their encampments and only dared venture to the Kimberley coast in sizable groups. Interracial conflict with outsiders, the tragic mark of the centuries to come, had commenced in the Kimberley.

But it was the inexorable proliferation of contact and conflict with Europeans, starting as a trickle and growing to a devastating flood, that was to change fatally Aboriginal life in the Kimberley for ever. In the space of barely a century, 50 000 years of gradual and continuous evolution was supplanted, as if in the passing of one tumultuous day, by a body blow of calamity and confrontation, disease and death.

In 1688, William Dampier, one of the first Europeans to encounter Aboriginal people, made a revealing and well-known observation regarding the inhabitants of the peninsula that was later to bear his name. He described the Aborigines there as the 'miserablest people in the world'.[16] His somewhat disdainful remark typifies the European view of Aborigines that has pervaded non-Aboriginal attitudes ever since. In its seventeenth-century sense, 'miserable' did not suggest sadness or unhappiness but was more likely to mean wretched, poor, pathetic or unfortunate. Dampier made his assessment in the confined context and knowledge of his own age and culture but it was a response backed by a belief that placed value in the tangible above all else. The opinion he formed of the land was sour, and his response to its people was equally so. Dampier saw a people doomed to roam an impoverished land without the benefit of crops, domestic animals or any of the comforts of his own world. He, and the other Europeans that followed, could not see lives that were carefully attuned to the seasons and the dictates of the land. The most easeful path to a sustaining, stable and ultimately fulfilling life was totally obscured from the European eye. The two cultures lacked any common ground. They were, each to the other, from an utterly alien world.

All has changed, changed utterly

North of Kalumburu, the fanciful shapes of sandstone outliers scatter across broad expanses of open sandy woodland. Viewed from atop one of these casual stone sculptures, the sparsely wooded plains stretch out in gentle repose towards the coast in the north and a low range of hills to the east. We pause to reflect and appreciate our surrounds in the company of Father Anscar McPhee from the Kalumburu Mission. Father Anscar's infectious enthusiasm for the landscape and life of the place knows no bounds. He talks of the old people of the Kalumburu Community with great love and affection; people like Mary Pandalo, the gentle matriarch amongst all the women. Mary claims to be the first child born at the original Mission at Pago, 30 kilometres north of Kalumburu. She spent much of her childhood in the bush, living the traditional way. Her knowledge of bush foods and the old life has been vital to the research of noted anthropologist Dr Ian Crawford, and she has been a central figure in more than one doctoral thesis. We had met Mary briefly on our visits to Kalumburu. Now an old woman, she had captivated us at every meeting with her friendliness, dignity and quiet strength; a strength no doubt indebted to her past.

We descend from our vantage point, scrambling through the charred remnants of dry-season fires, to a group of teetering boulders. Under a shallow rock overhang, Father Anscar points out a group of barely discernible rock paintings of unknown age. Anscar's ebullience for the present is matched by his fascination with the past. We discuss the paintings with gusto, speculating as to their origins, their meanings and the imperceptible links between ancient times and the more recent past. Whilst enjoying the paintings, we discuss our first visit to the Kimberley four years earlier. A dull feeling of unease, first felt at that time, returns. In the course of that earlier sojourn, our reaction to the landscape and rock art of the region had forced us to contemplate the completeness of this world in pre-European times. The recurring unease now reflects a growing comprehension of what has happened since that time. The land now seems somehow undone; the whole has been unravelled, its reconstruction insoluble. The traditional life has faded, confined now to the memory of a dwindling handful of old people like Mary Pandalo.

Father Anscar went on to talk of the courage and tenacity of the Benedictine monks who founded the original Drysdale River Mission at Pago in 1908. Not only did this handful of committed men endure the hostility of the Kimberley landscape, they also confronted the defiance of Aboriginal spears. Father Anscar related to us how the monks were attacked on several occasions, with one of their brethren, Father Alcalde, seriously wounded in a melee with over a hundred Aborigines in 1913.

Father Anscar's words brought back thoughts of another time in the Kimberley, just seven months past. We had spent that June day in the Kalumburu environs with Robert Unghango, one of the senior men of the Community. In the course of our wanderings, Robert had told us stories of Pago and the new Mission at Kalumburu. He told us of his times spent roaming the country in search of 'bush tucker'. He talked of the tumultuous days of World War II and how the people had returned for a time to live in the bush after the Japanese strafed the Mission in 1943. Near the end of the day, Robert said, 'Bad man from Drysdale, he shoot many of us. Lots. There were three, four heaps of people. A bad man.' Robert was talking of the killing of the people that occurred before his time, when white men with cattle came to the north in search of land and pasture for their beasts.

As the conversation with Father Anscar concluded, sombre thoughts crowded in: thoughts of the shadowed and sinister times that must have surrounded the massacres and similar undocumented events. Equilibrium was so abruptly replaced by tumult. In contrast to the spirit of others, the monks had come with peaceful intentions but for a while at Pago had

114

been hapless victims, caught on the edge of hostilities, close to the dark and tragic episodes that were unfolding across the Kimberley and throughout Australia.

All has changed, changed utterly.

1. It is interesting to note that Aborigines often state that their people have always been here. The oldest occupation evidence so far obtained in Australia is thought to derive from the Malakunanja II site in Arnhem Land. Dates of 45 000 +/– 9 000 years and 52 000 +/– 11 000 years were obtained using a technique known as thermoluminescence. The findings purport to indicate occupation in excess of 50 000 years but are still the subject of considerable debate amongst the archaeological community. R.G. Roberts, R. Jones and M.A. Smith, 'Thermoluminescence dating of a 50 000-year-old human occupation site in northern Australia', *Nature*, vol. 345, 1990. See also P. Hiscock, 'How old are the artifacts in Malakunanja II?', *Archaeology in Oceania*, no. 25, 1990.

2. Occupation dates of 40 000 B.P. have been obtained at Upper Swan near Perth and the Cranebrook Terrace near the Nepean River west of Sydney. M. Barbetti and R.H. Pearce, 'A 38 000-year-old site at Upper Swan, Western Australia', *Archaeology in Oceania*, no. 16, 1981; G.C. Nanson *et al.*, 'Chronology and palaeoenvironment of the Cranebrook Terrace (near Sydney) containing artifacts more than 40 000 years old', *Archaeology in Oceania*, no. 22, 1987.

3. S. O'Connor, 'New radiocarbon dates from Koolan Island, West Kimberley, WA', *Australian Archaeology*, no. 28, June 1989.

4. C.E. Dortch, 'Archaeological work in the Ord Reservoir area, East Kimberley', *Australian Institute of Aboriginal Studies Newsletter*, vol. 3(4), 1972.

5. I.M. Crawford, 'Traditional Aboriginal plant resources in the Kalumburu area: Aspects in ethno-economics', *Records of the Western Australian Museum*, supplement no. 15, Perth, 1982.

6. S. O'Connor, 'The stone house structures of High Cliffy Island north-west Kimberley, WA', *Australian Archaeology*, no. 25, December 1987.

7. J.L. Stokes, *Discoveries in Australia*, vol. 1, pp. 172–3.

8. G. Grey, *Expeditions in Western Australia 1837–1839*, vol. 1, p. 253.

9. J.R.B. Love, 'Notes on the Wororra tribe of north-western Australia', *Transactions of the Royal Society of South Australia*, vol. 41, 1917, p. 32. As a Presbyterian missionary for 17 years in the north-west Kimberley early this century, the Reverend J.R.B. (Bob) Love recorded detailed and insightful observations of Aboriginal life and custom in the region. His book *Stone Age Bushmen of Today* (Blackie, London, 1936) is a priceless collection of knowledge of Kimberley Aboriginal society shortly after first contact with Europeans. Love's time was spent at Kunmunya near Port George IV amongst the Wororra people. The Wororra's territory stretched from the Prince Regent River and Hanover Bay, south to Doubtful Bay, George Water and the Glenelg River, and east as far as Mt Lyell. Wild and wonderful country indeed!

10. A.P. Elkin, 'Social organisation in the Kimberley division north-western Australia', *Oceania*, vol. 2, no. 3, 1932. Elkin notes that it was remarkable to find so many tribes in such a comparatively small area as the Kimberley. For instance, according to Love, the Wororra people of the north-west numbered approximately three hundred tribe members and occupied a territory of roughly 500 000 hectares.

11. W.B. McGregor, 'The Kimberley Language Resource Centre', *Australian Aboriginal Studies*, no. 2, 1985.

12. Crawford, op. cit.

13. It is interesting to note that both Love and Grey comment on the edible grains occurring in Wororra territory. Grey is convinced of their agricultural potential: '... on an elevated basaltic ridge, ... there was a large crop of grain which we called wild oats ... When hungry, I have repeatedly eaten these oats, which in some parts grow in such abundance that several acres might be mown at once; and I have no doubt that this plant would, with cultivation, turn out to be a very great addition to our tropical grains' (op. cit., p. 197). Love is puzzled: 'A very remarkable peculiarity of the Wororra is that they do not gather any grass seeds for food. In most parts of Australia grass seeds constitute a very considerable part of the food supply ... The country of the Wororra is particularly well provided with grass seeds, some of which are as large as oats and densely abundant ... Yet the Wororra do not use this food' (*Stone Age Bushmen of Today*, p .77).

14. Stokes, op. cit, p. 112.

15. Love, 'Notes on the Wororra tribe', p. 25.

16. W. Dampier, *A New Voyage Round the World*, vol. 1, 1697.

Opposite: An ancient Bradshaw figure high above the Drysdale River seems to hover enigmatically over the entire Kimberley.

6

Shadows on stone:
Kimberley rock art

Enigmatic marks

As we stumble off the Carson Escarpment and down through the regrowth of last year's fires, the lanky stems and grotesquely large grey-green leaves of the Elephant-ear Wattle crash and rattle with our every footfall. Descending to a tangled gully of vines and stained black boulders, dry since the flash floods of the previous wet, we come to a huge rock in midstream. Though leaning downhill alarmingly, it has not shifted in thousands of years. Its tilt protects an ancient secret: facing the river several hundred metres below, a small, painted symbol barely discernible on the rockface. It remains only as a bleached stain under the angle of the boulder's protection. Roughly circular, with six short arms, its enigmatic simplicity hides from us any sense of meaning.

First encounters such as this with painted images from a long-distant antiquity are, for most, a compelling experience. For us, the Kimberley provides the experience in abundant measure. Those meetings and their recollection will always remain as privileged opportunities, seized as fragmentary but valued insights into a world so absolutely different from our own.

We scan the irregular walls and rough ceilings of the long-inhabited rock shelters lying close to the river. Where did the human hand end and nature begin? A jumble of faded marks and the occasional distinct painting cover most of the walls and many parts of the ceiling, some as high as the most inaccessible reaches. Unfortunately, these human marks are almost everywhere made more confusing by the marks of time and the overlay of natural process. This is after all a living environment, totally subject to the unalterable flow of life and decay. Paintings as old as many of the least decipherable have withstood countless wet–season deluges, rock falls and bushfires. Their preservation, even in such an imperfect state, is almost too much to believe.

Rust-coloured streaky watermarks, fringed in the dull-black then white concentric lines of organic stains and crystalline salts, flow in irregular pathways over the ceiling and down the walls. Like a slowly shedding skin, parts of the wall reveal random patches of fresh pale-grey and cream stone. Elsewhere, the weathered reds and dull oranges are dusted in powdery white salts exuding from the rock.

On the ceiling, wasps of several species have industriously daubed mud or constructed delicate grey clusters of intricate paper-nest tubes. Abandoned mud structures cling to the walls, like strange barnacles on the sides of a beached ship. At the rear of the shelter, spiders lie in wait amidst dusty webs threaded over dark shadows. From above, fine tendrils at the root ends of some distant Rock Fig force their way through the smallest of fissures, seeking further opportunities to secure footholds. Termite corridors, fine lines of mud that look like roots themselves, meander across rockfaces and run along tight corners.

The shelter floor is a confused jumble of rocks: from large slabs long ago dislodged from the ceiling, to newly fretted fragments strewn amongst the dust. Some of the larger slabs are polished to a cool smoothness by countless years of human occupation and the drop-by-drop deposition of silicates leaching from the rock above.

Whilst human occupation has ceased, the polishing continues as small animals, such as the Short-eared Rock-wallaby, continue to seek out shade and protection. Stirring in the shadows, bats dart out with almost noiseless flight, then wheel back in tight curves, not venturing into the glare of full daylight beyond the edge of the overhang.

Amongst the confusion of the indecipherable and the unintelligible, the poignant immediacy of a group of hand stencils of varying sizes is readily sensed. Sprayed in red ochre from the artists' mouths onto the almost immutable dull-orange bands of hard Kimberley sandstone, they have us eagerly trying to visualise the act of their creation. Such a casual and seemingly tender collective mark of an ancient family. The more we encounter humble images like these stencils, the greater the realisation that the world in which they were placed is now incomplete. As a natural environment, it was self-contained and as close to pristine as any in the country but it now lacks one vital and fundamental part: the active presence of those original artists and all who followed them.

Opposite: Alasdair McGregor, 'Frieze of Bradshaw figures, Drysdale River' (gouache on paper, 31 x 45 cm).

Top: Paintings adorning the walls of Kimberley rock shelters are often hidden from view, their presence not obvious at first glance. Drysdale River.
Left: Hand stencils and Bradshaw figures. Bundarwa, Drysdale River.
Right: Rock shelters are a favoured habitat for a variety of industrious wasp species. Drysdale River.

Outdoor galleries: the sacred and profane

Although much of the traditional life has now lapsed, pre-European cultural achievement lingers on through the astounding legacy of rock paintings occurring throughout the Kimberley. The region is one of the world's great repositories of indigenous art. As a massive outdoor art gallery, it rivals in richness, cultural complexity and sheer aesthetic achievement, more famous rock-art bodies in Europe, Africa and the Northern Territory. From overhanging rock shelters, not quite deep enough to be truly regarded as caves, to walls barely protected from the constant attack of sun, water and time, the Kimberley is emblazoned with art in literally thousands of locations. From off-shore islands to the semi-arid margins of the south, only the smallest number of sites have ever been seen by anyone other than the original creators and their descendants.

Whilst the Kimberley is richly endowed with rock art, its presence is subtle. Away from the overhangs or shelters themselves, clues to the existence of art are meagre. Empty shelters abound. Though devoid of paintings or any other signs of human occupation, each one remains as a testament to the suitability and richness of the physical surrounds for sustaining life. With an abundance of commodious living space, occupants of a region could be selective. Empty shelters remained perpetually so, being too far from food, water or easy access. Others that lacked prospect or a propitious spiritual atmosphere remained similarly unused and unadorned.

Many art sites were simply living shelters decorated with the casual record of social life. Whilst they were located by the demands of daily and seasonal existence, other sites were selected according to transcendental considerations. Here were depicted significant events and ideas associated with the spiritual beliefs of the people or the ritual disposal of their dead. The location of these sites was determined by fundamental acts of creation and destruction, as the cosmic struggle of spirit beings and Aborigines left its imprint on the landscape.

The full antiquity of Kimberley art is not known but it shares many similarities in its themes and development with the art of Arnhem Land. Both areas were likely to have once been closely linked as part of a wider, more unified cultural region stretching as far as Cape York. The earliest Arnhem Land paintings are thought to be at least 35 000 years old and appear as the imprint of human hands, grasses and thrown objects.[1] Considering the likelihood that the Kimberley was a beach-head for the very first immigrants to Australia, the earliest art of the region is probably at least as old as that of Arnhem Land. No definitive sequence has yet been finalised for the multitude of forms in Kimberley rock art. But it is probable that stylistic changes were contemporaneous with social development across all of northern Australia. The styles often appear as a puzzling jumble of random paint layers: large, naturalistic animals daubed over delicate, lifelike figures; hand-stencils obscured by indecipherable symbols, their meaning long lost. It is often difficult even to be sure which pigment preceded another in the successive layers of thin ochre. Through this untidy web of art, the evolution of Kimberley life can only be tantalisingly glimpsed.

Amongst the great diversity of Kimberley art, two styles exemplify the visual richness and diversity of the region: the little known, elegant Bradshaw figures of great antiquity, and the spectacular Wandjinas of recent times. The latter are still linked with contemporary Aboriginal custom and belief. Both have attracted the European eye because of their supposed 'non-Aboriginal' appearance.

The alien and the 'self-taught savage'

Kimberley paintings have on occasion endured a peculiar array of ethnocentric European appraisals, all doubting Aboriginal authorship. From the British explorer George Grey to the 'Bush Tuckerman', Kimberley art has either been ascribed to or said to be inspired by some very fanciful influences. Egyptians, African Bushmen, Portuguese navigators and visitors from other planets are amongst the more incredible sources claimed for Kimberley art.

Often postulated with scant regard for the ability of Aboriginal people over thousands of years to develop a rich and varied visual imagery of their own, these supposed influences

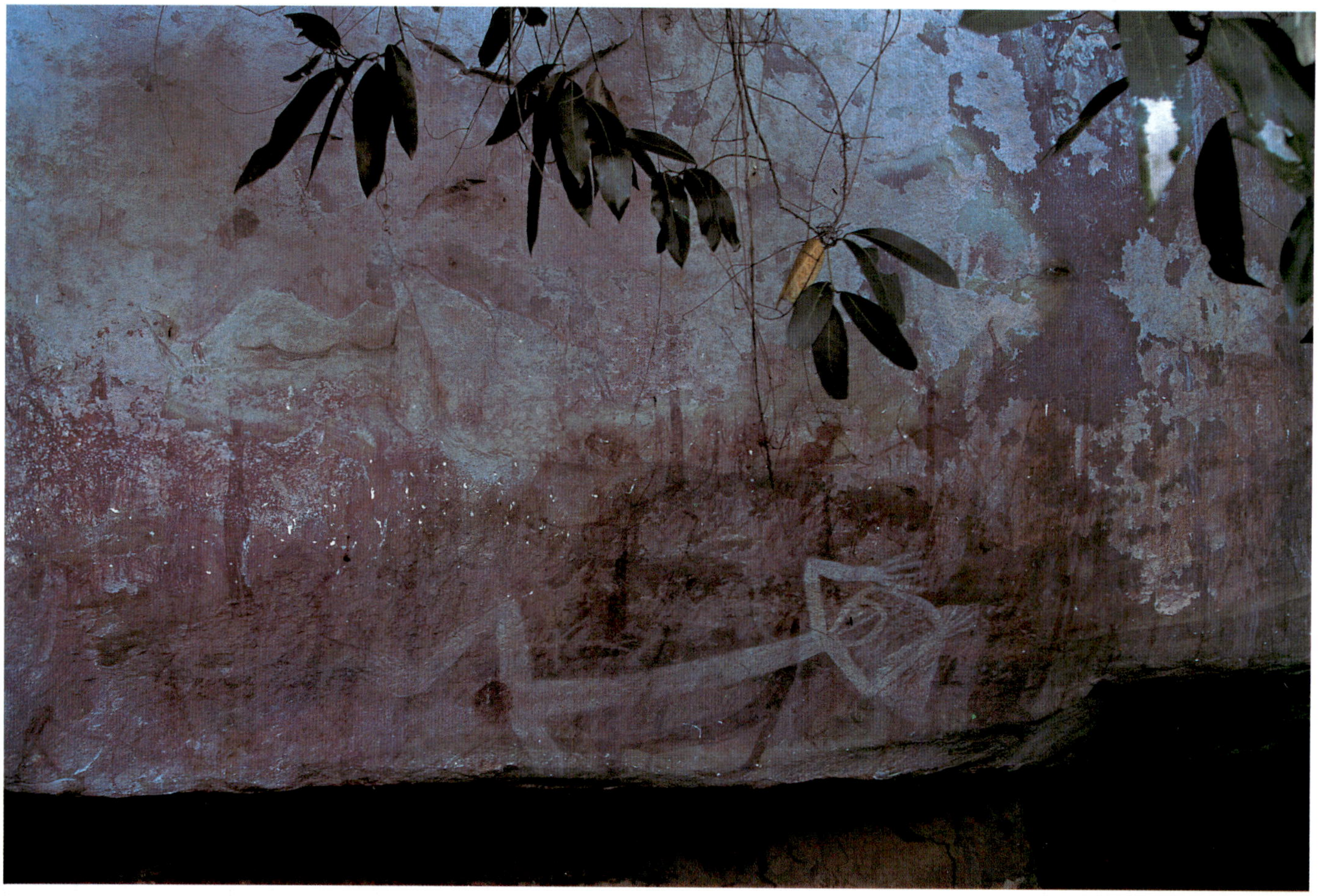

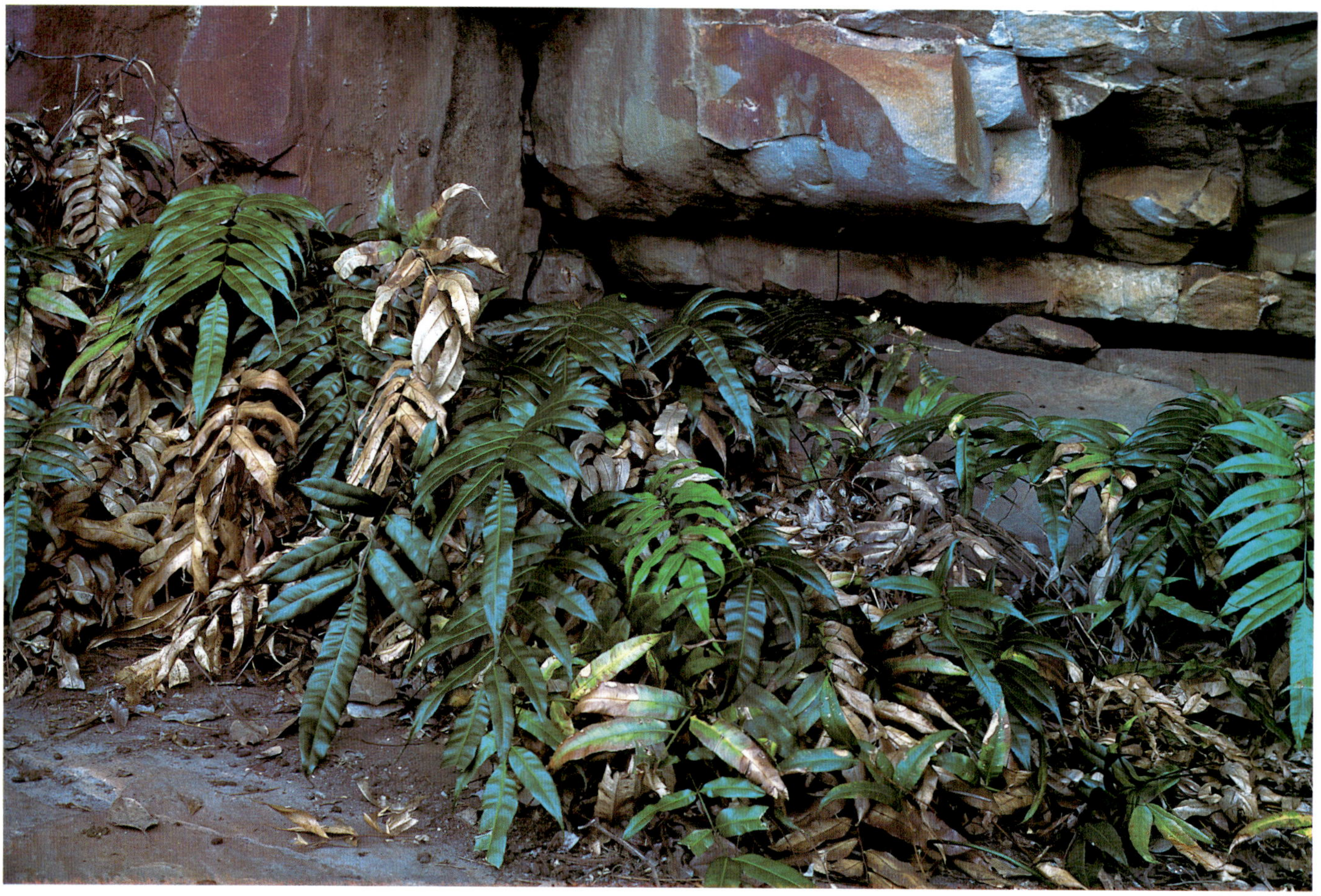

Top left: Nurini, Little Mertens Falls. Mitchell Plateau.
Left: Ferns adorn a damp corner of a shelter beneath the lingering remnants of a stencilled foot, Mitchell Falls.
Above: Sandstone terraces, Drysdale River.

121

Top: Anthropomorphs, Cockburn Range.
Above: The hunt. Balagulta, Drysdale River.

are generally easily dismissed. From first contact with the imposing Wandjinas and the widespread attention that followed, alternative explanations have been sought for their origins. Grey, in the course of his explorations of the Glenelg River region in 1837, was probably the first European to sight the Wandjinas. He was startled by what confronted him:

> ... my attention was drawn to the numerous remains of native fires and encampments which we met with, till at last, on looking over some bushes, at the sandstone rocks which were above us, I suddenly saw from one of them a most extraordinary large figure peering down upon me. Upon examination, this proved to be a drawing at the entrance to a cave, which, on entering, I found to contain, besides, many remarkable paintings ... [It] appeared to stand out from the rock; and I was certainly rather surprised at the moment that I first saw this gigantic head and upper part of a body bending over and grimly staring at me. It would be impossible to convey in words an adequate idea of this uncouth and savage figure.[2]

Grey at a later point in his narrative reflected: 'whatever may have been the age of these paintings, it is scarcely probable that they could have been executed by a self taught savage. Their origin therefore, must still be open to conjecture.'

The comments of Grey in doubting Aboriginal authorship for the Wandjinas are telling of nineteenth-century European attitudes to Aborigines and their culture. Grey himself did not proffer an opinion as to the origins of the paintings. However, numerous theorists and religious dreamers, spurred on by the mystery and excitement of Grey's discoveries, interpreted his sketches and writings in many ways. They concluded that the Wandjinas were variously the work of traders from the Red Sea, Malays, Sumatrans, Moors, Hindus or shipwrecked Japanese fishermen. All laboured under false assumptions drawn from Grey's sketches, which were inaccurate and stylised renderings, possibly produced from memory.

Whilst having no idea as to the meaning or origins of the Wandjinas, Grey was still moved by their powerful imagery and physical presence:

> ... the art and skill with which some of the figures are drawn, and the great effect which has been produced by such simple means, renders it most probable that these paintings must have been executed with the intention of exercising an influence upon the fears and superstitious feelings of the ignorant and barbarous natives: for such a purpose they are indeed well calculated.

Thunderheads and lightning

Wandjinas are pre-eminent in the most recent art tradition and are dispersed over large parts of the region, principally in the west, north-west and central Kimberley. They share many common elements of style and mythology with the Lightning Brothers who appear in the Victoria River District of the Northern Territory, and with the vaguely 'Wandjina like' lightning figures in various parts of the Kimberley itself. In fact, the Wandjina tradition can be linked with the development of multi-coloured art throughout northern Australia. Reaching its height in the last few thousand years, it is represented in Arnhem Land by the spectacular X-ray paintings of predominately animal forms and in Cape York by enormous naturalistic figure paintings.

Wandjinas appear in a variety of forms and embellishment. They are generally large, human-like figures depicted in frontal pose, and often show only the head and shoulders or a half torso rather than the full body. Their size can be startling, individual figures sometimes measuring more than two metres. The palette consists of a white background, with red, orange and yellow ochres plus black charcoal defining the body parts.

The most arresting feature of the Wandjinas are their pallid faces, staring with a wide eyed and portentous gaze over the world in which they hold sway. Eyes are depicted as full circles or ovaloid shapes, and are sometimes joined to form one long horizontal form. They are solid red or black and are outlined in red ochre. Eyelashes are often added. The nose appears in a variety of shapes from a thin line dividing close set eyes to a red or black bulbous form. Both the eyes and the nose may be abraded to form shallow depressions in the surface of the painting.

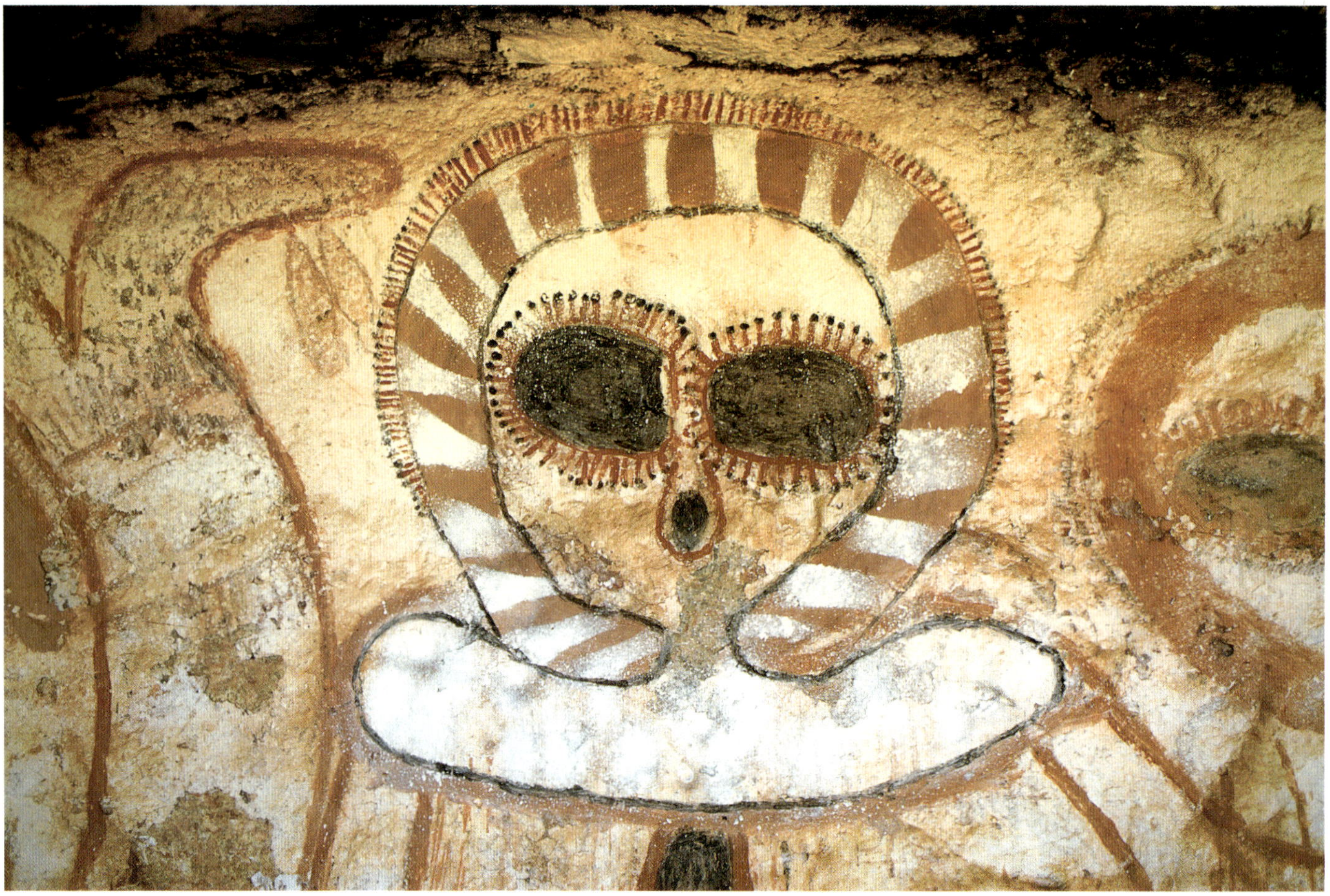

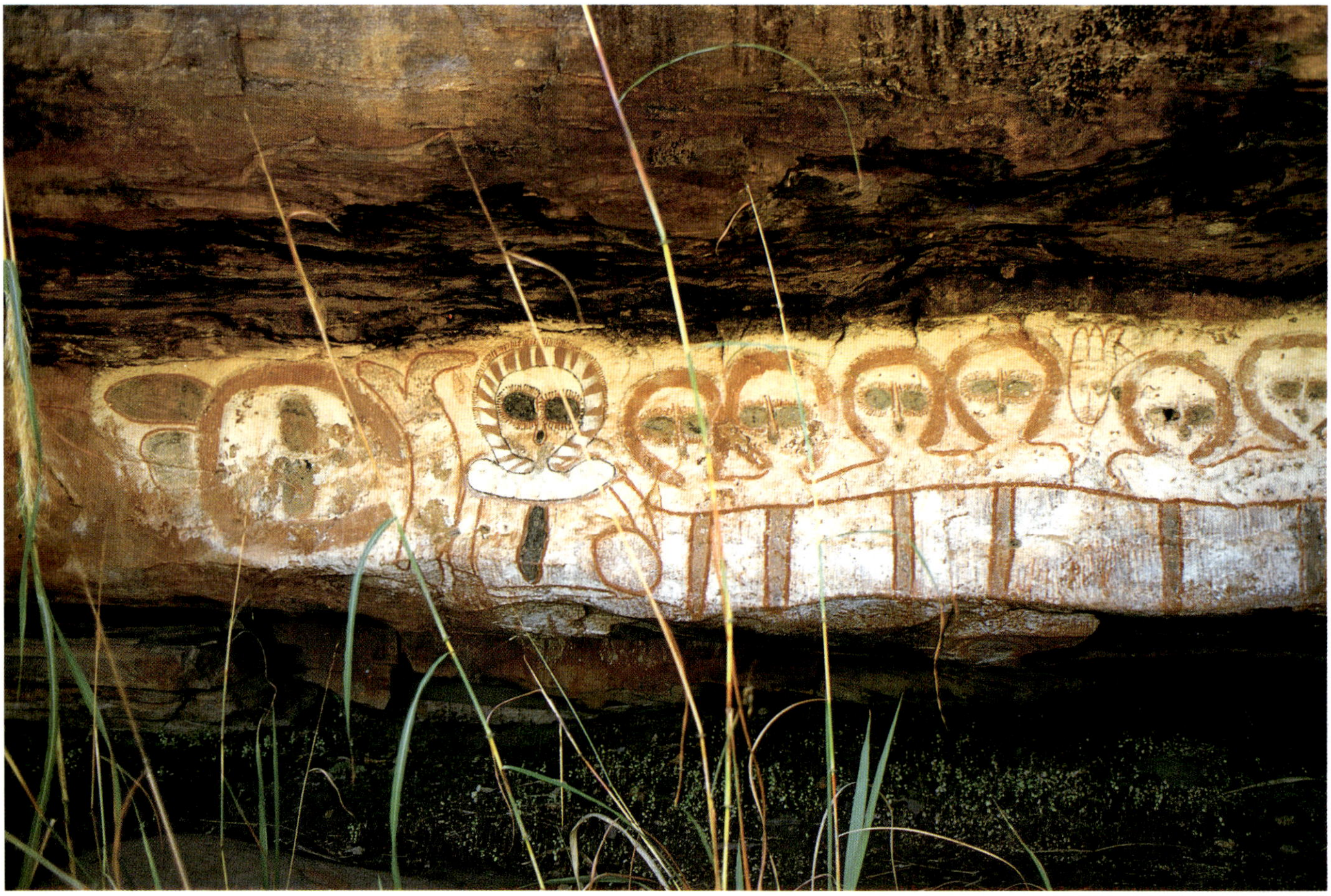

The vision of the Wandjina in mute malevolence is heightened by the universal absence of a mouth. Like a scream from a nightmare that can't be uttered, the Wandjina's mouth is permanently sealed. Common Aboriginal belief insists that the mouth must not be painted. To do so would be to destroy the painting's potency and invite unrelenting rain.[3]

The Wandjina's face is surrounded by one or more halo-like bands. Variously coloured, infilled or cross banded, these halos are said to depict clouds or lightning. A fringe of hair is usually shown, and the head may be further adorned with feathers which are also believed to represent lightning. Lightning may also emanate from the Wandjina's shoulder.

From Grey onwards, European observers of the Wandjinas have been puzzled by their apparent depiction as clothed figures wearing what seems to be a loose fitting shirt, waist belt and trousers. This paradoxical state of attire, compared to the nakedness of pre-European Aboriginal society, has done much to stir the imaginations of those who have doubted an Australian origin for the Wandjina. However, the 'clothed' appearance can also be interpreted as the result of artistic convention. Animals appearing in the same panels will often be depicted with segmented extremities; that is, individual parts of the body being drawn in complete outline. The Wandjina's body, being also divided into such portions, therefore appears to be clothed.

In complex examples of the style, vertical stripes may be included on the torso, below the yoke of the shoulders. These stripes are said to depict ceremonial body decorations, falling rain, or long beards. In the centre of the Wandjina's chest, an oval-shaped decoration often appears. Early interpreters concluded that it was the Wandjina's breastbone, but it may also be the heart or liver — the source of power and potency within the body.

Despite being ascribed gender in their associated mythology, most Wandjinas are depicted asexually. Sexual detail is infrequent. Genitals and breasts are usually omitted, although associated female figures called Djilinja display sexual characteristics in graphic form. An arrangement of smooth stones on a shelter floor in front of the Wandjina is said to be his testicles.

Grey's encounter with the Wandjinas was startling. Our first contact with them, whilst not as dramatic, is truly unexpected. Our party had been surveying rock-art sites along the Drysdale River for more than a week. In an area abounding with easy rock terraces, abundant water and shelter, evidence of a high concentration of Aboriginal occupation over a great length of time was likely.

One of the first intensive surveys of Kimberley rock art was carried out in 1938 by the Frobenius Institute of Frankfurt, Germany. The Institute came to Australia to study the culture of three north-west Aboriginal tribes: the Ngarinyin, Wororra and Unambal. Amongst the members of the Frobenius Expedition, Agnes Susanne Schulz produced fine watercolour facsimiles as a record of many significant Wandjina sites in the west Kimberley. Along with an extensive photographic collection, the paintings were exhibited in Frankfurt on the eve of war and in Britain in 1947.

Top left: Wandjina (detail). Panda-Goornya, Drysdale River.
Left: Wandjinas. Panda-Goornya, Drysdale River.
Above: Wandjinas, vicinity of Mt Hann. Watercolour by Agnes Susanne Schulz, Frobenius Institute.

Wandjinas and animal totems near Mt Hann. Watercolour by Agnes Susanne Schulz.

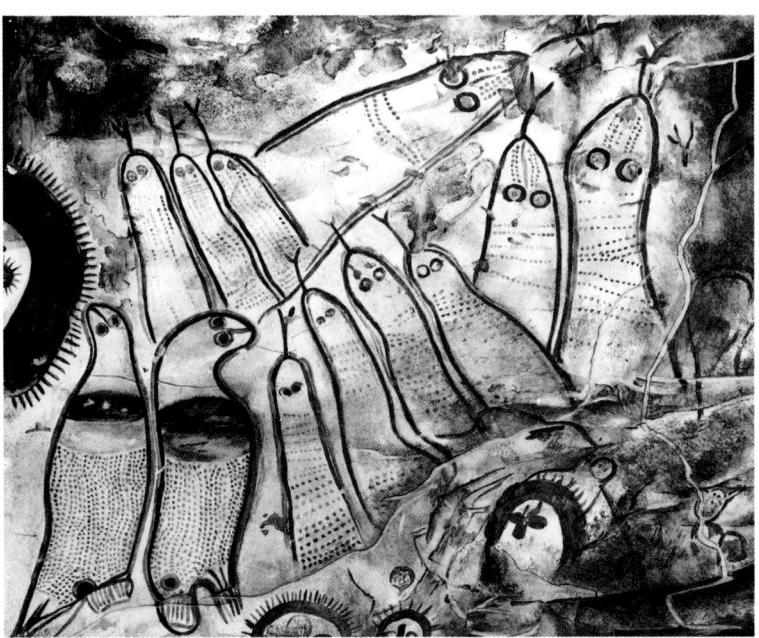

Ungud (serpents), Edkins Range. Watercolour by Agnes Susanne Schulz, Frobenius Institute.

It is late April and the wet season is over. One brief thunderstorm has produced the only rain in three weeks. The river's floodtide fury has passed. The Drysdale is gently settling into the languid repose that is to be its state for the remaining months of the dry season.

Despite the enervating climate and the annoyances of plants that scratch, cling, entangle or ensnare, our search for rock art becomes relatively easy in time. The key to success seems to lie in attempting to read the country the way the original inhabitants might have done — a presumptuous ambition perhaps, but we soon become aware of sites likely to have been favoured for occupation, such as rock shelters close to water and located along the easier stretches of river terrain.

Stepped terraces of water-hewn sandstone, the colour of sienna, run as an assortment of jumbled angular blocks and spacious flat pavements along both sides of the river. These rocky shores have a look of casual order about them, with the striking linear bedding so common in Kimberley geology being very much in evidence. The seasonal violence of the river has tossed enormous boulders about with implausible ease, leaving them strewn about in disarray, but the underlying horizontal look of the terraces prevails. They step up quite steeply on the eastern side to a stretch of pavement barely above the black stain of the flood line. Here we find numerous small shelters containing a variety of very faint paintings, many in the Bradshaw style. Interspersed with the monumentality of rock, melaleuca-fringed sandy reaches slip gently into tepid waters glowing amber in the shallows, then on into the depths of long, placid pools. On the opposite bank, wide, unevenly vegetated terraces climb the hillside to a broken and ragged skyline. There, the occasional filigreed crown of a Livistona Palm bends compliantly against a ridge-top breeze. On that side of the river we find an abundance of fine living shelters and a profusion of art.

Never more than about 200 metres from the river runs a wide, elevated terrace, dotted with rock outliers and fancifully eroded sandstone mushrooms. The largest of these outliers and rocky complexes were once home to what seems to have been a considerable concentration of people over untold years. Art abounds, though other cultural evidence is rare. Only one ochre grindstone, used in the preparation of pigments, is found in any of the dozen or so significant shelters that we locate.

The paintings are strewn over the walls and ceiling in a graffiti-like confused array of styles and motifs. Most give the impression of being very old. Hand-stencils, animal and human forms, indecipherable motifs, and many Bradshaw figures cover all but the most recently weathered surface. Whilst we find numerous examples of what are probably recent paintings, large monochrome animals for instance, there appear to be no Wandjinas in the area. That seems odd. This part of the northern Kimberley, whilst on the eastern margins of Wandjina territory, is certainly within its bounds.

Wandjina sites are found on the King Edward River close by to the west and at Kalumburu immediately to the north-west. In the central Kimberley to the south, in the vicinity of the Drysdale River, is the major Wandjina painting and burial site known as Panda-Goornnya. Wandjinas tend to be less dispersed than other Kimberley art forms. Perhaps this part of the region was not significant in Wandjina mythology? Although it appeared that life and art flourished along the river in the distant past, the Wandjinas may not have cast their shadow over the rocks of the Drysdale.

However, when least exposed, there are the faces of three Wandjinas staring through the narrow, slotted opening of what appears to be only an annex of a major shelter complex. A large slab, once part of the roof, forms the lower half of a giant visor through which these mysterious apparitions peer. Like Grey at his first encounter, we are taken aback. Two Wandjinas are painted on their sides, heads at opposite ends of what may have been a shared body. All three are badly decayed. Unusually, only red pigment remains. Nearly all traces of their pallid white faces have washed away. The red pigment itself has run, diffusing to a faint stain at the base of the narrow band of wall. In undiminished impact, the washed-out appearance of these three Wandjinas seems only to intensify their melancholic pout.

The mythology and meaning surrounding Wandjinas is marvellously complex and dramatic. The Wandjina paintings are believed to be the shadows of ancestral beings cast against the rock in the course of their travels across the land. At the end of each Wandjina's active life its spirit became part of the earth, its shadow on stone becoming a painted image at the place of its death.

They came from the sea or the sky to the north and north-west, and moved over the country, hunting, fighting and teaching Aborigines, whilst creating minor features of the landscape such as lines of stones, rock shelters and trees. It is believed that they originated in the Dreamtime, yet they arrived in a populated world, the features of which already existed. Their creative acts were less momentous than those of the great animal spirits of the Dreamtime, in particular the rainbow serpent, known in the Kimberley as Ungud. For this reason Wandjina myths have probably been grafted onto the more ancient rainbow serpent beliefs that stretch through the Kimberley, across northern Australia and into the desert. The serpent appears in Kimberley art, often associated with Wandjinas.

Wandjinas may not still be living amongst Aborigines but their spirits remain,

Previous page: Dry-season evening, Drysdale River.
Top: Wandjinas and animal totem. Munuro, King Edward River.
Above: Wandjina and waterstains. Mulcutinari, Drysdale River.

influencing the course of events on earth. They control life itself through their mastery of the elements. They are the bringers of the monsoon, the great storms and cyclones that flood the land and regenerate life. They are the very essence of water, their heads haloed in the billowing cumulus clouds and lightning bolts that summon the start of the rains. Fertility and increase are gifts from the Wandjinas, as they send down life spirits to inhabit the billabongs and rivers. Supplication of the Wandjinas is thought necessary to ensure success in hunting and pregnancy. This is often achieved through ritual repainting of the figures and associated animal forms.

The Wandjinas' energies are also destructive. They fought with Aborigines, uniting on one occasion to punish their wrongdoings in a massive conflict in the Central Kimberley. The great Wandjina, Wodjin, and the other members of his band who took part in the battle were transformed into paintings at Wanalirri, a site that is central to all Wandjina mythology.

Whilst the Wandjinas can be prevailed upon to provide bounty, they can also be invoked to cause the death of others. By painting a caricature of the intended victim beside or near a Wandjina's head, disease and painful death will befall one's hapless opponent. The malevolence of the Wandjinas should not be dismissed. Their wrath when displeased can be made manifest through floods and lightning. The paintings themselves are sacred and whilst rarely secret or restricted, command the utmost respect. So as not to startle them, visitors to a Wandjina site are required to announce their approach by calling out. Frivolous behaviour in the Wandjinas' presence is disapproved of and touching the paintings, forbidden. To ensure the Wandjinas' continued good favour, the paintings should be annually renewed during the wet season. Retouching outside that time is not allowed.

Each Wandjina has a living representative amongst a clan group, usually an older man who bears the name of the Wandjina who gave him his life spirit. He is responsible for the custodianship of that Wandjina's site. Far from being a static belief, the Wandjina mythology is structured to allow change through direct communication with the spirit beings themselves. Some men are able to communicate with Wandjinas in dreams, bringing new stories and ritual into a living and evolving tradition. As a result of this flexibility of belief, aspects of Christianity found their way into Wandjina mythology with the advent of Europeans in the Kimberley.

Elegant art

Despite further searching, the three washed-out figures were the only Wandjinas encountered near the Drysdale River on our first visit. On our return three years later, further Wandjinas are located in nearby shelters. Two of these were major living complexes completely overlooked on our previous visit. So much for thinking we could read the country! None of these galleries contains many Wandjinas, their representation restricted to just a few heads in each. What these shelters do exhibit though, is the astonishing array and contrast of forms in Kimberley art from the simplicity of a hand-stencil to the intense power of the Wandjina.

Across the tangled courtyard of one of these shelter complexes, overgrown almost to eye level with pungent smelling, viscid spinifex, the refreshing gloom of a cleft of deep shadow looks inviting. Investigation reveals more than welcome shade: the wall of the shelter is adorned with an exquisite frieze of human figures utterly unlike the Wandjinas on the ceiling of the shelter opposite.

Possibly a dozen graceful, attenuated individuals of various sizes, most in an advanced state of decay, are assembled in a statuesque line. In muted colours, from faded dull red to dark brown, they appear to be posed for some ancient form of group or family portrait. Outfitted in complex finery, they are even attended by indeterminate minute animal forms hovering above the heads of two of the more prominent figures. The intricate feathery nature of their fine garb perfectly echoes the drooping fibrous skirts of dead fronds that swathe the base of *Livistona* Palms growing hard against the far end of the shelter.

These are Bradshaw figures, part of that ancient, enigmatic body of art bearing the

Above: Elegant art — a frieze of Bradshaw figures. Barten, Drysdale River.
Left: Fan Palms (Livistona loriphylla *) sway and rustle in the warm breezes of the dry season, their skirt of dead fronds almost mimicked by the Bradshaw figures.*

132

unfortunate epithet of the first European to describe them. The name Bradshaw is such an awkward tag for a body of art that is so mannerly and refined, but in the absence of any apt descriptive label it has come to be loosely applied to a variety of closely related small monochrome figurative styles, all of considerable antiquity. They are widely dispersed in the north and north-west Kimberley, where Joseph Bradshaw explored in 1891 while searching for viable grazing land. Commenting on the figurative paintings he found in the vicinity of the Prince Regent River, Bradshaw noted:

> We saw numerous caves and recesses in the rocks the walls of which were adorned with native paintings, colored in red, black, brown yellow, white and pale blue. Some of the human figures were life size. The bodies and limbs were attenuated and represented as having numerous tassel shaped adornments appended to the hair, neck, waist, arms and legs, but the most remarkable fact in connection with these drawings is that wherever a profile face is shown the features are of a most pronounced aquiline type, quite different from those of any natives we encountered. Indeed, looking at some of the groups one might think himself viewing the painted walls of an Egyptian temple. These sketches seem to be of great age, but over the surface of some of them were drawn in fresher colors, smaller and more recent scenes, and rude forms of animals, such as the Kangaroo, Wallaby, Porcupine, Crocodile, etc ... [4]

As with the Wandjinas, European observers have been quick to compare Bradshaw figures with non-Aboriginal art forms and in more fanciful moments ascribe authorship to other groups. Any resemblance of the Bradshaws to African Bushmen's art or the regal posturings of Egyptian tomb paintings should be regarded as a fine example of cross-cultural coincidence and admired as such, but nothing more. Within the context of an Australian origin for the Bradshaws, further conjecture exists. Because they are seemingly so unlike any other Kimberley art form, suggestions have often been made that they were executed by some extinct racial group, long since absorbed or overrun by the ancestors of contemporary Aborigines. The paucity and nature of Aboriginal explanations of the Bradshaws' origins have also encouraged such speculation.

Bradshaws are not part of the visual representation of any aspect of contemporary Aboriginal custom or belief. They are regarded as insignificant and frivolous beside the potent Wandjina. It is commonly believed that they were the work of birds, not of people, and therefore their secrets cannot be deciphered. Aborigines say that they are very old, depicting people long before their time. Limited mythology associates the existence of these people with the creative acts of the first Wandjinas.

The fully developed classic form of the Bradshaws is an astonishing testament to the artistic skill of their creators. The Bradshaw artist coping with the disadvantage of working against the irregularities of natural stone, produced works of the finest draftsmanship. Their execution would do great credit to any painter labouring over the finest prepared wall or canvas. Deft and graceful fine lines were achieved with brushes of unknown construction. Perhaps they used feathers? The chewed end of a twig or a piece of canegrass, often used for the detail on Wandjinas, would most likely have been too coarse for such fine delineation.

Bedecked in an array of fine regalia and body ornament, the people depicted in Bradshaw paintings appear to be imbued with a highly developed regard for their own self-image and importance. Dancing, swaying and drifting across the rock as if in suspended flight, they portray a sophisticated people not satisfied with just recording aspects of mere survival. Most Bradshaw figures measure less than 60 centimetres; however, in the course of our Drysdale River surveys we encountered larger examples, including one imposing figure that measured 150 centimetres.

Within various permutations of style, they are rendered with a remarkable degree of consistency; from shelter to shelter and throughout their range. It sometimes occurred to us whilst viewing Bradshaws, that they were the work of a select group of skilled painters, thoroughly versed in a restricted range of artistic conventions. Did they work from some sort of ancient style manual?

The head is almost always shown in profile, as are the feet. With the body opposed in frontal view, they often assume that vague Egyptian-like aristocratic appearance alluded to by Bradshaw himself. Where hands are delineated, palms and fingers are also shown in open

detail. The feet point slightly down and mostly face the same direction. Sexual detail is almost nonexistent. An occasional figure posed unconventionally with knees bent and legs apart displays what may be a penis but is more likely to be simply part of the Bradshaw regalia. What could be diminutive breasts are portrayed unconvincingly as small bulges on either side of the upper torso on an extremely small proportion of figures. Apart from relative size, which could also indicate age or rank, no other possible indications of gender are shown.

Most of all it is the assortment of head-dresses, tassels, skirts, armlets, bracelets, epaulets and accoutrements that epitomise the Bradshaw style. The head-dress can be as long as the body itself. Arching back in extravagant sweeping curves, punctuated by a great flourish of adornment at the end, they must surely have been intended as an outrageous caricature of style.[5] Alternatively they may appear tight and compact, dragged back from the head in a pendulous bun crowned with a spray of feathers. A conical cap reminiscent of the headgear of medieval aristocratic women is yet another variation.[6] Diminutive wings sprout from heads or form epaulets fluttering on shoulders as wispy tassels hang from elbows and waists. The decorative permutations are endless.

The Bradshaws' accoutrements provide some of the most useful clues as to their age. In addition to dilly bags, fans, digging sticks and batons, Bradshaws are often depicted wielding weapons. They commonly carry boomerangs and occasionally a multi-barbed spear. This form of spear has been absent from the weaponry of northern Australia for at least 3 000 years.[7] In a radical technological shift, an array of new tools and implements were introduced to common usage in the Kimberley at about that time. Included among them were finely worked single stone spearheads now known as Kimberley points. Bradshaw figures themselves may have evolved into a bichromatic art style that also displays multi-barb spears, usually depicted with two prongs. It is therefore likely that the Bradshaws and particularly their earlier, less embellished variants are considerably older than 3 000 years.

The paraphernalia and adornment of the Bradshaw has much in common with that of an ancient form of Arnhem Land art known as the Dynamic Figures style. These energetic, vital little figures sprint, hunt and fight their way across the rock, brandishing similar spears and boomerangs, whilst clad in fantastic skirts and head-dresses. It is probable that the Dynamic Figures share a similar antiquity with their Kimberley equivalent. Estimates of their age suggest that they were painted somewhere between 9 000 and 20 000 years ago.[8]

Decay, disintegration and preservation

Apart from their relict weaponry, the advanced state of deterioration amongst Bradshaws is a telling sign of their age. They were successively overpainted by generation after generation of shelter occupants. If they were placed on the most protected or expansive rock surfaces, chances are that successive artists favoured those locations also. Bradshaws are found in many of the major Wandjina sites, so it is certain that many Bradshaws remain hidden under several millimetres of Wandjina ochre.

The processes of nature have also exacted their price from the Bradshaws. Water, sunlight, mineral salts, wasps, termites and the gradual exfoliation and breakdown of the rock surface itself has reduced the Bradshaw population to a pale and crumbling shadow of its past brilliance. Any remains of the original pigments have long ago vanished; the paintings only persist as stubborn iron-oxide stains, varying in colour from terracotta-red to brown-black. Unlike the Wandjinas, they appear not to have been repainted at any time.

Incredibly, some Bradshaw figures have survived the centuries in good condition. Secreted away from the elements and the casual hand of generations, they remain almost as clear now as the day they were painted. In a paradox of nature, they have actually been protected by physical processes. Dissolved silicates moving through the body of rock combine with the remaining pigments of a painting lying below the surface. When they migrate to the atmosphere and evaporate they leave behind a deposit of silica. This deposit

Opposite: Bradshaw figures, almost perfectly preserved. Goyon, Drysdale River.

A Bradshaw figure, resplendent in head-dress, tassels, skirt and epaulets, springs from the rock, wielding boomerangs in its right hand. Jerungurri, Drysdale River.

Morning light floods the rear 'courtyard' of a shelter-complex high above the Drysdale River.

Above: Bichrome figures. Only the tenacious red-brown pigments rich in iron remain. All other colours have long-ago faded or been washed away, leaving the figures incomplete. Borolga, Drysdale River.

Left: A site repainted as part of a Commonwealth funded cultural revitalisation program in 1987. Ngornjar, Mt Elizabeth region.

138

forms a permanent and impenetrable protective skin over the paintings themselves and postpones their disappearance to the time when the rock surface itself breaks down.[9]

We find one near-perfect Bradshaw figure after climbing through the vine-forest entanglement towards a sweeping arc of overhang and the lip of a shelter. For 50 metres, the walls of this huge gallery are stained by a random band of indistinct and decaying paintings. A hand here, the staccato cross-hatching from the tail of a long vanished kangaroo there. The ceiling is rough and uneven, and similarly decorated. As the western sun drops rapidly in the tropical sky beyond the Drysdale River floodplain, the shelter rebounds with light.

Towards the outer edge of the ceiling, in the middle of its impressive length, we find a Bradshaw figure quite alone. Washed by the reflected glow of the oncoming evening, its features clear and intact, this 45 centimetre long figure could have been painted yesterday! In action pose, legs bent and arms outstretched, still imbued with its original vitality, it almost springs from the rock. The passage of time appears to have been fooled.

How was it that this figure survived so well when so much more recent art had gone? It is now only 150 years since George Grey made his startling discoveries, yet in that short time much of the glory of the Wandjinas has gone. Water has been central to the power of the Wandjinas, yet in devastating irony, it is water that is the essential agent of their demise as they are scoured from the shelter walls. Just as the complex but fragile traditions and mythology that backed them have been irreparably harmed and changed, so the Wandjina paintings have been left to the mercy of nature and the damage that results. As the people were killed or dispossessed, so the old ways have faded along with their art.

Whilst the Wandjinas erode, a few Bradshaw figures linger in stubborn persistence. An ancient and unknown tradition survives and communicates through art alone, as a powerful and living imagery withers and dies within the space of a few generations.[10] Which will survive the longer as the great and total body of art in the Kimberley disappears? A natural anomaly perhaps, but also an indication of the fragility of the remaining rock-art heritage. A miraculous legacy, a narrative of the continuous cultural development of preliterate people over thousands of years, is inexorably passing from view. Such is the state of Kimberley art today. Without massive conservation efforts, the fate of much of this heritage remains uncertain.

We came as privileged observers, looking but never touching. We left greatly enriched. It is hoped that all who view Kimberley art likewise fall to its spell, respecting it for the insights it offers and caring for its future.

1. G. Chaloupka, *From Palaeoart to Casual Paintings*, Monograph Series no. 1, Northern Territory Museum of Arts and Sciences, Darwin, 1984.
2. G. Grey, *Journals of Two Expeditions of Discovery in North-west and West Australia during the Years 1837 to 1839*, T. & W. Boone, London, 1841.
3. J.R.B. Love thought that the omission of the mouth may be just an artistic convention. When elderly members of the Wororra tribe were asked by Love to draw animals or people, they omitted the mouth as a matter of course. Younger people, exposed to a mission education, portrayed figures with mouths. Love, 'Rock paintings of the Wororra', *Journal of the Royal Society of Western Australia*, vol. 16, 1930.
4. J. Bradshaw, 'Notes on a recent trip to Prince Regent's River', in *Transactions of the Royal Geographic Society of South Australia*, vol. 9, pt 2, 1892, pp 90–103.
5. Ibid. It is interesting to consider Bradshaw's description of contemporary Aborigines encountered on his Prince Regent River expedition: 'Two or three of them had imposing head-gears, made, I imagine, of the pliable bark of the papyrus tree. We noticed one man in particular who had two huge appendages extending upwards and obliquely outwards from the top of his head, about 3 ft long; but whether they were made from the wings of a large bird, or were pieces of bark we could not ascertain, as he kept in the background far up the range.' The depiction of regalia in Bradshaw paintings was perhaps an accurate portrayal of everyday attire in large measure unchanged at the time of European contact.
6. Everyday practice amongst the men of the Wororra tribe was to bind their hair with string into a tight conical arrangement drawn back from the head. Into the apex of the cone, a plume of emu or white cockatoo's feathers was inserted. (J.R.B. Love, 'Notes on the Wororra tribe of North-Western Australia', *Transactions of the Royal Society of South Australia*, vol. 41, 1917). Love also describes a ceremonial head-dress worn by Wororra men for the dugong dance, 'balgudja': 'The Wororra head-dresses get remarkable effects from very simple material ... The dugong head-dress is a sheet of soft paper-bark about two feet square. This is bound round the forehead, and the string continued up and round the bark, tying it up into a tall cone. To the top of this cone is fixed a light reed, two feet long, surmounted by an imitation of the divided tail of the dugong.' (J.R.B. Love, *Stone Age Bushmen of Today*, Blackie, London, 1936).
7. I.M. Crawford, *The Art of the Wandjina*, Oxford University Press, Melbourne, 1968.
8. Chaloupka, op. cit.
9. Ibid. The mobility and deposition of silica is aided by dry conditions. Such conditions occurred at the height of the last glacial period 18 000 years ago. This may be a pointer to the age of early paintings and also may help in explaining their preservation.

10. Much controversy has occurred in recent years over the retouching of Wandjina paintings. Several of the major Kimberley sites were repainted in 1987. Federally funded by a Community Employment Program, young unemployed Aborigines of both sexes were enlisted for the project. Although overseen by tribal elders, their efforts and the organisation of the work have been much criticised. An agonising dilemma exists. Are the rights of Aboriginal people to control their heritage, its preservation and cultural evolution greater than the wider concerns associated with the conservation of world-heritage art in a traditionally faithful manner? G.L. Walsh, *Australia's Greatest Rock Art*, E.J. Brill/Robert Brown & Associates, Bathurst, 1988; D. Mowaljarlai and A. Watchman, 'An Aboriginal view of rock art management', *Rock Art Research*, vol. 6, no. 2, 1989; and D. Mowaljarlai and C. Peck, 'Ngarinyin cultural continuity: a project to teach the young people the culture, including the re-painting of Wandjina rock art sites', *Australian Aboriginal Studies*, no. 2, 1987.

Authors' Note

We thank Hector and Austin Unghango for providing names for art sites in the vicinity of the Drysdale River, Mitchell Plateau and King Edward River.

Opposite: A stubborn legacy — Bradshaw paintings close to the banks of the Drysdale River have survived the wet-season torrent through indeterminate millennia.

7

Five fathom tides:
The Kimberley coast

It starts as a trickle: a thin wedge of silty-brown saltwater that drives up into the outflow of the Isdell River. The wedge widens and gathers speed as it advances across the mudflats. In three hours the inundation is nearly complete. What was a wide bed of silt at the base of the Isdell gorge is now submerged beneath eight metres of saltwater. Six hours later all will be revealed once more.

On the Kimberley coast the tide moves like a flood. It does not flow and ebb, so much as charge, baulk and flee. It surges up rivers and rips through island passages. Wherever there is a constriction of land the massing water generates truly potent forces. So the tide can be seen to curl down around headlands and cascade off reefs. In its most outrageous displays the water whirls into deep hollows and 'boils over' to form rolling domes.

There are places where the tide can outrun a boat travelling at 10 knots. Small craft have been known to disappear completely into the convulsing waters. At its peak the measure between low and high tide exceeds 11 metres. The volume of water passing through some narrows rivals anything humans have done to engineer similar forces.

The first Europeans to explore this coast found themselves at the mercy of tidal currents they were often powerless to evade:

> We soon reached Whirlpool Channel, through which again the tide hurried and whirled us with almost frightful rapidity; we were in one part of it shot down a fall of several feet, the boat's bow being fairly buried in the boiling current.[1]

At low tide the disposition of the shore is radically altered. An inviting beach lapped by turquoise waters is transformed into a derelict mudflat only a crab could enjoy. A clean wall of orange quartzite suddenly appears with a 10 metre ebony-black skirt of stone trailing into the water. On the Isdell River low tide drops our boat almost out of sight from our camp, leaving it stuck fast on its keel in the mud. The river looks just as though somebody has pulled the plug.

A changing shore

This restless tide washes a coastline which itself is always on the turn. A succession of broad capes and deeply indented gulfs make this the continent's most serpentine shore. One estimate suggests it is 4 340 kilometres long, which is two and a half times longer than the New South Wales coast.[2]

The Kimberley presents a jagged face to the world. As well as gulfs and open bays, the coast is broken by harbours and sounds, basins, inlets and passages. River estuaries snake deep inland. Offshore the waters are studded with reefs and more than 3 000 islands. The only hazard not faced by navigators is monotony.

An intimate mix of habitats fringes the coastline, reflecting abrupt changes in soil type, drainage and aspect. Low, rocky headlands give way to sprawling mangrove flats. Crescent shaped beaches are shadowed by 80 metre high sandstone cliffs. Moist vine thickets abut dry spinifex ridges and screes with sentinel Boabs.

The coast is also where the great agents of natural change converge. The sway of the tides is matched by the prodigious outflow of the rivers during the wet season. Their floodwaters break free to the ocean, surging along narrow sea gorges and toppling hundreds of metres down black-streaked waterfalls.

Throughout these months the coast bears the brunt of the monsoonal storms. Thunderheads roam inland from the sea, bringing torrential rain that blankets the ranges and plateaux. Cyclones traverse the seaboard, making brief but brutally destructive incursions over the land.

As the storms withdraw and the cloud masses disperse, the coastline is exposed to a bleaching sun. For month after month it dries out the land and withers the vegetation. Floodplains bake and crack. During this long dry spell grass-fires dot the coast, continuing the cycle of clearing and regrowth that has been occurring since before human contact.

Yet, for all this tempest and spectacle, the coast is also a place of quiet refuge.

Opposite: Alasdair McGregor, 'Harlequin coast, Yampi Sound' (gouache on board, 33 x 40 cm).

Left: Low tide in the estuary of the Isdell River, just over a kilometre downstream from where salt meets fresh.

Above: The black skirt of the tideline is a distinctive feature of the Kimberley coast. Talbot Bay.

Right: One of 'The Gaps' at Talbot Bay, where twice a day the incoming tide rushes through two narrow passages.

In sheltered bays Dugongs (Dugong dugon) graze and breed on the beds of sea grass. Pockets of resplendent monsoon forest nestle in spring-fed gullies on the ridges of King Leopold Sandstone. As the tide retreats hermit crabs scrabble in their thousands across shelly beaches. Nearby Great Bowerbirds diligently fashion and adorn their bowers.

Meanwhile all along this wandering and diverse shore the Kimberley's pre-eminent predator, Crocodylus porosus — the Estuarine Crocodile — basks and waits. Just as the crocodile embodies its domain, so the coast itself is a fitting countenance for an entire region: a landscape marked by contrasts.

Rising seas

Watching the rise and fall of the tide, and gazing out to the islands and weathered headlands, the shore has an ancient, time-worn presence. But the distinctive cast of land and sea is a relatively recent phenomenon. In its long history the Kimberley coastline has been subjected to profound shifts and extremes of climate.

From such a perspective the range of the tides can seem like a faint echo of the changes in sea level that have occurred over the last two million years. As the massive global ice sheets advanced and retreated, so the sea level alternately dropped and rose across the shallow continental shelf that fringes Australia's northern perimeter.

At the onset of the most recent period of intense glaciation, 30 000 years ago, the sea was already 50 metres lower than present levels. By the time glacial conditions peaked, around 20 000 years ago, the sea level had dropped a further 90 metres. This lowering exposed much of the shelf of the Timor Sea. A perch overlooking the coast today would have then been a dry inland ridge swept by chill winds. To reach the sea would have meant making a daunting 200 kilometre trek.

With the subsequent melting of the icecaps the vast coastal lowlands were once again inundated by rising ocean levels. Over a 12 000 year period the seas reclaimed the land and rose 140 metres to their present height. The encroaching waters isolated areas of outlying high ground, leaving the islands that now cluster the coastline.

The sea also advanced up the rivers and formed long, drowned valleys. Like so many of the Kimberley's greatest rivers, the Isdell makes its journey to the sea along a sinuous gorge. These deep corridors of stone are stark, confronting places.

Where salt meets fresh

The tide has fled. We leave to walk up the Isdell gorge. Thin streams of fresh water braid the river mud. From our camp at the upper limit of navigable water it's a short walk to where fresh meets salt. But the going is far from straightforward. Broken cliffs flanking the gorge rise straight up out of the river. A fall into the mass of oozing grey mud would leave us immobilised from the waist down. So we skirt along narrow ledges and lunge on handholds to pass the bulging ribs of rock.

On the drained riverbed below, mudskippers flip across the silt. The only other signs of life here are the schools of mullet that ruffle the film of water mid-river. The rest of the gorge remains still in the blistering light of a November morning. It's an immense enclosure that presses in on the river. In a few weeks' time the storms will return. Floodwaters, churning with silty gravel, will scour and polish the sandstone.

We are lured upstream by the sound of water hushing through a scree of black boulders. This is the point of convergence. Above the scree is a large pool of clear emerald water; below there's a finger of glossy mud marking the tide's ultimate reach. We cool off in the small intermediary ponds of fresh water, sharing our baths with snooping Black Bream.

A series of steep ramps zig-zags up from the river to the ridgetop. Dead vines and mats of spinifex drape the outcrops. The rim of the gorge is capped by massive wind-scalloped blocks.

Above: Sheltered waters and mangrove flats near Talbot Bay. Right: Named for William Dampier, the Buccaneer Archipelago presents much the same prospect to the modern navigator as the shore on which he first landed in 1688.

From these vantage points the rocky margin between fresh and salt waters has an other-worldly appearance, as though it were the result of some cataclysm, like a mudslide or eruption from underground. Down below, the tide is rippling up the gorge.

The ridge top is deadly dry and recently singed by fire. Yet life is abundant. Scattered Boabs are sprouting their large parasol-shaped leaf clusters. Occasionally there are pink-flowering hibiscus and small groups of *Livistona* Palms. Along stone-terraced gullies the powdery-white trunks of the Snappy Gums shade small palms and ferns.

This is broken, rocky country. What meagre topsoil there is lies in shallow pockets. Water is plentiful in the gorge below but the vegetation on these ridges has to endure what is in effect an annual eight-month drought. Then every few years grass-fires strip the ground bare. In spite of all this the place hums with activity. A trio of Great Bowerbirds darts about in a huge sprawling fig. In the foreground a jet-black beetle makes off with the remains of a spider. Skinks rattle through the leaf litter, their tails curling high in the air.

Back down the scree slope to the river. A thin sheet of cloud filters the sun. Even so, at midday the gorge is a cauldron. The slabs radiate a fierce heat, and each handhold seems more scorching that the last. Saltwater swarms upstream, threatening the line of ledges and couch-matted banks that lead back to camp. Over the gorge an eagle turns on the climbing tide of warm air.

By nightfall the river is high. The tide has brought some passengers up into the gorge. Out of the darkness comes the sound of thrashing water. We look down from our rock-shelf camp and with torch-beams pick out three pairs of flame-red eyes glaring from the surface of the river. If we needed a reminder of where we were, and the essential wildness and antiquity of the place, this was it.

Wholesale gastronomers

The Kimberley coast is the realm of the saltwater crocodile. These exemplary opportunists exploit the margins between land and sea, estuary and river, freshwater and saltwater, like no other creature. Their primeval presence and ability to endure have made them inextricable with our sense of this landscape.

Crocodiles loom large in local legends, both ancient and modern. Their ochre portraits adorn rock-art sites, and they are a recurring source of fear and dread in the journals of the white explorers. Wherever there is a campfire in the Kimberley the conversation turns, inevitably, to crocs.

Among storytellers the two species that inhabit Australia's Top End are called 'freshies' (the Freshwater Crocodile, *Crocodylus johnstoni*) and 'salties' (the Estuarine or Saltwater Crocodile, *C. porosus*). These names imply a neater division of habitats than is often the case. In the larger river systems Saltwater Crocodiles have been found 100 kilometres upstream. At the other extreme their distribution can also encompass islands a similar distance offshore.

Both species are widespread, though surveys suggest that Saltwater Crocodile numbers are still less than half the population that existed prior to commercial hunting. The subsequent protection of both species has seen a steady increase in population numbers, though the precise picture in the Kimberley is still not clear.

While there is some overlap of habitats, the two species have their distinguishing characteristics. Saltwater Crocodiles are much bigger than Freshwater Crocodiles; indeed they can lay claim to being the world's largest living reptile. Adult males can exceed seven metres in length and weigh more than a tonne.

A Freshwater Crocodile feeds mainly on insects and fish, whereas a mature Saltwater Crocodile generally takes larger prey like mud crabs, birds, turtles and assorted mammals — even large cattle — and its snout is broader, with an array of sturdy conical teeth set in muscular jaws. Crocodiles don't chew their food. Instead prey is crushed and torn, then gulped whole.

Being on top of the food chain gives crocodiles the freedom to eat what, where and when they please. Aside from the task of establishing and maintaining territory, they enjoy a leisurely life. Much of their time is devoted to lying in the shallows and basking on mud banks.

Above: Clear flowing waters meet the silt-laden tidal reaches at the confluence of salt and fresh on the Isdell River.
Left: The Desert Cave Gecko (Heteronotia spelea), a reptile found in arid parts of Western Australia and the Northern Territory. Pasco Island, King Sound.

*Above: A three-metre Saltwater or Estuarine Crocodile (*Crocodylus porosus*) basks in the shallows of Helpman Island in King Sound.*
Below: Cape Domett and Shakespeare Hill lie at the very northen end of an area of Cambridge Gulf known as the False Mouths of the Ord. It is the most extensive mudflat and tidal waterway complex in Western Australia.

Their metabolism is remarkably efficient. Crocodiles digest virtually all they eat, including bones, and convert over half the energy contained in their food into fat reserves. They eat a major meal on average only once a week and conserve energy while, in effect, sitting and waiting for food to come to them.

When the moment does come to strike at prey, Saltwater Crocodiles move with formidable speed and force. From well-camouflaged positions at the water's edge they lunge and charge at anything enticing that approaches the shoreline. Saltwater Crocodiles can leap more than a metre out of the water to snap at prey on steep riverbanks. Once seized the victim is either devoured whole, or dragged into the water where it is drowned before being ripped into swallowable pieces.

For all this fearsome predatory skill, a Saltwater Crocodile is itself acutely vulnerable in the earliest stages of its life. Over three-quarters of eggs laid are lost through a combination of environmental factors like floods and temperature change, together with attacks by predators, most notably goannas and birds. The fate of hatchlings is no less problematic. Though watched over by an attentive mother, the hatchlings emerge into an exposed environment where they are at risk from aquatic predators as well. Less than 10 per cent will survive the first year of life.

Saltwater Crocodiles lay their eggs during the wet. They build nests on rafts of vegetation or in mounds near permanent water such as billabongs. As with Freshwater Crocodiles, the sex of Saltwater Crocodile embryos is determined in the early stages of the incubation by the egg's environment. A steady temperature close to 32 degrees Celsius will produce male embryos. Any fluctuation of two or three degrees above or below this temperature will result in females. Greater extremes usually kill the embryo.

While salties are wide ranging they are also highly territorial and protective of nesting sites. The need for an equable and protected breeding habit means they are most at home in estuarine environments like tidal creeks and mangroves.

One of the Kimberley's many locations for salties is the dense maze of mangrove creeks that fret the shoreline of King Sound. During the 1838 survey of this area John Lort Stokes described returning to a creek where a few days earlier he and fellow officers had nearly lost their lives to the rising tides.

> … we saw an alligator[3] slide his unwieldy carcase from the soft mud-bank, upon which he had been lazily reclining, into one of those creeks we had so much difficulty in crossing. We could not but feel grateful that even the existence of these monster reptiles in this river was then unknown to us, as the bare thought of a visit from one of them would have added to the unpleasantness of our position, while the actual presence of so wholesale a gastronomer would perhaps have given another and less auspicious name to Escape Point.[4]

Munificent mangroves

Mangroves dominate the muddy margins of river estuaries and sheltered inlets all along the Kimberley shoreline. These communities play a crucial role in the coastal ecosystem. They offer food and sanctuary to a remarkable pyramid of life, with *Crocodylus porosus* at its apex.

Fifteen species of mangrove have been recorded in the region: a diversity reflecting the marked variations in salinity and tidal influence. The dense mangrove root structures promote a build up of sediment and nutrients which might otherwise be lost through tidal movement, river currents or wave action.

This repository supports a complex food chain, including fish, crustaceans and the richest mangrove bird fauna in the world with some sixteen endemic species. Closed mangrove forests provide a secure nesting and feeding habitat for a variety of waders, terns and flycatchers. They are the home of the Collared (or Mangrove) Kingfisher (*Halcyon chloris*) and Kimberley (or Brown-tailed) Flycatcher (*Microeca tormenti*) as well as a diverse bat fauna.

Extensive mangrove forests cover the tidal reaches of rivers like the Ord and Fitzroy. Large stands border the enclosed waters of the St George Basin and Walcott Inlet. But mangroves also colonise narrow fringes along rocky sea gorges, offshore islands and coastal clifflines.

A drainage channel snakes through the mangroves that fringe much of Prince Frederick Harbour.

A river in the sea

We depart with the tide. Our boat sweeps down the final bends of the Isdell sea gorge. We leave behind the flanking walls of orange sandstone, and emerge suddenly into open flood-plains. These flat, alluvial expanses lie bleached and dry. Willy-willys rage across the plain raising conical plumes of dust and canegrass.

The landscape has a desolate, unruly kind of beauty. Even so it seems faintly absurd to think that, until recently, a tourist resort was being contemplated for this exposed corner of land near the mouth of the Isdell.

The river runs east then makes a final short turn west before the corridor of mangroves parts and the water spreads open into Walcott Inlet. We bank left, still travelling with the tide, but a stiff westerly breeze works against the current and licks the murky grey–green water into a steep chop.

Walcott Inlet is 30 kilometres long and 11 kilometres across at its widest point. In shape it resembles a flattened bottle. The neck of the inlet is fed by the Isdell, Calder and Charnley rivers, as well as a number of smaller creeks. This vast estuary is virtually land locked, apart from the slenderest of openings, an 800 metre aperture called Yule Entrance.

From the middle of the inlet we look out across two contrasting horizons. To the south, beyond the broad tidal mudflats, stand ranges of King Leopold Sandstone, rising from the plain in blocky orange bluffs and steep ridges. To the north the gentle hills and dark brown screes of Carson Volcanics are capped by a flat-topped escarpment of Warton Sandstone.

Walcott Inlet forms the boundary between these graphic examples of the two dominant geomorphological groups of the northern Kimberley. In earlier times, where now we are chasing the tide, a river once drained to the ocean. The surrounding landforms have changed little since the sea rose to inundate this broad valley. And the landscapes wear an ancient armour of rock and scarp no less proudly than the two species of *Crocodylus* that populate the mangroves and rivers nearby.

By late afternoon the waves begin to ease. Approaching the western extremity of the inlet we come across a large turtle. From a distance it appears to be floating dead in the water, its shell covered in green algae and a curtain of weed. When we draw alongside, the turtle flaps its flippers feebly. It seems powerless to escape and we are left with an image of this forlorn creature spending its final days being shunted in and out of the inlet by the tide.

The inlet narrows. Even though the outgoing tide is beginning to slacken, the current is still forceful enough to slew our boat sideways without warning. The silt-laden waters of the inlet swirl in wide arcs. We plow down into churning depressions, barely able to steer a straight course towards the entrance. Where the whirlpools collide, the water erupts into foaming ridges. The boat is swept on, one moment gliding forward, the next lurching with the rogue currents. Then suddenly we are in the mouth of the inlet, and our boat is shot out into open water like a cork from a champagne bottle.

Beyond Yule Entrance the tide keeps driving straight out to the ocean. It carries the silt-laden water some six kilometres out into Collier Bay, creating a cloudy brown river in a brilliant aquamarine sea. The opposing wind carves sharp waves and whitecaps in the surface of this river. We veer south into clear water that is mercifully calm. The night is spent at anchor in the lee of the Fletcher Islands, just offshore from a swathe of mangroves. Distant lightning flashes in the eastern sky presage storms that will rain down on the catchments of the rivers: storms that will liberate another burden of sediment for the tide to bear out to sea.

Not waning but drowning

Walcott Inlet is but one of many inlets and harbours created by the drowning of the Kimberley coast. The tide turns on similar displays in entrances to a host of enclosed estuaries, most notably the St George Basin and George Water.

It's no surprise that there has been keen interest in harnessing this twice-daily release of energy. But proposals to build tidal power stations near the mouths of such inlets have not

been acted on, principally because of the huge distances between the potential power-source and the consumer.

Forty kilometres to the west of Walcott Inlet is Talbot Bay. This convoluted cluster of flooded valleys and islands bites deep into the Yampi Peninsular. Steep, sparsely wooded ridges surround the bay with prominent outcrops of sandstone breaking the slopes. The sheltered waters of Talbot Bay make it a prime habitat for Dugongs and also one of the world's best sites for commercial pearling.

But Talbot Bay is best known for two spectacular gorge narrows, where the tide breaches parallel ridges to engulf the intervening valleys. Sheer cliffs of white–orange stone flank the two openings, which are acutely narrow: approximately six and 15 metres respectively. A fast incoming tide gathers before these ridgelines and mounts a charge through the gaps. The turquoise water hurtles into white ridges that crash off the walls. Even before the last of the inbound water has passed through the second gap the tide begins to retreat out of the first. At its peak the difference in levels is some four metres.

This shore line was fashioned by the relentless rise in sea levels, between 18 000 and 6 000 years ago.

In northern parts of the continent the early Aboriginal inhabitants would have been confronted by waters advancing across their coastal lowlands at the rate of about a metre each week and rising approximately 15 millimetres each year. Aside from the obvious need to relocate inland onto higher ground, the social impact of this inundation, occurring over thousands of years, can only be guessed at.

The consequences for the environment at large were no less dramatic. Rising sea levels were associated with a progressively warmer and wetter climate. By about 8 000 years ago the vegetation cover had expanded to include large areas of monsoon rainforest. The remnants of this now form one of the most ecologically important habitats for rare species of flora and fauna.

Islands in the stream

Of equal significance for long-term nature conservation was the creation of the islands studded all along the coast, most conspicuously in the waters between Cape Londonderry and Cape Leveque.

This vast congregation includes the Bonaparte and Buccaneer Archipelagos which form the fragmented outer perimeter of the coast. Islands also crowd the more enclosed waters, especially in Vansittart Bay, Napier Broome Bay, Admiralty Gulf, Prince Frederick Harbour and Collier Bay. Lying well offshore are a formidable array of coral-fringed reefs, rocky shoals and oceanic islands.

Represented in this collection is a rich variety of landforms, vegetation and wildlife, often reflecting the environment on the adjacent mainland. Most islands are dominated by an elevated plateau of dissected sandstone or laterite, with a shallow mantle of skeletal soils. These plateaux fall away to broken sandstone cliffs or steep basaltic scree slopes. The surrounding shoreline is typically rocky, with prominent headlands, the occasional sheltered sand or shell beach, and extensive tidal flats.

Markedly seasonal rainfall and thin, sandy soils govern the plant communities on the islands. Hummock grasses prevail and are usually associated with sparse eucalypt woodlands. Vine thickets often adorn the scree slopes, and moist gullies may contain small pockets of rainforest. On larger islands like Augustus and Bigge there are broad valleys supporting open shrubland, and freshwater creeks lined with pandanus and cadjeputs. Sandy shorelines are dominated by *Spinifex longifolius*, with dense bands of mangroves, most commonly *Rhizophora stylosa* and *Avicennia marina*, fringing most inlets.

The separation of these areas from the mainland has preserved a diversity of animal life that is effectively isolated from the depradations of humans and introduced species.

Previous page: Dry-season fires flare on the precipitous slopes of the McLarty Range, above The Gaps and the drowned valleys of Talbot Bay.

The sea gorge of Casuarina Creek, a tributary of the Berkeley River.

157

The sea gorge of Casuarina Creek, a tributary of the Berkeley River.

Top: Looking south-west from the Harding Range, over the expanse of Walcott Inlet.
Above: Steep Island, near Raft Point, Doubtful Bay.

Cone Bay, an expansive waterway at the north-eastern end of King Sound. Numerous freshwater springs flow from the hills of King Leopold Sandstone on the southern side of the bay.

Islands form the refuge for a variety of small mammals like the Warabi, Scaly-tailed Possum and Golden Bandicoot. Rock-wallabies, Rock-rats, Dingos, Tree-rats, Quolls and several bat species are also prevalent.

The more outlying islands boast large colonies of seabirds such as the Least (or Lesser) Frigatebird (*Frigate ariel*), the Brown Booby (*Sula leucogaster*) and the Red-tailed Tropicbird (*Phaethon rubricauda*). Closer to shore, Ospreys (*Pandion haliaetus*) and White-bellied (or White-breasted) Sea-Eagles (*Haliaeetus leucogaster*) frequent the cliffs and headlands all along the coast. Other island bird fauna include kingfishers, honeyeaters and flycatchers. More specialist habitats such as remnant rainforests are home to birds like the Rose-crowned Fruit-Dove (or Rose-crowned Pigeon) (*Ptilinopus regina*) and Rainbow Pitta (*Pitta iris*).

Smaller reptiles like skinks, geckos and dragons are abundant on most islands. Occasionally their much larger relative, the Saltwater Crocodile, also cruises these offshore waters to feed and bask on the golden sands of the archipelagos. Beaches are a vital link in the breeding patterns of turtles. The sandy margin of Browse Island, 350 kilometres north of Derby, is the nesting site for thousands of turtles. Green Turtle (*Chelonia mydas*) rookeries are found all along the coast, from the Lacapede Islands to Cambridge Gulf. More elusive are the Dugongs that graze and breed on sea-grass beds along the length of the Kimberley shore.

As even the wildest quarters of the mainland become exposed to external disturbance, so the Kimberley islands offer one of the best opportunities for conserving the remarkable life that distinguishes the region.

Shingle and sandflies

The island has no name. It is one of several hundred in the Buccaneer Archipelago off the Yampi Peninsular. The boat eases onto a steep shingle beach and the tide draws away as we unload for the night. The shingle rises in shelves and ridges to a line of driftwood marking the limit of the storms and spring tides.

Rounded promontories covered with low spinifex enclose the beach. In the lee of this rocky isthmus a dense mangrove forest extends across the tide-washed mud. Siltstone cliffs front the seaward faces of the headlands. These decrepit walls, tottering before the waves, are vividly coloured in umber-yellows and plum-reds, with solitary figs striking out from seepage cracks in the cliff. The sharp, fractured blocks contrast with the rounded shingle underfoot. The beach composes itself into accidental patterns, the smooth mauve-coloured stones decorated with the occasional orange mangrove leaf or tumbled shell.

Off the eastern headland the beach gives way to a platform of grey rock. The tide has vacated this wave-cut apron, leaving silted pools where crabs rear up at any intruder. Oysters encrust the water's edge and mark the upper range of the tide.

Gravel ramps lead up to overhangs scooped out by the waves. High on the cliff a sea-eagle bursts from its nest. Below stands a row of young mangroves rising from a strip of mud skirting the platform. From such humble beginnings the coast is recast, as Admiral J.L. Stokes noted in his inimitable style: 'As they rise, the mangrove, the pioneer of such fertility as the sea deposits, hastens to maturity, clothing them with its mantle of never fading green and thus bestowing on these barren reefs the presence of vegetable life.'[5] Such changes can also be seen as another small turn in the erratic cycle of reclamation and erosion that is continuous along this shore.

The wind drops and in the evening light the beach shingle glows a luminous purple. For several hours after sundown the still air is massed with sandflies. The tide is on the way in, rushing through the narrow straits of the archipelago.

For millennia these islands stood as the front line for changes that transformed the land. Just as the sea level has fluctuated so the human involvement with the region has, until recently, ebbed and flowed inland from the coast.

For the first Europeans investigating this corner of the continent, the shore was at once alluring and forbidding. They sailed from the misery of mosquito-infested mangroves to luxuriant creeks where fresh water fell to the sea in 'glittering cascades'. One moment the experience bouyed them with hope; the next it left them drained and despairing. Yet still they

Top: Ipomoea macrantha *trails over the upper edge of bare shingle beaches on Ballast Island in Yampi Sound.*
Left: Beach debris, Napier Broome Bay.
Right: The Loggerhead Turtle (Caretta caretta), *an endangered but widespread species, is found along Australia's western and eastern coasts. Near Broome.*

161

persevered, borne on by a vision as flawed as it was resilient. Stokes echoes this optimism as he set out to explore the Buccaneer Archipelago after several weeks of 'mud and misery' in King Sound:

> It was thus again our good fortune to enjoy the exciting pleasure of anticipated discovery; perchance again to wander over the face of a country, now the desert heritage of the solitary savage, but fated, we hope, to become the abode of plenty and the land of peace.[6]

It is a measure of the power of the landscape that, for all this promise, the coast even today resists attempts to claim it for purely human benefit. The tide continues to wash a shore which stands as one of the wildest left on earth. As the push for change — to open up, to subdue, to extract — comes from overland, so the coast bears a new set of hopes: to preserve some of what remains.

1. J.L. Stokes, *Discoveries in Australia, With an Account of the Coasts and Rivers Explored and Surveyed During the Voyage of the H.M.S. Beagle in the Years 1837–43*, T. & W. Boone, London, 1846.
2. J. Harris, *The Kimberley — The Slide Towards Extinction*, Wilderness Society (W.A.), Perth, 1990.
3. Stokes's 'alligator' was in fact a Saltwater Crocodile.
4. Stokes, op. cit., pp. 153–4.
5. Ibid, p. 166.
6. Ibid, p. 162.

Left, top: Fancifully eroded siltstone forms, Strickland Bay.
Left: Shingle on Ballast Island, Yampi Sound.

8

False promises, changing fortunes:
European exploration and settlement

Islands in time

From the eastern tip of Cockatoo Island the view west extends across an opal-blue sea to the Irvine and Bathurst islands. The knolls and islands lie low in the water, their rounded backs sloping down to wave cut cliffs. For millenia Bardi, Djawi and Wororra people plied these waters. They roamed on rafts among the islands to fish and forage along the shores. They lived with the turning winds and seasons, visiting shelters in rocky coves where they retold stories that sustained their belief in the land.

Three hundred years ago William Dampier voyaged twice to this shore. A century later the French navigators Baudin and Hamelin briskly skirted the coast, barely within sight of land. Then the British returned to examine the islands and inlets. They took soundings and drew charts. They attached new names to the capes and harbours, sketched and gathered plant specimens, and wrote journals recording their observations of a strange country and its inhabitants.

In the early years of this century two of the world's richest deposits of iron ore were surveyed on Cockatoo Island and its immediate neighbour, Koolan Island. During the last 40 years nearly 90 million tonnes of iron ore have been extracted from these deposits. The southern flanks of the islands were carved into long, open-cut terraces with tailing screes sweeping down into the waters of Yampi Sound. The mining of the islands saw roads and airstrips graded, wharves constructed and villages built to house workers in their hundreds.

Cockatoo Island is now virtually deserted, at least temporarily. But all the evidence of the mining days remains. There was an attempt in the late 1980s to turn the mining village into a luxury tourist resort. The houses were painted a lolly pink, a swimming pool was installed, the worker's club was decorated with lattice, and hundreds of palms were planted on the stony hillsides. Meanwhile mining at Koolan Island is due to end in 1993. The 800 workers will leave behind another village, another island irrevocably changed.

In 1985 a much smaller excavation took place in a rock shelter above a protected bay at the western end of Koolan Island. The search was not for iron ore but for archaeological evidence. A total of five square metres of material was removed, including sediment, a small amount of charcoal, and particles of bone and shell. Radiocarbon dating of the shell established that this shelter was in use more than 27 000 years ago, the oldest date yet *confirmed* for human presence in the Kimberley.[1]

The historical legacy of these islands suggests some problems of perspective when considering the region's past. From one vantage point there is a 2 000 million year old landscape that became the life-force of a great tribal culture evolving over thousands of years; from another vantage point this corner of the continent is an arena to which explorers came to survey, appropriate and 'civilise'. In recent times the area has been re-cast by the struggle for development. A dogged frontier culture has gouged and grazed its own brand of prosperity from the north-west.

The gulf of time separating the deep past from documented events is immense. So in many ways it is absurd to talk about the Kimberley's last 200 years in terms of discovery and exploration, when the region has already been successfully inhabited for thousands of years. And yet the original explorers — the Aborigines — did not construe their experience simply in terms of dates and defined spans. Instead much of it became compressed into myth.

The problem is not just one of scale. The cultures and their values are so divergent as to make their histories almost irreconcilable. One is an elusive oral tradition based on a cycle of intimate associations with the country. It is nurtured by ritual songs, stories and spiritual art. The other is driven by the acquisition of knowledge and wealth. It is underpinned by a belief in human capacity to remake the natural order for personal gain and the common good; a tradition wedded to notions of progress and to the written record.

Overshadowing these distinctions are the consequences of the clash between the two cultures. It is imperative to respond to the injustice of what has occurred to Aboriginal

---

Opposite: Alasdair McGregor, 'Ord River Valley' (gouache on paper, 31 x 45 cm).

Above: Sunset over a myriad of islands in the Buccaneer Archipelago.
Left: The transformed southern face of Cockatoo Island, Yampi Sound.

people in the Kimberley. But this does not mean that the period since the European occupation can simply be categorised as one of violent conflict. The original inhabitants were most certainly dispossessed, often brutally. Without doubt their culture was all but devastated. But to pour all the recent past into a well of sorrow is to deny the earnest endeavours of many newcomers. More importantly it masks the ability of Aboriginal people to adapt and survive, against all the odds.

In the broadest sense of the word the exploration of the Kimberley continues. The existence of large tracts of undisturbed country makes it possible for people to journey into places about which little is known. There are still 'discoveries' to be made. For Aboriginal people much of their original landscape remains, and with it the power to connect with aspects of their tradition. For others there is the opportunity to bear witness to this relationship and to listen. And there is also scope to imagine the impact of the Kimberley on the first Europeans to see it: to appreciate how at key moments the land confronted them with their own mortality and the transcendent power of place.

Charting the coast

The British settlement at Port Jackson was into its third decade before the north-western coast of the continent was surveyed at close-quarters. The man appointed to the task was Phillip Parker King, the 26 year old son of the New South Wales Governor. The Lords of the Admiralty advised the young captain: 'The chief motive of your survey is to discover whether there be any river on that part of the coast likely to lead to an interior navigation into this great continent.'[2] They also gave him an exhaustive list of other aspects to report on, including the region's climate, topography, geology, flora and fauna, and native tribes.

It was a daunting brief and it took King four separate voyages to complete his survey. The first in 1818 with the 84-ton cutter *Mermaid* was largely devoted to the coast around Northwest Cape and Bathurst and Melville islands. The following year King returned via the east coast, retracing his survey past Bathurst Island, before sailing south-west into Joseph Bonaparte Gulf. Reaching Lacrosse Island at the head of Cambridge Gulf, King noted: 'The character of the country here is entirely changed.'

King and his men explored Cambridge Gulf, venturing up the west arm as far as The Gut, where they sighted and named Mt Cockburn. They made frequent landings and saw ample evidence of Aboriginal occupation but nowhere did they locate a source of much-needed fresh water. King reluctantly abandoned his investigation of this 'extraordinary inlet'.[3]

Beyond Cape Londonderry the coastline became increasingly broken. By the middle of October the *Mermaid* had successfully negotiated the 'labyrinth of islands and shoals' that crowd the waters between Cape Londonderry and Cape Voltaire. Along the way they had witnessed numerous fires but their only direct encounter with the 'natives' was in Vansittart Bay. In Admiralty Gulf the green, luxuriant upper reaches of Port Warrender were explored but still no water was found. With a sick crew and a shortage of provisions King made for Timor.

Less than 12 months later King and the *Mermaid* resumed the survey at Cape Voltaire. After examining Montague Sound they entered Prince Frederick Harbour. Here King and his men roamed the harbour's spectacular reaches, including the Hunter and Roe rivers. They found an abundance of fresh water, and the 'indefatigable' botanist Allan Cunningham collected plant specimens from the densely forested slopes.

A worsening leak in the cutter soon forced King to careen the *Mermaid*. Fresh water was discovered near the chosen beach but in spite of favourable conditions the repairs took nearly three weeks to complete.

Departing Careening Bay, they entered St George's Basin and the Prince Regent River. The square profiles of Mt Trafalgar and Mt Waterloo stood to the north-east. King took the *Mermaid* 20 miles up the mangrove-lined Prince Regent, passing an impressive set of cascades on the way . But on the return from the river the *Mermaid* was once again leaking badly and King had little choice but to call a halt to this voyage.

Repairing the cutter Mermaid. *Wash drawing by Phillip Parker King, c.1820.*

In July 1821 King continued his survey with a new vessel, the 170-ton brig *Bathurst*. Visiting Careening Bay revived memories for King and his men. They located the large Boab that bore the inscription 'H.M.C. *Mermaid*' from the previous year's stay, and King commented prophetically that it 'seemed likely to bear the marks of our visit longer than any other memento we had left'.[4]

King took advantage of a favourable wind and tide to make for the cascades by the Prince Regent River. While his men gathered water, King and the ship's surgeon Andrew Montgomery scaled the tiers of the cascades. King describes the scene:

> On reaching the summit, I found that the fall was supplied from a stream winding through rugged chasms and thickly-matted clusters of plants and trees, among which the pandanus bore a conspicuous appearance and gave a picturesque richness to the place.[5]

This more buoyant mood prevailed during their time on the Prince Regent. Pulling upriver in whaleboats they negotiated rapids, sighted crocodiles and reached the upper limit of the tide, beyond which lay 'a beautiful fresh-water rivulet'.

Departing the river the force of the tide swept the brig on a perilous course. 'The vessel was at times unmanageable from the violent whirlpools through which we passed, and was more than once whirled completely around upon her keel,' noted King.[6]

Reaching Hanover Bay on 6 August, they encountered Aboriginals face to face for the first time since the standoff in Vansittart Bay nearly three years before. Curiosity enticed King and his party to shore. After a successful exchange of gifts with two Aboriginal men, the meeting ended abruptly in confusion during which spears were thrown and Mr Montgomery was wounded. When the Aboriginals appeared again the following day, King decided they 'were intent upon some mischief' and muskets were fired, wounding one of the Aborigines. King then had all their possessions confiscated, including 'water baskets, tomahawks, spears, throwing sticks, fire-sticks, fishing lines, and thirty six spears'.[7]

After this episode the survey continued with more routine tasks, charting the coast and islands south from Camden Sound to Collier Bay. Hazy weather, strong tides and the lack of a

Above and left:
Cockburn Range.

169

second anchor forced King to postpone close examination of the Buccaneer Archipelago until after a resupply voyage to Mauritius.

In the final leg of this voyage King penetrated the cluster of islands that fronts Cygnet Bay (later renamed King Sound) and sailed the western shore. Further exploration of the archipelago was inconclusive but not without incident. Navigating through the narrow island straits King and his men had several near disasters as the *Bathurst* was tossed and whirled by the brute power of the tides. The weather once again closed in, and with unfavourable easterly winds prevailing, King was forced to return to Port Jackson.

These surveys represented a major breakthrough in European knowledge of Australia's north-western shores. Circumstances may have prevented King from identifying any of the major rivers in the region, although he sailed in close proximity to the Ord and Fitzroy. But he had nevertheless successfully charted the continent's most formidable coastline. In doing so King and his men endured the debilitating climate, fearsome tides and a landscape they regarded with an equal measure of fascination and repugnance.

Searching for the rivers

When the British again found it expedient to explore the region, they chose to return to the islands and shores that had occupied the thoughts of Dampier and King. The dream of finding great rivers and inland riches persisted.

In July 1837 the sloop *Beagle* under the command of Captain John Clemments Wickham sailed for Australia. On board were Lieutenants Stokes, Grey and Lushington. At Cape Town the latter pair chartered another vessel, the *Lynher* and made directly for Hanover Bay, at the entrance to the Prince Regent River. Meanwhile the *Beagle* continued to the colony at Swan River before commencing its survey of the Buccaneer Archipelago.

Lord Glenelg, the Colonial Secretary, had instructed the 26 year old Grey to lead an exploration of the country south from the Prince Regent, working towards the uncharted opening behind Dampier Land. 'You will use the utmost exertions to penetrate from thence to the Swan River,' advised the Secretary optimistically.[8]

The *Lynher* dropped anchor by Entrance Island on 2 December. Eager to get a feel for the country, Grey, Lushington and four others went ashore to walk overland to Hanover Bay. In a foretaste of what was to come, they were immediately overwhelmed by the heat, rugged terrain and a shortage of fresh water. Only by good luck did they manage to re-join their ship.

For the next month Grey and his men were occupied with moving stores onto land. On 9 December they hoisted the British flag and 'went through the ceremony of taking possession of the territory in the name of her heirs for ever'. While the *Lynher* sailed to Timor to collect supplies, Grey made tentative forays into the surrounding country. In spite of wet-season storms, the rocky terrain and unnerving encounters with the local Aborigines, Grey was always willing to succumb to the wonder of the landscape:

> The romantic scenery of this narrow glen could not be surpassed ... on each side rose cliffs of sandstone, between three and four hundred feet high, and nearly perpendicular; lofty paperbark trees grew here and there, and down the middle ran a beautiful stream of clear, cool water, which now gushed along, a murmuring mountain torrent, and anon formed a series of small cascades ... Cockatoos soared, with hoarse screams, above us, many-coloured parakeets darted away, filling the woods with their playful cries, and the large white pigeons, which feed on the wild nutmegs, cooed loudly to their mates, and battered the boughs with their wings as they flew away.[9]

After several hapless attempts to move laden ponies through the deep gorges, progress was slowly made inland. Then on 11 February Grey and two companions were attacked by a group of spear-wielding Aborigines. In the flurry of battle, Grey was speared in the hip . He managed to regain his feet and retaliated by shooting his fleeing assailant. 'The effect was electrical,' wrote Grey, 'not another spear was thrown, not another yell was uttered.' But that night Grey's sleep was broken by the 'piercing shrieks of wailing women and the mournful cries of native men, sorrowing over him who had fallen that day by my hand'.[10]

It was two weeks before Grey's wound healed sufficiently to allow the party to cross into

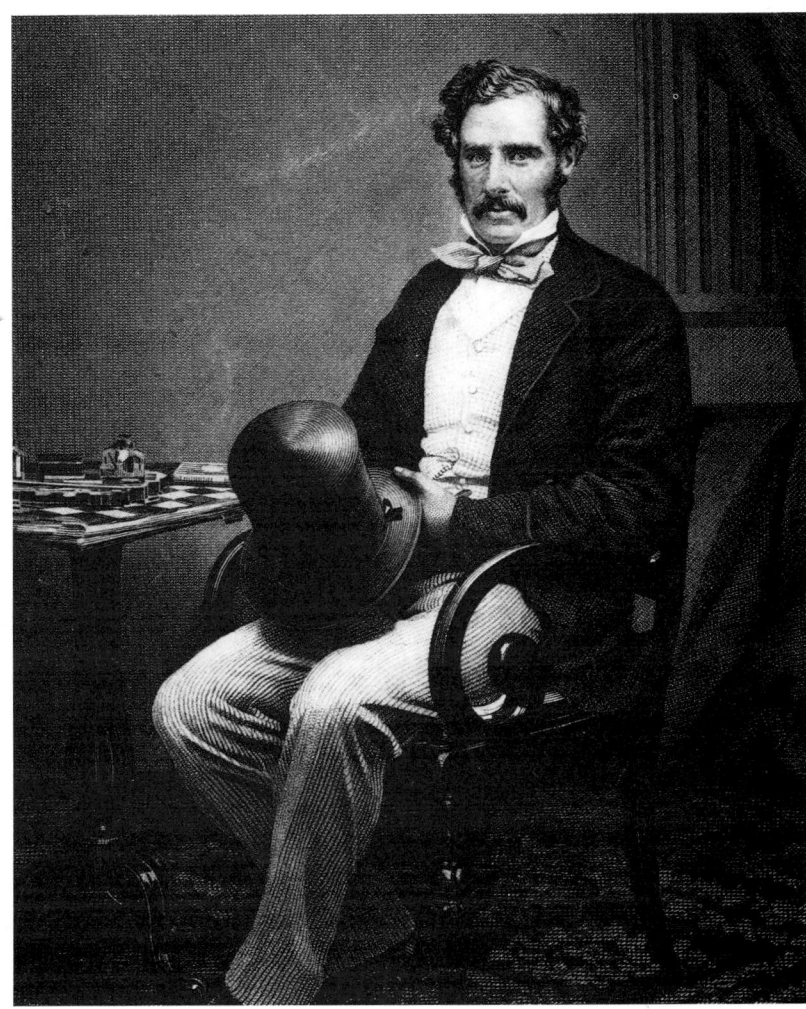

Sir George Grey was one of the Kimberley's most enthusiastic explorers. He later became the Governor of South Australia, New Zealand and Cape Colony.

open, basalt country. 'Since I have visited this spot, I have traversed large portions of Australia, but have seen no land, no scenery to equal it,' he enthused.[11]

The discovery of the Glenelg River gave the party fresh hope and they spent several days exploring the densely vegetated river fringes . Grey wrote, 'I could not but feel we were in a land singularly favoured by nature.'[12] Yet this sanguine outlook was constantly being subverted by the ravages of storms that swept in without warning. The marshy lowlands were often impenetrable, and Grey was also haunted by signs of Aboriginal presence. Only by climbing isolated summits could he regain his grasp of the larger landscape and the vision of fertile country, navigable rivers and fine harbours.

They moved upriver into broken sandstone country, where Grey made his famous rock-art discoveries. These inspired 'a wide field of conjecture', and he pondered 'the timid character of the natives' and their 'anomalous position in so fertile a country'.[13] Yet Grey's own position was itself becoming even more anomalous: his health was declining, his men were enfeebled, and stores were dwindling. After an advance party led by Lushington had returned Grey started the march back to Hanover Bay. Arriving there on 15 April they found both the *Lynher* and the *Beagle* waiting at anchor.

During the previous three months the *Beagle* had been engaged in a detailed study of the coast to the south. When Lieutenant Stokes arrived at Roebuck Bay on 15 January the view from the masthead convinced him that speculation about an opening connecting the bay with the waters of the Buccaneer Archipelago was unfounded. For the next month the *Beagle* hugged the shores of the Dampier Peninsula. Bays and headlands were named, and there were many intriguing, and usually friendly, encounters with Aborigines. But no good sources of fresh water were found, and the terrain appeared desolate and 'barbarous'.

Top: Sunset over the coastline near Raft Point — named by Stokes for the Aboriginal craft he sighted in the area.
Left: King Cascades adjacent to the Prince Regent River's sea gorge. Located by Phillip Parker King in 1820, the cascades provided a welcome source of abundant fresh water.
Right: The lower Fitzroy River. John Lort Stokes saw the river as his longed-for path to the inland.

For all this bleakness their arrival at Point Cunningham brought them to the brink of unknown waters and the prospect of great discoveries. Stokes climbed to the masthead to spy the expanse of King Sound which he would survey with a boat party. As with Grey, an elevated view seemed to prompt Stokes to a rush of enthusiasm and lofty rhetoric:

> ... nor can I describe with what delight, all minor annoyances forgotten, I prepared to enter upon the task of exploring waters unfurrowed by any preceding keel; and shores, on which the advancing step of civilisation had not yet thrown the shadows of her advent ...[14]

Setting out on 24 February, Stokes and his men crossed the sound and made for the eastern shore. They pushed further south into the narrowing until the ebbing waters tasted nearly fresh. After all his fervid anticipation Stokes had discovered a significant river and was moved to name it the Fitzroy, in honour of his revered former commander. But the mouth of this great river is a diabolical place. That night the incoming tide formed a charging wall of water that nearly capsized the boats. The following day Stokes and two others risked a sortie on the muddy shore only to find themselves hopelessly trapped by the advancing tide. As the rising waters topped their shoulders they were rescued by the boat party.

In spite of such trials, and constant harassment by mosquitoes, Stokes was indefatigable. After returning to the *Beagle* he persuaded Captain Wickham to help him resume the investigation of the river. In Stokes's view they indulged, 'in the golden anticipation that the Fitz-Roy would yet convey our boats some distance into the interior of that vast and unknown continent'. His captain was less enthusiastic and soon ordered the quest be abandoned.

The *Beagle*'s survey work continued up the eastern flank of King Sound. From Port Usborne, Stokes again left the ship and took a boat to explore the islands and deeply indented bays as far north as Bathurst Island. The rugged hills, cliffs and sandy coves on this shore were a relief after the monotony of the Fitzroy. Stokes was also fascinated by an Aborigine who met them 'with all the confidence of an old acquaintance'. The bearing of this lone figure greatly impressed, though his 'listless' departure seemed baffling. Stokes was moved to generalise that with the 'native Australian ... wonder is rarely expressed, curiosity seldom apparent — yet their indifference is not stupidity, or their simplicity cunning.'[15] On Bathurst Island there were more discoveries, including elaborate Aboriginal huts, a large raft framed from the trunk of a mangrove tree and on the summit of the island 'rocks containing iron'.

After Stokes rejoined the *Beagle*, it was decided to sail north in the hope of meeting with Grey's expedition near Hanover Bay. While the others searched for Grey's party, Stokes chose once more to cross the threshold into the unknown. Taking a boat party he ventured down along the coast as far as Walcott Inlet. But their investigations, both here and in Doubtful Bay to the north, failed to reveal the great opening they imagined would lead to the heart of the continent.

Stokes returned to the *Beagle* on 16 April to find the battered but unbowed figure of Grey on board: 'Badly wounded and half-starved, he did, indeed, present a melancholy contrast to the vigorous and determined enthusiast we had parted from at the Cape, to whom danger seemed to have a charm, distinct from success.'[16]

As the two ships prepared to depart, Grey and Stokes spent memorable nights poring over charts and sketches. Grey was impressed by Stokes's descriptions of Camden Sound, 'as being one of the finest he had ever seen; and such being the case it must undoubtedly be the most important position on this part of the coast'.

Even after all their respective ordeals, both men were reluctant to leave these shores. In material terms their discoveries can be judged as minor. But their travels reflected a willingness to engage the landscape imaginatively. Their enthusiasm was for the experience of the coast and its people.

Before leaving, Stokes gazed upon Grey's deserted camp at Walker's Valley and noted, 'the rugged and lofty cliffs that frown down upon the valley — the flitting shadows of the watchful eagles soaring far above my head — and the hoarse murmurs of the tide among the rocky masses on the beach.'[17]

Grey chose to muse upon the more humble image of the pumpkins and coconut palms he had placed in the ground with his own hands. 'I would very gladly have passed a year or two of my life in watching over them ... now they must be left to their fate,' he wrote.

*Above: The King
Leopold Ranges,
north-west from
Mt Broome.
Left: Reflections,
Richenda River.*

A quarter of a century later, ships bearing settlers and sheep from the south started landing at Camden Harbour. They came to fulfil dreams conjured from the pages of Grey's journal. But the pioneers were singularly unprepared for the rigours of the country. Arriving at the end of the dry season, water was scarce and many people died in the heat. Ships and provisions were lost to the tides. Thousands of sheep perished from thirst and the lack of suitable pasture. Meanwhile an unknown number of Wororra people were casualties of the fight to defend their traditional lands. After barely six months the settlement was abandoned. Grey's seeds of empire were crushed even before they had taken hold.

Surveying the inland

The failed attempts to settle the far north-west served to postpone further close examination of the region for a decade. In 1879 the surveyor Alexander Forrest set out on an expedition to investigate the country north from the Fitzroy River. He was funded by the Western Australian government to assess the potential of the region for cultivation and cattle grazing.

After crossing the Dampier Peninsula from Beagle Bay Forrest's party of nine reached the Fitzroy River on 8 May. 'The magnificent Fitzroy. A beautiful stream to behold, and still running strong,'[18] wrote Forrest in his journal. Another member of the party, Arthur Hicks, noted that the river banks were 'covered with eucalyptus, banksia, and acacias. Ducks, turkeys, and cockatoos were there in countless numbers ... When game was plentiful and on the menu, our flour and bacon remained intact.'

Over the next month the expedition worked its way along the alluvial plains of the Fitzroy basin, thick with grass after the wet season. Near the junction of the Fitzroy with the Margaret River they broached the Oscar Range. Beyond lay the imposing barrier of the King Leopold Ranges. A direct passage north seemed improbable and the leader was frustrated by a terrain that 'completely shut us in with bold, high ranges'.

They trekked to the north-west for two weeks in search of a way through the ranges. Reaching the coast near Walcott Inlet they struggled in vain to force a route north. Hicks wrote, 'For the following ten days we were battered about making road bridges and passes through some of the roughest country horses ever travelled.'[19]

With the loss of several horses and illness affecting half his party, Forrest was forced to return to the Fitzroy. 'It is a bitter disappointment,' wrote the leader, 'I have never exerted myself so much in my life as I have within the last ten days, and I may say the same of the whole of my party.' In an audacious move Forrest decided to push east in the hope of making the newly built Overland Telegraph Line, nearly 600 kilometres away.

From the Margaret River they pressed on into unknown territory. By the end of July, as rations became increasingly limited, the weakest horses were killed for meat which made, in the words of Hicks, 'a most unpalatable, hard and tough repast'.

Yet in spite of these privations, the sweep of country beyond Mt Barrett showed great prospects. To Forrest, 'it was the most splendidly grassy plain it has ever been my lot to see'.[20] Shortly after they came to the upper reaches of an impressive river which was named the Ord after the then Governor.

When crossing into the Northern Territory, conditions became more extreme for Forrest's party. By 29 August, the way forward offered little hope of water. Forrest decided to leave the main party at the last waterhole and make a dash with Hicks to the telegraph line. They marched for two days before finally reaching a dry creekbed where, as night fell, their horses collapsed. Forrest resolved that they must rally themselves and travel through the night to make the line. 'I knew we should never be able to do so in the heat of the day, for even when riding, our tongues became so dry and parched that it was almost unendurable.'[21]

They dragged themselves forward and stumbled upon the telegraph line less than a mile further on. 'The night rang with our cheers,' wrote Forrest. Turning north they soon reached a full water tank, where they enjoyed a celebratory meal. After a further three days' trek they encountered a party of linesmen who supplied fresh provisions and horses for the pair's return journey to the waiting group. A week later the expedition was reunited and together they began the long haul north to Darwin and safety.

Left: Alexander Forrest's epic traverse of the southern Kimberley in 1879 sparked a rush of interest in the grazing potential of the region.
Right: 'Frank Hann with his Aboriginal boy Talbot.' Hann was one of the first Europeans to find a passage across the King Leopold Ranges to the spectacular headwaters of the Prince Regent River.

In the next three decades there would be further survey expeditions to the Kimberley, many of which would penetrate the ranges that had defied Forrest. But nothing would kindle the expectations of budding settlers across the continent quite like the reports that came with Forrest's return. As well as noting the rivers he had traversed, Forrest estimated that the region boasted 'an area of 20 millions of acres of good, well-watered country, suitable for pastoral purposes, besides a large area suitable for the culture of sugar, rice, or coffee'.[22]

The grab for land

Even before Alexander Forrest had departed from Darwin, the Commissioner of Crown Lands in Perth had received a flurry of applications for land around the Fitzroy River. In March 1881 grazier George Paterson arrived at the river to establish Yeeda Station, having travelled overland with a herd of sheep from Beagle Bay. Others, including members of the Kimberley Pastoral Company, soon followed to take up further large holdings along the Fitzroy and Meda rivers. In the space of two years over five million acres had been leased in the west Kimberley.

As a result of the Western Australian Government's efforts to promote the region there was a scramble for land, attracting both a rash of speculators and more committed pastoralists. Between 1883 and 1886 a series of now legendary cattle drives to the Kimberley were initiated from distant properties in the eastern states. These remarkable overland journeys across great expanses of unknown country and in the face of floods, droughts and disease, helped to forge much of the popular folklore about the Kimberley and its pioneering families.

The redoubtable bushman and drover Nat Buchanan was the first to cross into the eastern Kimberley, arriving in 1884 with 4 000 head of cattle at what was to become Ord River Station. In September of the following year the Durack brothers converged on the black-soil plains to the north. This dynasty undertook the development of Argyle Downs, Lissadell, Dunham River and Ivanhoe stations. The longest cattle drive of all was completed in June 1886 when the MacDonald brothers arrived at Fossil Downs station near the Margaret River after an epic three-year journey of 5 600 kilometres from Goulburn in New South Wales. Their neighbours were to be the renowned Emanuel family who founded Go Go, Liveringa and Noonkanbah stations on the plains of the Fitzroy River.

For all the success of these pioneers, the sudden spread of settlers with their horses and cattle had drastic consequences for Aboriginal society along the plains of the Ord and Fitzroy. At stake was their very means of survival: the waterholes, foraging grounds and hunting territory. Even more significant was the threat to their ancestral attachment with the particulars of place, those external contours and fixtures of an inner, spiritual landscape. It was as though the Aborigines were about to lose everything — their land, their livelihood, their cathedrals of grass and stone.

Tribal groups along the Ord and the Fitzroy fiercely resisted the invasion. Hundreds of cattle and sheep were speared. Droving camps were raided, stores and equipment were stolen. The settlers themselves came under direct attack, several dying from spears that came whistling out of the grass. Such incidents inevitably led to retaliation from the drovers and pastoralists: many were hard-bitten characters who dispensed rough justice with repeating rifles. For the Aborigines the incursion of the cattlemen and their herds was bad enough. But barely before the dust from the hooves had settled, another equally threatening wave of intruders began to arrive.

Chasing the weight

In 1882 prospectors Philip Saunders and Adam Johns retraced Forrest's route along the Fitzroy, and found small traces of gold near the upper tributaries of the Ord River. During the next two years a government-appointed geologist Edward Hardman led survey expeditions which eventually confirmed the existence of payable quantities of gold in the same vicinity. Then in August 1885 Charles Hall and John Slattery returned to Derby with 10 ounces of gold. The news of their find spread, and within 12 months the contagion that is gold fever lured nearly 2 000 prospectors into the area around Halls Creek.

These pilgrims of the pick and pan made arduous treks from the shanty towns of Derby and Wyndham. Many did not survive the overland journey. Those that did reach the diggings had to contend with blinding heat and chronic food shortages. Diseases like typhoid fever, dysentery and scurvy claimed many prospectors even before they had seen a glint of gold. It was as harsh a frontier as could be imagined, with the usual mixture of rogues, drinkers and determined fortune-seekers.

Yet this population rapidly dwindled. By 1890 less than a hundred diggers remained. The yield from the gullies around Halls Creek could never fulfil the dreams of the 10 000 fossickers who passed through the district in its heyday. The mining boom may have been shortlived, but the government and mercantile presence remained. The port towns of Wyndham and Derby became well established, along with police stations and telegraph and mail services.

For the Aboriginal population, the flood of miners into their country presented a jarring new challenge and led to an escalation of violence. Almost from the outset there were Aboriginal attacks on the invaders. Barney Lamond describes one ambush:

> There were five spears thrown. Billy Keelan who was with them escaped with a spear through his hat. Fred Marriot was speared in the heart. Sam Johnson had a spear cut across the forehead, and the blood blinded him for a time.[23]

The reprisals were swift and devastating. Another gold-seeker, George Hales, described in a letter home the response to an earlier attack:

> Having bailed up a large number of blacks in a gully who showed fight, they proceeded to slaughter them with repeating rifles. It is certain a great many of them were killed, some say at least a hundred. The blacks could not understand why their comrades dropped one after another, although they could see nothing coming towards them.[24]

Above: The upper reaches of the Charnley River's sandstone gorge — typical of the obstacles encountered by Frederick Brockman.
Left: Wandjinas, King Edward River.
Right: Basalt and Boab country, lower Calder River.

Pushing back the frontier

While European settlement continued apace in the western and eastern Kimberley, the country to the north of the King Leopold Ranges remained essentially unknown. In 1884 the bushman Harry Stockdale launched an ill-fated expedition from Cambridge Gulf. His party of seven traversed the stony ranges around the Forrest River. But dissent within the group forced the leader to abandon his plans. Two members, Ashton and Mulchay, 'lost all heart' and refused to continue. Stockdale was forced to leave them camped by the Laurence River. The two men were never found.

With the advent of the port at Wyndham others would inevitably have more success in their journeys westward. Joseph Bradshaw and six others set out in March 1891 to explore the source of the Prince Regent, with an eye on the value of the country for pastoral activities. The expedition crossed the Drysdale River and by the end of March was in the gorge country between the Prince Regent and Roe rivers. It was here that Bradshaw made his now famous discovery of the rock-art style that bears his name.

There were numerous sightings of Aboriginal groups who followed the progress of the expedition with great curiosity. Most of the time these onlookers kept their distance, but at one camp Bradshaw noticed 'about sixty dusky forms scattered along the face of the range'.[25] After attempts to find a passage west to the Glenelg, the expedition carried out a series of forays towards St George's Basin and the Roe River before returning to Wyndham in mid-May.

The pastoralist and bushman Frank Hann travelled into this same area around the headwaters of the Prince Regent in 1898. His expedition was the first to investigate the country further to the south. In doing so he discovered the Isdell and Hann rivers and made the first successful crossing of the King Leopold Ranges.

Hann's reports stirred the government into commissioning an extensive survey of the northern Kimberley. In May 1901 Frederick Brockman set off from Parry's Creek near Wyndham with a team which included Charles Crossland as his deputy and the naturalist Dr F. M. House. The expedition started along the Chamberlain River until Brockman located a pass through the Durack Range to the vast tableland beyond. Compared with the lush plains Brockman had spied to the east, he found the new terrain sparse and unpromising.

By 13 June, they had reached the Hann River and from there began a detailed investigation of the Isdell and Charnley rivers. While a party led by Crossland pushed south to investigate the Isdell, Brockman veered north into basalt country to locate the Calder River. Further exploration included the sandstone ranges around the Sale and Glenelg rivers and the upper reaches of the Prince Regent.

On 5 September, Brockman set out with a party of four to head north beyond the Roe River, which he noted was bounded on the west by high sandstone ranges. 'They [the ranges] rise to a great altitude and apparently extend westward to the coastline; whilst on the east it is flanked by high, undulating, beautifully-grassed basaltic country.'[26] Here he discovered the Moran River and further north a larger river he named the King Edward. For the next two months Brockman and his men roamed the shores of Vansittart and Napier Broome Bay. They pushed east to the Drysdale River and the undulating grasslands of the Barton Plain before ultimately returning to Wyndham.

In his report Brockman estimated the region had 'between seven and eight million acres of valuable pastoral country'.[27] Of the Aborigines he noted that they seemed to be less numerous than expected and those encountered 'were terrified at our approach and immediately ran for cover'. Of particular interest to both Brockman and Dr House was the abundance of Aboriginal paintings 'on almost every available smooth, vertical face to be found in the sandstone ranges'.[28] Echoing earlier opinions House ventured that the paintings 'are finished with greater care and attention to detail than one would expect to find in such a primitive race, and apparently they value them considerably'.[29]

Footholds of faith

On the western side of Napier Broome Bay, near a small pandanus-lined creek, are the remains of several stone walls. Tall, leafy mango trees shade the ruins. Where once other buildings stood, only broad stone slab floors survive, with lush grass sprouting from the cracks. In the midst of the clearing squats a solitary, venerable Boab. Two bare Cypress Pine uprights nearby are the frail remnants of a two-storey monastery. Eighty years ago Benedictine monks would have stood on the upstairs verandah and looked across the bay where every few months boats would arrive with news and supplies from a distant world. To the east and south the view was of wild sandstone country: the domain of the Kwini, Kulari, Walmbi and Arrawari people, to whom the monks had come to preach their civilising gospel of salvation.

Pago Mission was founded in August 1908 by the Right Reverend Fulgentius Torres, Order of St Benedict, Abbot of New Norcia. Working from the report of Brockman's expedition, Abbot Torres chose the coastal plain behind Mission Bay, after first considering the Barton River. During the early years the missionaries lived in a state of siege as they struggled to establish their buildings and gardens, as well as befriend the local people. There were numerous attacks and one diary entry reads: 'We are in the chapel saying our prayers, with the Rosary in one hand, and the revolver in the other.'[30]

During the next 30 years the monks were gradually accepted by the Aborigines and had increasing success with their evangelical work. By the time the mission was relocated to nearby Kalumburu in 1938 it had become an integral, if not central, part of the district.

During latter stages of the last century, missions had become a conspicuous feature of European influence in the remote corners of the Kimberley. The earliest attempt to establish a mission was by Father Duncan MacNab at Cunningham Point on King Sound in 1885. His battle with illness and the intractable problems of conveying his Catholic message to the local people ended two years later when the Father returned from a tour of the Halls Creek goldfields to find his mission burnt to the ground.

In 1890 a more durable outpost on the Dampier Peninsula was founded by Bishop Gibney at Beagle Bay. This later transferred to the control of Pallotine Fathers in 1901. Meanwhile in 1897 the Church of England was persuaded by Sydney Hadley to attempt a mission on Forrest River. After an initial failure the Church resumed its efforts in 1913 under Reverend E. R. Gribble. The Reverend Hadley went on to set up his own mission on Sunday Island at the entrance to King Sound in 1899, adopting a libertarian and controversial approach to his vocation and the local people.

Further to the north a Presbyterian mission was founded at Port George IV in 1912 by Robert and Frances Wilson. Three years later the mission was relocated to a more suitable inlet to the south at Kunmunya. This was to become the base for J.R.B. Love and his noted work among the Wororra people.

Stories of individual fortitude and perseverance on the part of these missionaries are legion. Alongside this rich history it is now commonplace to question the long-term effects of their work. If indeed the missions helped to create a culture of dependence and a breakdown of tribal traditions, then it is also true that they offered sanctuary from the violent turmoil that raged in other quarters. In doing so the missions represented a rare example of European culture's capacity for benevolence towards Aboriginal people. For many years the practical help provided by the missions forestalled the wholesale eradication of Aboriginal tribes by massacre and disease. During the grim decades it was the missionary voice that pleaded for a more just, humane treatment of the original inhabitants.

'T. Yalag-umeri (Kulari), V. Ran-tja (Walmbi) and Paul M. Yuroa (Kwini).' The men were all members of different tribes (noted in brackets), brought together at the Drysdale River Mission, Pago, circa 1920. Each man bears ochre body decorations and ritual scarring (cicatrices).

Quietening the country

Later that bloke came up with the wagon and started mustering all the black-fellers, and quietening them all down. This is how they started Ord River Station. My grannie was a young girl then camping at the creek where the Racecourse is now ... The white man came there and made the camp. They had tents everywhere, and were quietening down all the bush black-fellers. They'd get all the young girls and young boys for the work ... and they didn't want to fight. The mob from Dunham River down to Wyndham and over at Gordon Downs were cheeky. They used to spear the whites, but not around this way They thought he was a devil all the time until my father came. He had a bit of language and he'd say, 'This a different mob of people. They're black and we're white, that's gotta be our company in this world.'[31]

By the turn of the century there were more than 400 000 cattle and sheep in the Kimberley. Pastoralists gradually pushed north to take up holdings in the outlying areas identified by government surveys. The more established properties along the Ord and the Fitzroy slowly built up their herds and secured their grip on the land, notwithstanding the manifold problems of isolation, drought, wet-season floods, and diseases like cattle tick and redwater fever.

Localised Aboriginal resistance to white occupation of traditional lands continued. The most notorious figure was Sandamarra, better known as Pigeon, an Aborigine who for over two years waged a personal campaign of vengeance and murder before finally being captured. Direct attacks on settlers did gradually become less frequent but the punitive expeditions that followed were still often bloody and indiscriminate. By the 1890s the cattle and sheep that drove out traditional game, ravaged waterholes, and disturbed foraging grounds had become the main target of raids. Cattle were speared, mobs were chased, and pastures were set on fire. In this period Aborigines also sabotaged the telegraph line, turning the insulators into spear points.

As this harassment persisted the penalty for cattle killing was increased to three years' gaol with whipping. The responsibility for enforcing this law now fell on police patrols emanating from Wyndham, Derby and Halls Creek. A system was introduced whereby police were entitled to claim a standard payment for each prisoner's rations. By allowing the police the scope to profit from arrests, this system may have contributed to a decline in the number of indiscriminate killings. But it also instituted another injustice as large groups of Aborigines were arrested, chained together neck to neck, and marched into the towns.

Meanwhile massacres were still perpetrated. One of the most publicised occurred as late as 1926 when a group of police and others set out from Wyndham to hunt down an Aborigine responsible for the killing of a stockman near the Forrest River Mission. There is no accurate figure on the number of Aboriginal deaths that resulted but estimates range from 20 to over a hundred. Most of the slain were burnt and then buried. The public outcry prompted a Royal Commission, which led to the arrest on murder charges of the two Police involved. They were tried and acquitted.[32]

The spiral of vengeance and reprisal between black and white was just one product of European settlement. On the other side of the frontier there was a hidden history of hardship, as tribal groups strove to maintain their traditional life. Competition increased for the land and food sources that remained within Aboriginal control, which led to intertribal fighting and, in some areas, malnutrition. But the most insidious effect of the white invasion was foreign disease. Influenza, measles, tuberculosis, smallpox, whooping cough, typhoid, leprosy, mumps, diphtheria, pneumonia and venereal disease all contributed to a substantial decline in Aboriginal population in northern Australia.

In the eyes of many at the time this decline only served to support the notion that 'the dark race is doomed to extinction'. The popular opinion among European onlookers was that Aborigines were treacherous and hostile savages beyond redemption, and all that remained was to 'smooth the dying pillow'. Underlying such notions was a belief in white destiny and supremacy echoed by Nat Buchanan's son Gordon:

This is now the only continent under the hegemony of one people; and with the best British pioneering traditions to live up to, it should, in such favourable and unprecedented opportunities, lead the van of Christian civilisation ... [33]

Over the next 50 years the changing realities of life in the Kimberley gradually eroded the burden of this argument, if not its ingrained prejudice. Many Aborigines who endured the initial period of conflict became involved with the work of the cattle properties. For some it was a matter of choice; for others it was more a form of enslavement. Either way, through their unique knowledge of the country and their ability to adapt their skills to station life, Aboriginal men and women played a central role in the survival of the fledgling pastoral industry.

So began a period of paternalism that continued up to and in some areas beyond the Second World War. In return for their labour, Aborigines were usually fed and clothed, though rarely paid a regular wage. Living and working conditions varied greatly, and there is little doubt that on many stations employees were mistreated. Yet for all its manifest faults this semi-feudal existence did at least offer a more peaceful, secure alternative. In the wake of so much despair and barbarism, here was an opportunity for workers, both black and white, to develop some degree of mutual trust and understanding. Aspects of this new life were grafted onto Aboriginal culture and social relationships were recast, often to the benefit of Aboriginal women. At the same time the cycle of cattle work gave people scope to go bush in the wet months and relate to their land and culture in more traditional ways.

The Kimberley may have been 'pacified' by force, but over time the vagaries of life in such an isolated and distinctive region wrought unexpected changes. If there was a pioneering tradition, it evolved largely from the character of the land and the people who responded best to its rhythms.

Side by side

Among many of the elderly Aborigines who survive from this era, there is a nostalgia for what is seen as a 'golden age'. As Amy Laurie, a bushwoman and now Kununurra resident says, 'I reckon I had my best days because of cattle work. Droving is the best.'[34] This nostalgia can be seen in part as a reaction to the social upheaval of the post-war years. The collaboration between black and white in the cattle industry became increasingly precarious with the advance of new technology, fluctuating beef markets and government policy towards Aborigines.

The war years 1942–43 had a major effect on coastal settlements. Broome, Derby and Wyndham were all the victims of Japanese bombing raids. The mission at Kalumburu was almost devastated. Large numbers of Aborigines fled inland and took refuge in bushcamps. Broome suffered two air raids in March 1942. Around 70 people were killed, and several ships and aircraft destroyed. The local pearling industry was especially hard hit, both from the loss of luggers and the internment of 500 Japanese workers. Meanwhile on cattle properties, the shortage of white labour during the war years shifted additional responsibility to Aboriginal stockmen and women.

This elevated role was however mostly short-lived and usually unrecognised. Beyond what was known as the 'Japanese war', the patterns of life in the Kimberley were steadily transformed. From being a highly contained and self-reliant region, it was drawn into the outside world by improvements in transport and communication. As early as 1941 the Ord River was being surveyed for possible dam sites as part of the push for post-war reconstruction and as a bulwark of northern settlement.

After decades of silence, government agencies attempted to grapple with their response to the exploitation and abuse of Aboriginal people. The policies of assimilation and integration sought to give Aborigines some basic rights and encourage them to meld into the wider community. Along with improved access to social welfare, there was pressure on pastoralists to guarantee payment to their workers, something they were often unable or unwilling to do. By the time award wages became enshrined in the Pastoral Act of 1968 there was a widespread drift of Aboriginal workers and families from the stations and the bush to the outskirts of the towns. The effects of this dislocation, with its loss of belonging and purpose, and the complications of grog and welfare money, are still being felt in many areas.

Out of the tensions of the new social order there has slowly emerged a stronger Aboriginal voice. What has been interpreted by outsiders as a fatal despondency has often disguised the underlying resilience and pride of the people themselves. If discontent is more evident, that reflects both a greater confidence by Aboriginal groups to speak out and equally an overdue willingness of others to listen.

Underlying the Aboriginal demands is an acceptance of the realities of their new world, and a wish to co-exist 'together' and 'side by side'. If the traditional bush life has all but vanished that does not mean that the culture it spawned — its ethics, art and stories — is not still potent and malleable to the times. What is needed most is the freedom to share the country and to see it afresh. The unique history of the Kimberley and the lingering power of its unspoilt landscapes makes that a real possibility.

1. S. O'Connor, 'New radiocarbon dates from Koolan Island, West Kimberley, W.A.', *Australian Archaeology*, no. 28, June 1989.
2. E. Favenc, *The History of Australian Exploration*, Turner & Henderson, Sydney, 1888.
3. P.P. King, *Narrative of a Survey of the Intertropical and Western Coast of Australia, Performed Between the Years 1818 and 1822*, vol. 1, John Murray, London, 1827, p. 291.
4. Ibid, vol. 2, p. 44.
5. Ibid, p. 46.
6. Ibid, p. 61.
7. Ibid, p. 67
8. G. Grey, *Journals of Two Expeditions of Discovery in North-West and Western Australia 1837–1839*, vol. 1, T. & W. Boone, London, 1841, p.3.
9. Ibid, pp. 93–4.
10. Ibid, pp. 150–56.
11. Ibid, p. 162.
12. Ibid, p. 180.
13. Ibid, p. 207.
14. J.L. Stokes, *Discoveries in Australia, With an Account of the Coasts and Rivers Explored and Surveyed During the Voyage of the H.M.S. Beagle in the Years 1837–43*, vol. 1, T. & W. Boone, London, 1846, p. 121.
15. Ibid, p. 170.
16. Ibid, p. 208.
17. Ibid, p. 216.
18. A. Forrest, *North-West Exploration: Journal of Expedition from De Grey to Port Darwin*, Perth, 1880.
19. A. Hicks, 'The Kimberleys explored: Forrest expedition of 1879', *Early Days*, vol. 1, Oct. 1938, pp. 11–19.
20. Forrest, op. cit.
21. Ibid.
22. Ibid.
23. G.H. Lamond, *Tales of the Overland*, Hesperian Press, Perth, 1986.
24. N. Green, 'Aborigines and white settlers', in *A New History of Western Australia*, ed. C. Stannage, University of Western Australia Press, Perth, 1981, p. 115.
25. J. Bradshaw, 'Notes on a recent trip to the Prince Regent River', *Transactions of the Royal Geographical Society of South Australia*, vol. 9, 1892.
26. F. Brockman, *Report on Exploration of North-West Kimberley*, 1901, p. 7.
27. Ibid.
28. Ibid.
29. Ibid, Appendix C.
30. E. Perez, *Kalumburu, The Benedictine Mission and the Aborigines, 1908–1975*, Kalumburu Benedictine Mission, 1977.
31. From the interview of Amy Laurie by Ann Magrath, in *Fighters and Singers: The Lives of Some Australian Aboriginal Women*, eds I. White, D. Barwick and B. Meehan, Allen & Unwin, Sydney, 1985, pp. 80–82.
32. B. Elder, *Blood on the Wattle: Massacres and Maltreatment of Australian Aborigines Since 1788*, Child & Associates, Sydney, 1988.
33. G. Buchanan, *Packhorse and Waterhole*, Angus & Robertson, Sydney, 1934, p. 84.
34. Laurie, op. cit.

9

Shifting ground:
Kimberley prospects

The view at the falls

The wooden signpost at the turnoff has been vandalised, but a message scrawled in chalk on a 44-gallon drum alongside reads, 'The Mitchell Falls 12 k — and well worth it'. We heed this advice and drive on through the palm forest, passing gravel scrapes heaped with sun-bleached cans and garbage bags. The sandy track narrows, then drops sharply off the plateau. We engage low range and lurch down the rutted, gravel incline. At the bottom a young couple in their four-wheel drive wait for us to clear the track and then give encouraging smiles as we pass by.

Across a grassy flat we come to a clearing and six vehicles parked in a ragged circle. The numberplates are all from distant parts: two from Queensland, one South Australian and three Victorian. Large tents and annexes occupy plots of flattened canegrass in between the four-wheel drives. Most of the owners are out wandering. But in the shade of one awning a middle-aged couple, wearing only swimming costumes and sunglasses, are seated in folding chairs reading.

We park our vehicle and set off on foot down the track to Mitchell Falls. The mid-morning humidity is oppressive, even in the pools of shade cast by the eucalypts. The path is well-trodden and marked with small, stone cairns and coloured tapes. We meet an elderly man ambling back up the hill, his round red face shining under a large canvas hat. 'I think I avoided the worst of the heat,' he says. 'It's an extra good show down there.'

The track winds across to Mertens Creek, where the smooth walls of caves and overhangs are embellished with paintings of serpent shapes, wallabies and angular human forms. Water from the creek trickles over the lip of the falls and drops free, down the overhanging face of the narrow gorge. We cross stone pavements and skirt around a low spine of rock to the main Mitchell Falls. There are a dozen or so people bathing and dozing at the pools above the falls. In the distance there are yahooing voices reverberating off the walls and the sound of rocks being lobbed into the void.

We leave our rucksacks and sidle around the terraces and overflow runnels to a lookout with a commanding view back to the tiers of stone and the torrent of white water crashing into a deep pool below. On the skyline there are figures moving about at the rim of the falls, their profiles blurred by rising spray.

Beyond our perch to the north the river gorge is flecked with orange light. Two hundred metres immediately below, a tiny speck — an Azure Kingfisher perhaps — drops from the branch of a paperbark and pierces the dark, lacquered surface of a waterhole. Amidst all the clamour of the falls and the visitors, this fleeting glimpse of unperturbed nature seems somehow reassuring.

By the time we make it back to our campsite the crowds have departed. We use the last of the light to swim in the river. At a series of cascades upstream we let the warm water drum over our heads. It is a relief to have the falls to ourselves, to listen to the rushing music of the river, free from jarring notes.

In such moments there is a temptation to regard the presence of humanity as an affront to the dignity of a place like the Mitchell Falls. And when that presence becomes so numerous or mindless as to damage the surroundings, then it is time to call for rules and restrictions.

During our stay at the falls there were many occasions to rue the conduct of our fellow travellers. It may be true that the creeks are being polluted and the campsites degraded. It could also be said of most visitors that 'they came, they saw, they took videos'. And yet to wish these visitors out of existence might be more than self-delusion. Like us, these people had travelled thousands of kilometres across the continent to reach this spot. Their appreciation of the place, however imperfect it appears to us, may count for more than the depradations they inflict. When the time comes to decide on the destiny of the plateau, their voices and their votes may be crucial.

Previous page: Alasdair McGregor, 'Afternoon in the stone country, Drysdale River' (gouache on paper, 45 x 31 cm).

*Above: The Mitchell
Falls in dry-season flow.
Left: The Mitchell
River close to its sea
estuary.*

Four-wheeled frontier

After the pastoralists and settlers, after the miners, the pearlers and the engineers, come the tourists. Each dry season they arrive in their thousands to ride camels along Cable Beach, to hook barramundi on the Ord River, to whirl in helicopters around the Bungle Bungle Range and to bump along the Gibb River Road in four-wheel drives, camping in the gorges and making the pilgrimages to wonders like the Mitchell Falls. The latest incarnation of the Kimberley frontier is as a tourist destination.

The precise number of annual visitors to the Kimberley remains a mystery. There is little doubt however that the figure is increasing rapidly. Over the last decade the number of people using commercial accommodation in the region has more than doubled to over 250 000.[1] But this statistic does not include the innumerable safari-style tour groups, the independent travellers in private vehicles, or the self-sufficient visitors who fly into the region or cruise the coastline. For many people who have journeyed through Cape York and the Northern Territory's Top End, the Kimberley represents the next stop, the new 'outback' destination.

A host of factors has contributed to this flurry of interest, including the sealing of Highway One in 1986, the publicity surrounding the Ord River Scheme, the promotion of Broome as a tourist town, and increased prominence in the media of the region's natural history and Aboriginal heritage. But no element has been more influential than the national publicity lavished on the Bungle Bungle Range in 1982–83. Hailed as a mysterious lost world, this 'discovery' was instantly appropriated as part of the Kimberley's scenic wealth — tourist gold. Sightseers soon began arriving by the thousands and, in the wake of the 1986 Bungle Bungle Working Group Report, the Purnululu National Park and Conservation Reserve was declared the following year.

For some, this flooding tide of visitors is a curse. Others see tourism as a salvation, the new industry that will bring money and jobs into the region. Along the travellers' trails, cattle properties like El Questro, Home Valley, Drysdale River, Mt Barnett and Mt Elizabeth now rely increasingly on tourist trade to contribute to their livelihood. Pastoralists have found themselves in the business of selling fuel and supplies, guiding tours, maintaining camping sites and providing homestead accommodation. The cattle kings are opening their castles to an ever curious public.

Shifting ground, changing people

The old homestead at Mt Elizabeth Station sits abandoned on the banks of the Hann River. Within the weathered paling fence stand giant mango and orange trees. They shade over-grown garden beds, neatly bordered with upturned rum bottles. Purple Bougainvillea arches over the rough, white-washed walls of the house. Inside it is cool and dark. We prise open the iron shutters and look across to the river slipping by. What was once a long, deep pool is now almost full of buff-coloured silt washed down from the sandstone ridges upstream.

In December 1946, close to the height of the wet season, Frank Lacey made a tortuous overland journey by truck to take up his lease at Mt Elizabeth. After 23 years of cattle droving to all corners of the Kimberley, he had found a place to begin a new life. The house was built using local stone, posts hewn from the heartwood of the native pines, and a mortar made out of the pounded remains of anthills mixed with water. The roof was thatched with the grass that grew tall by the river.

Frank Lacey's son Peter spent his early childhood at this homestead, growing close to nature and learning the ways of cattlemen. Now, as he leads us around the old house, Peter sucks thoughtfully on his pipe, peering into the rooms, the corners of his past. 'I haven't been back here for a while,' he says. In the kitchen he gently slaps his palm on one of the upright posts and adds with a slight smile, 'I reckon the old place should hold together for a bit longer.' By the look of things, at least another 46 years.

Above: One of many sandstone archways in the Purnululu National Park.
Left: Livistona *Palms tower above thermal springs. El Questro Station.*

189

Top: Dry-season burning, Dunham River valley.
Above: Overgrazing, Fitzroy River.
Right: Rainforest margins, Mitchell Plateau.

Meanwhile, 10 kilometres to the south, Peter and his wife Pat have built a new homestead. The roof may be iron and steel, and the floor standard-issue concrete, but the walls are unmistakably local, a siltstone in rich shades of pink and gold. The homestead is both the hub of a 200 000 hectare pastoral property and the base for a variety of tours that Peter and his family now lead into the country around Walcott Inlet and Bachsten Creek. 'The money from the tours helps to keep us going,' says Peter. 'It seems to get busier every year — perhaps a little too busy around mustering time.'

As on most stations, life is changing at Mt Elizabeth. Many of the Aboriginal families who used to live and work closely with the Lacey family have moved off. They have gone to new out-station communities and into town, taking advantage of what is sometimes called 'sit-down money'. Gone too is the freedom to visit areas like the Prince Regent River, now a World Biosphere Reserve and accessible only for 'approved' scientific research.

There is still a lot of fine country at the Laceys' back door. However, like many pastoralists, they are unsure what to make of the new pressures now being made on the region and their impact on a way of life which itself is bending to the times.

In spite of its reputation as one of Australia's great cattle-producing regions, Kimberley pastoralists like the Laceys have always had to contend with formidable difficulties. There has been a history of erratic seasonal conditions which, combined with long periods of depressed beef prices, have reduced the viability of many properties. High operating costs and the distance to major markets have compounded these lean times. But the most serious challenge has centred on the land itself and how it has been used.

Some 50 per cent of the Kimberley is held under pastoral lease. But only 7.6 per cent of this land is considered to be high quality for grazing, and this is mostly concentrated along the Ord and Fitzroy river valleys. The remaining usable areas, especially in the northern Kimberley, have only moderate or low stock-carrying capacity.[2]

On the vast majority of properties, cattle roam wild on the open range for most of the year. As a result, pastoralists have limited control over the breeding or grazing of stock. The lack of fencing and artificial sources of water has caused serious over-grazing of river frontages and alluvial flats. A 1972 State Government report suggested that 30 per cent of the prime western Kimberley was in poor range condition and stated that 'the worst areas of degradation and erosion are found on the most valuable pastoral lands'.[3] Similar problems in the eastern Kimberley have resulted in a marked drop of the land's capacity to carry cattle.[4]

There was evidence of land degradation in the Kimberley as early as the 1930s, but it was not until studies in the 1960s revealed that 22 million tonnes of soil were being washed down the Ord River each year, that regeneration was attempted in the form of a reserve comprising several resumed properties along the Ord.

Over the last two decades there have been other efforts to improve land-management practices within the region. But there is no doubt that the problems of over-stocking, soil erosion, feral cattle, pasture degradation, and uncontrolled burning are still threatening the long-term future of many properties throughout the Kimberley. Predictably these problems have also spread across property boundaries into adjacent crown lands, parks and reserves, often with dire consequences for native wildlife populations and plant communities in these areas.

The high turnover in the ownership of station leases highlights the extent of the troubles afflicting the pastoral industry. It is generally acknowledged that many existing leases are, at best, marginal operations. In recent years several properties have been taken on by Aboriginal communities to provide living areas and an income from cattle. Others have been abandoned, incorporated into other leases or resumed by the Government.

Against this background, the influx of visitors and the calls for improved conservation of the region's natural heritage are reshaping attitudes towards land in the Kimberley. It is inevitable that many unsustainable leases, and tracts of ecologically significant country on other, viable properties, will become part of a much more representative collection of national parks and conservation reserves.

A long-awaited step in this direction occurred with the purchase in 1991 of the Mt Hart pastoral lease by the Department of Conservation and Land Management (CALM). This

Top: Flanks of Mt Broome, King Leopold Ranges.
Left: Waterfall, Richenda River.
Right: Animal architecture. Mud-wasp's nest, Mitchell Falls.

Previous page: Moonrise, Mirima National Park (Hidden Valley), near Kununurra.
Top left: The hide of the land. Ripple patterns, Cockburn Range.
Top right: Crocodile motifs, Drysdale River.
*Above: Freshwater Crocodile (*Crocodylus johnstonii*), Carr Boyd Ranges.*

property in the south-west Kimberley includes a large stretch of the King Leopold Ranges, and is destined to form the basis of a major national park incorporating features such as Bell Creek, Bold Bluff, the Isdell River and Lennard River Gorge.

Procrastination or pro-conservation?

Mt Hart is but one of many parks proposed for the Kimberley. Around four per cent of the region is currently protected within national parks and nature reserves. These include the Drysdale River National Park, Purnululu National Park, Prince Regent Nature Reserve, and a group of handkerchief-sized parks such as Windjana Gorge, Tunnel Creek and Geike Gorge in the limestone country, and Hidden Valley (Mirima) on the outskirts of Kununurra.

It is 25 years since the Conservation Through Reserves Committee first published its report recommending that some 14 parks and reserves be established in the Kimberley. Since then the proposals have been refined, updated, endorsed in principle, and added to. However, hardly any of the recommendations have been acted on. The only sizeable park to be declared during this period was Purnululu. This was largely in response to promotion and public pressure, and was not one of the original recommendations.

In 1991 CALM published a detailed report (known as the System 7 Update) on these proposals, which recommended additions to five existing parks and reserves, a further 13 new parks and reserves, and put forward 15 other areas worthy of investigation. The report noted that the region provides an opportunity, 'to proclaim a truly representative series of nature conservation reserves in keeping with the World, National and State Conservation Strategies'.[5]

The System 7 Update's key proposals in the south-west include enlarging the Point Coulomb Nature Reserve to create the Dampierland National Park, and forming a larger Devonian Reef National Park that incorporates the existing small parks in the Oscar and Napier ranges. To the north the report recommends a national park for the Walcott Inlet, together with a series of marine and nature reserves for the coastal islands and surrounding waters. The report also suggests enlarging the Prince Regent Nature Reserve, changing its status to that of a national park, and extending its boundaries northward to link up with the areas around the Hunter River and Mitchell Falls. New national parks are also suggested for the Lawley River along the eastern flank of the Mitchell Plateau, and at Cape Londonderry, the northern most tip of the state.

Of the north Kimberley the authors of the System 7 Update remark, 'the opportunity to protect these intact ecosystems is of international significance and should not be lost. Their proper management has some urgency'. This point has not escaped the attention of conservation groups who have argued that the report does not go far enough in securing the natural heritage of the area and makes dubious concessions to other mining and development interests.[6]

The current epicentre of these concerns is the Mitchell Plateau. While the two national parks suggested by CALM embrace the scenic splendours of the Mitchell and Lawley rivers, and include important areas of monsoon forests and mangroves, the bulk of the plateau and its palm forest is set aside for mining. Rights to the extensive bauxite deposits are held by a joint venture controlled by Comalco and Alcoa.

Meanwhile the region is also the focus of intense interest by the Aboriginal groups who claim traditional ownership of the plateau. Of specific concern are living areas near Camp and Crystal creeks. Protracted negotiations between the Government, miners and Aborigines over these areas have proved inconclusive. According to one Mowanjum elder, Laurie Utemorrah, 'We're talking about the land. We're not talking about any other thing ... we want the land.' His wife Daisy says, 'We want to go back and look at stones and the trees and everything that is in our country. We love our place because it is very dear to us. We come from there.'[7]

As the negotiations continue, tourists, like us, keep on arriving. There is little doubt the volume of traffic into the area requires better management, and that visitors should be encouraged to treat the country with more wisdom and understanding. But there is more at stake than simply the protection of the bush, its fauna and rock art. The delays and disarray are also testing the goodwill of the plateau's original custodians. In June 1991 Aborigines reacted angrily to the suspected looting of their outcamp at Camp Creek. Roadside protest signs were put up in the vain hope of restricting entry to the plateau to only those with an Aboriginal permit.

In 1991 a much more far-reaching claim for native title over a vast area of the north-west Kimberley, including the Mitchell Plateau, was lodged with the High Court on behalf of the Wororra, Wunambal and Ngarinyin people. David Mowaljarlai, a key figure behind the claim, says, 'We've got to fight this situation ... our heart, our whole body is there.'[8]

Then in March 1992 the Wilderness Society launched a proposal for a new park covering much of the area of the Aboriginal claim and a great deal more. To some the idea will be seen as unwieldy as its title: A World Class Aboriginal-owned Wilderness National Park and Marine National Park in the North Kimberley Region of Western Australia. Included in the 4 500 000 hectares are existing parks, Aboriginal Reserves, vacant crown land and smaller sections of pastoral leases. An additional 3 500 000 hectares is taken up by a marine national park. As a single entity, it would be the largest park in Australia and one of the biggest in the world.

The key to the concept is the suggestion that the Aboriginal claim and the park proposal are 'mutually achievable'.[9] It remains unclear to what extent the aspirations of the Wilderness Society and those of the many different Aboriginal groups encompassed by the park would be compatible. Perhaps the greatest value of such a proposal is as a symbolic and legal entity rather than as an answer to the management of the region's natural heritage.

If anything, the proposal is a recognition that the Kimberley's natural features are too diverse and dispersed to be approached in conventional terms. The things that make the region so distinctive — its size, isolation, sparse population, marked seasons, and above all else its great wildness — are the very things that make divining its future such a challenge. The nub of the problem is not a confrontation between idealistic conservationists and enterprising developers but a failure of will, a failure of imagination.

The Kimberley recommends itself as a place where the prime responsibility for working out ways of protecting the land should rest with the people who live there. Much more needs to be known about the natural landscape, and the existing knowledge needs to be better shared. But for anything to work it has to engage the pastoralists, the tour operators, the townspeople, the miners, the crop farmers and most of all the Aboriginal people in solving the equation. All have a role in creating a different land ethic. In the Kimberley it is not so much a case of framing new laws as seizing the potential to adapt old lore.

Going back

From the crest of a range, 400 kilometres south of the Mitchell Plateau, we look down into the dry bed of Carolyn Creek. The valley of spinifex below is encircled by a palisade of rock walls at the heart of the St George Ranges. Further south, across the nineteenth parallel, lies the Great Sandy Desert. This is the edge of the Kimberley. Beyond, the land vanishes beneath a sprawl of dunes and pink, aeolian sand.

The St George Ranges rise from the floodplain of the Fitzroy River. Clumps of spinifex colonise the land like a mass of spiky berets. Along the creekbed to the north the sunlight reflects off the glazed rocks, creating a mirage of shining pools. It is a place of storm-scoured gullies and gaunt, cupola-shaped hills. In any other corner of the continent this area would be a national park. In the Kimberley it remains a footnote in the catalogue of the conservation estate.

We quit the heights and descend into the shelter of a gulch. The afternoon is stifling. We wait till the sun slips behind the range before starting back to camp. In this desiccated hollow among the hills, signs of life are scarce: lizard tracks, a far-off bird cry, wasps hovering in fissures among the boulders. The landscape appears forbidding and empty.

Walls of fire, Cockburn Range. This range is the site of tourist development and is mooted by some as a potential national park.

Above: Late afternoon, St George Ranges.
Left: Vine thicket and rock art, Drysdale River.

200

At times it stuns the imagination to merge the fierce aspects of such a place with a record of human habitation. Yet for scores of centuries there were people living around these ranges. And now they are returning. Less than five kilometres away, at the foot of the rocky spurs, is an outcamp of the Nookanbah community.

The previous afternoon we had driven to Andrews Bore, down narrow sandy tracks flanked with tall grass. We passed a building, half-finished and seemingly abandoned, surrounded by pipes and bright sheets of corrugated iron. Further on, in a dusty clearing above a waterhole, there were a large tent, tables and a row of beds open to the sky. Three or four families appeared to be in residence. We talked with the people of the settlement and with their permission drove a short distance cross-country to set up our own camp on their land. Though our encounter with the community was brief, the mere presence of this outpost had the quiet strength of a declaration.

Now, in the stillness of the evening, we make our escape from the ranges. The heat continues to waft up from the dark hills. To the west, smoke plumes into the sky from fires out of control on grazing country near Go Go Station. We amble down the gorge and onto river flats plush with grass, where the first of the evening air moves through the trees. In the distance, braying donkeys herald the cool of the coming night. At camp we guzzle mugs of tea and sit watching the ranges. The brows of stone on the skyline are banded with shadow and light. We have come to the brink of the desert, having traversed a land of unfathomable beginnings. We have glimpsed the promise of a world without end.

1. Western Australia, Department of Regional Development and the North West, and Department of Planning and Urban Development, *Kimberley Region Plan Study Report*, 1990, p. 81.
2. Western Australia, Department of Agriculture, *Kimberley Pastoral Industry Inquiry* (the Jennings Report), October 1985.
3. Western Australia, Department of Agriculture, *Technical Bulletin*, no. 42, May 1979.
4. R. Davies, 'Kings in baked clay castles', *Habitat*, August 1987.
5. A. Burbidge, N. McKenzie and K. Kenneally, *Nature Conservation Reserves in The Kimberley*, W.A. Department of Conservation and Land Management, Perth, 1991.
6. Wilderness Society, *The Kimberley, The Slide Towards Extinction*, Wilderness Society (W.A.), 1990.
7. As quoted in the *Sydney Morning Herald*, 6 July 1991.
8. Ibid.
9. Wilderness Society, *A Proposal for A World Class Aboriginal-owned Wilderness National Park and Marine National Park in the North Kimberley*, Wilderness Society (W.A.), 1992.

Bibliography

Allen, J., Golson, J., and Jones, R. (eds), *Sunda and Sahul: Prehistoric Studies in South-East Asia and Melanesia*, Academic Press, London, 1977.

Andrews, M., and Wightman, G., *Plants of the Northern Territory Monsoon Vine Forests*, Conservation Commission of the Northern Territory, Darwin, 1989.

Australian Heritage Commission, *Australian National Rainforest Study*, vol. 1: *The Rainforest Legacy*, Special Australian Heritage Publications Series, no. 7 (1), Australian Government Publishing Service, Canberra, 1987.

Australian Water Resources Council, *Review of Australia's Water Resources*, Australian Government Publishing Service, Canberra, 1976.

Basedow, H., 'Narrative of an expedition of exploration to north-west Australia', *Transactions of the Royal Geographical Society of Australia, South Australian Branch*, vol. 19, 1916–17.

Berndt, R.M. and C.H. (eds), *Aborigines of the West: Their Past and Their Present*, University of Western Australia Press, Perth, 1979.

Beard, J.S., *Vegetation Survey of Western Australia: Kimberley 1:1 000 000 Vegetation Series and Explanatory Notes*, University of Western Australia Press, Perth, 1979.

Beard, J.S., and Clayton-Greene, K.A., 'The fire factor in vine thicket and woodland vegetation of the Admiralty Gulf region, north-west Kimberley', *Proceedings of the Ecological Society of Australia*, vol. 13: *Ecology of the Wet-Dry Tropics*, eds M.G. Ridpath and L.K. Corbett, 1985.

Benterrak, K., Muecke, S., and Roe, P., *Reading the Country*, Fremantle Arts Centre Press, Fremantle, 1984.

Bishop, K.A., and Forbes, M.A., 'Freshwater fishes of northern Australia', in *Monsoonal Australia*, eds C.D. Haynes, M.G. Redpath and M.A.J. Williams, A.A. Balkema, Rotterdam, 1991.

Bowdler, S., and O'Connor, S., 'The dating of the Australian small tool tradition with new evidence from the Kimberley, W.A.', *Australian Aboriginal Studies*, no. 1, 1991.

Bowler, J., and Jones, R., 'Struggle for the savanna: northern Australia in ecological and prehistoric perspective', in *Northern Australia: Options and Implications*, ed. R. Jones, Australian National University, Canberra, 1980.

Blundell, V., and Layton, R., 'Marriage, myth and models of exchange in the West Kimberley', *Mankind*, vol. 11, 1977.

Bradshaw, J., 'Notes on a recent trip to the Prince Regent's River', in *Transactions of the Royal Geographic Society of South Australia*, vol. 9, pt 2, 1892.

Brandl, E.H., *Australian Aboriginal Paintings in Western and Central Arnhem Land*, Australian Institute of Aboriginal Studies, Canberra, 1982.

Brock, J., *Top End Native Plants*, John Brock, Darwin, 1988.

Brockman, F.S., *Report on Exploration of North-West Kimberley, 1901*, (Appendices by C. Crossland and F.M. House), Report to Minister for Lands, Western Australia, Perth, 1901.

Buchanan, G., *Packhorse and Waterhole*, Angus & Robertson, Sydney, 1934.

Burbidge, A.A., and Kabay, E.D. (eds), *A Biological Survey of the Drysdale River National Park, North Kimberley W.A. in August 1975*, Wildlife Research Bulletin of Western Australia, no. 6, Department of Fisheries and Wildlife, Perth, 1977.

Burbidge, A.A., and McKenzie, N.L., 'Patterns in the modern decline of Western Australia's vertebrate fauna: causes and conservation implications', *Biological Conservation*, vol. 50, 1989.

Burbidge, A.A., McKenzie, N.L., and Kenneally, K.F., *Nature Conservation Reserves in the Kimberley Western Australia*, W.A. Department of Conservation and Land Management, Perth, 1991.

Burt, J., *The Kimberley: Australia's North-West Frontier*, Houghton Mifflin, Melbourne, 1989.

Carnegie, D.W., *Spinifex and Sand*, C.A. Pearson, London, 1898. (Facsimile edn, Hesperian Press, Perth, 1982).

Chaloupka, G., *From Paleoart to Casual Paintings*, Monograph Series no. 1, Northern Territory Museum of Arts and Sciences, Darwin, 1984.

Chappell, J., 'The quarternary environmental record', in *Proceedings of the Global Change Conference*, Australian Academy of Science, Canberra, 1988.

Clark, M., and Traynor, S., *Plants of the Tropical Woodland*, Conservation Commission of the Northern Territory, Darwin, 1987.

Cogger, H.G., *Reptiles and Amphibians of Australia* (4th edn), Reed, Sydney, 1986.

Conigrave, W.P., *Walkabout*, Dent, London, 1938.

Crawford, I.M., 'Aboriginal cultures', in *A History of Western Australia*, ed. C. Stannage, University of Western Australia Press, Perth, 1981.

Crawford, I.M., *The Art of the Wandjina*, Oxford University Press, Melbourne, 1968.

Crawford, I.M., 'The relationship of Bradshaw and Wandjina art in north-west Kimberley', in *Form in Indigenous Art*, ed. P.J. Ucko, Australian Institute of Aboriginal Studies, Canberra, 1977.

Crawford, I.M., 'Traditional Aboriginal plant resources in the Kalumburu area: aspects in ethno-economics', *Records of the Western Australian Museum*, supplement no. 15, Perth, 1982.

Cusack, M. and S., *Year in the Wilderness*, Viking O'Neill, Ringwood, Victoria, 1990.

Dampier, W., *A New Voyage Round the World*, London, 1697.

Dampier, W., *A Voyage to New Holland in the Year 1699*, vols 1 & 2, London, 1703 and 1709.

Davies, R., 'Kings in baked clay castles', *Habitat*, August, 1987.

Dortch, C., 'Archaeological work in the Ord Reservoir area, East Kimberley', *Australian Institute of Aboriginal Studies Newsletter*, vol. 3, no. 4, 1972.

Dow, D.B., and Gemuts, I., *Geology of the Kimberley Region of Western Australia*, Geological Survey of Western Australia, 1969.

Durack, M., *Kings in Grass Castles* [1959], Corgi Australia, 1990.

Elder, B., *Blood on the Wattle: Massacres and Maltreatment of Australian Aborigines Since 1788*, Child & Associates, Sydney, 1988.

Elkin, A.P., 'The rainbow-serpent myth in north-west Australia', *Oceania*, vol. 1, 1930–31.

Elkin, A.P., 'Rock paintings of north-west Australia', *Oceania*, vol. 1, no. 3, 1930.

Elkin, A.P., 'Social organisation in the Kimberley division north-western Australia', *Oceania*, vol. 2, no. 3, 1932.

Favenc, E., *The History of Australian Exploration*, Turner & Henderson, Sydney, 1888.

Figgis, P. (ed.), *Rainforests of Australia*, Weldons, Sydney, 1985.

Flannery, T., 'The impact of humans upon the biota of Australasia', *Journal and Proceedings, Royal Society of New South Wales*, vol. 124, 1991.

Flood, J., *Archaeology in the Dreamtime* (2nd edn), Collins, Sydney, 1989.

Flood, J., *The Riches of Ancient Australia*, University of Queensland Press, St. Lucia, Qld, 1990.

Forrest, A., *North-West Exploration: Journal of Expedition from De Grey to Port Darwin*, Perth, 1880.

Gellatly, D.C., and Sofoulis, J., *Drysdale River and Londonderry, W.A., 1:250 000 Geological Series: Explanatory Notes*, Bureau of Mineral Resources, Canberra, 1971.

Gemuts, I., and Plumb, K.A., *Precambrian Geology of the Kimberley Region, Western Australia* (Excursion Guide no. 44C), International Geological Congress, Canberra, 1976.

Gould, J., *Birds of Australia*, London, 1848.

Green, N., 'Aborigines and white settlers', in *A New History of Western Australia*, ed. C. Stannage, University of Western Australia Press, Perth, 1981.

Grey, G., *Journals of Two Expeditions of Discovery in North-West and Western Australia 1837–1839*, vols 1 & 2, T. & W. Boone, London, 1841. (Facsimile edn, Hesperian Press, Perth, 1983).

Griffin, T.J., and Grey, K., 'Kimberley basin', in *Geology and Mineral Resources of Western Australia*, Geological Survey of Western Australia, Perth, 1990.

Hallam, S.J., 'The first Western Australians', in *A New History of Western Australia*, ed. C. Stannage, University of Western Australia Press, Perth, 1981.

Hann, F., 'Exploration in Western Australia', *Proceedings of the Royal Society of Queensland*, vol. 16, 1900.

Harris, J., *The Kimberley: The Slide Towards Extinction*, Wilderness Society, Western Australia, Perth, 1990.

Haynes, C.D., Ridpath, M.G., and Williams, M.A.J. (eds), *Monsoonal Australia*, A.A. Balkema, Rotterdam, 1991.

Hicks, A., 'The Kimberleys explored: Forrest expedition of 1879', *Early Days*, vol. 1, Oct. 1938, pp. 11–19.

Hiscock, P., 'How old are the artifacts in Malakunanja II?', *Archaeology in Oceania*, no. 25, 1990.

Hordern, M., *Mariners are Warned! John Lort Stokes and the H.M.S. Beagle in Australia 1837–1843*, Melbourne University Press, Melbourne, 1989.

Kerr, A., *Australia's North-West* (2nd edn), University of Western Australia Press, Perth, 1975.

King, P.P., *Narrative of a Survey of the Intertropical and Western Coasts of Australia, Performed Between the Years 1818 and 1822*, vols 1 & 2, John Murray, London, 1827.

Kok, B., and Petheram, R.J., *Plants of the Kimberley Region of Western Australia* (2nd edn), University of Western Australia Press, Perth, 1986.

Lamond, G.H., *Tales of the Overland*, Hesperian Press, Perth, 1986.

Laurie, A., interviewed by Ann Magrath, in *Fighters and Singers: The Lives of Some Australian Aboriginal Women*, eds I. White, D. Barwick and B. Meehan, Allen & Unwin, Sydney, 1985.

Long, J., *Nomadism; John Wolseley; Twelve Years in Australia — Paintings and Drawings*, University Gallery, University of Melbourne, 1988.

Love, J.R.B., 'Notes on the Wororra tribe of north-western Australia', *Transactions of the Royal Society of South Australia*, vol. 41, 1917.

Love, J.R.B., 'Rock paintings of the Wororra', *Journal of the Royal Society of Western Australia*, vol. 16, 1930.

Love, J.R.B., *Stone Age Bushmen of Today*, Blackie, London, 1936.

McGonigal, D. (ed.), *The Kimberley*, Australian Geographic, Sydney, 1990.

McIntyre, K.G., *The Secret Discovery of Australia: Portuguese Ventures 200 Years Before Captain Cook*, Souvenir Press, Medindie, South Australia, 1977.

McKenzie, N.L., Johnston, R.B., and Kendrick, P.G. (eds), *Kimberley Rainforests*, Surrey Beattie, Sydney, 1991.

Marchant, L.R., *An Island Unto Itself: William Dampier and New Holland*, Hesperian Press, Perth, 1988.

Moon, R. and V., *The Kimberley: An Adventurer's Guide*, Kakirra Adventure Publications, Chelsea, Victoria, 1989.

Mowaljarlai, D., and Peck, C., 'Ngarinyin cultural continuity: A project to teach young people the culture, including the re-painting of Wandjina rock art sites', *Australian Aboriginal Studies*, no. 2, 1987.

Mowaljarlai, D., and Watchman, A., 'An Aboriginal view of rock art management', *Rock Art Research*, vol. 6, no. 2, 1989.

Nanson, G.C., Young, R.W., and Stockton, E.D., 'Chronology and palaeoenvironment of the Cranebrook terrace containing artifacts more than 40 000 years old', *Archaeology in Oceania*, no. 22, 1987.

Bibliography

Nixon, M., *The Rivers of Home: Frank Lacey — Kimberley Pioneer*, Vanguard Press, Perth, 1978.

O'Brien, B.J., (ed.), *Environment and Science*, WA Sesquicentenary Celebration Series, University of Western Australia Press, Perth, 1979.

O'Connor, S., 'New radiocarbon dates from Koolan Island, west Kimberley, W.A.', *Australian Archaeology*, no. 28, June 1989.

O'Connor, S., 'The stone house structures of High Cliffy Island, north-west Kimberley, W.A.', *Australian Archaeology*, no. 25, Dec. 1987.

Olsen, J., Durack, M., Serventy, V., Dutton, G., and Bortignon, A., *The Land Beyond Time*, Macmillan, Melbourne, 1984.

Palfreyman, W.D., *Guide to the Geology of Australia*, Australian Government Publishing Service, Canberra, 1984.

Perez, Fr. E., *Kalumburu, the Benedictine Mission and the Aborigines, 1908–1975*, Kalumburu Benedictine Mission, 1977.

Reynolds, H., *The Other Side of the Frontier*, Penguin, Melbourne, 1982.

Ridpath, M.G., 'Ecology in the wet–dry tropics: How different?', *Proceedings of the Ecological Society of Australia*, vol. 13: *Ecology of the Wet–Dry Tropics*, eds M.G. Ridpath and L.K. Corbett, 1985.

Roberts, R.G., Jones, R., and Smith, M.A., 'Thermoluminescence dating of a 50 000-year-old human occupation site in northern Australia', *Nature*, vol.35, 1990.

Royal Australasian Ornithologists Union, 'List of recommended English names', *The Emu*, vol. 77 (supplement), May 1978.

Sainty, G.R. and Jacobs, S.W.L., *Waterplants in Australia*, Sainty & Assoc./Royal Botanic Gardens, Sydney, 1988.

Schilder, G., *Australia Unveiled*, Theatrum Orbis Terrarum, Amsterdam, 1976.

Schodde, R., and Tidemann, S.C. (eds), *Readers Digest Complete Book of Australian Birds* (2nd edn), Readers Digest, Sydney, 1986.

Schulz, A.S., 'North-west Australian rock paintings', *Memoirs of the National Museum of Victoria*, vol. 20, 1956.

Stannage, C. (ed.), *A New History of Western Australia*, University of Western Australia Press, Perth, 1981.

Stokes, J.L., *Discoveries in Australia, With an Account of the Coasts and Rivers Explored and Surveyed During the Voyage of the H.M.S. Beagle in the Years 1837–43*, vols 1 and 2, T. & W. Boone, London, 1846.

Storr, G.M., *Birds of the Kimberley Division, Western Australia*, Western Australian Museum Special Publication, no. 11, Perth, 1980.

Stow, R., *To the Islands* [1958], Picador, Sydney, 1983.

Strahan, R., *The Australian Museum Complete Book of Australian Mammals*, Angus & Robertson, Sydney, 1983.

Sutton, P., *Dreamings: The Art of Aboriginal Australia*, Viking, Ringwood, Victoria, 1988.

Thom, J.H., 'Kimberley region', in *Geology of Western Australia*, Western Australian Geological Survey, Perth, 1975.

Walsh, G.L., *Australia's Greatest Rock Art*, E.J. Brill/Robert Brown & Associates, Bathurst, NSW, 1988

Walsh, G.L., 'Rock painting sizes in the Kimberley and Victoria River district', *Rock Art Research*, vol. 8, no. 2, 1991.

Webb, G. and Manolis, C., *Crocodiles of Australia*, Reed, Sydney, 1989.

Welch, D., 'The bichrome art period in the Kimberley, Australia', *Rock Art Research*, vol. 7, no. 2, 1990.

Western Australia, Department of Agriculture, *Kimberley Pastoral Industry Inquiry*, Perth, 1985.

Western Australia, Department of Agriculture, *Technical Bulletin*, no. 42, May 1979.

Western Australia, Department of Regional Development and the North West and Department of Planning and Urban Development, *Kimberley Region Plan Study Report*, Perth, 1990.

White, I., Barwick, D., and Meehan, B. (eds), *Fighters and Singers: The Lives of Some Australian Aboriginal Women*, Allen & Unwin, Sydney, 1985.

Wilderness Society, *The Kimberley, The Slide Towards Extinction*, Wilderness Society (W.A.), Perth, 1990.

Wilderness Society, *A Proposal for a World Class Aboriginal-Owned National Park and Marine National Park in the North Kimberley*, Wilderness Society (W.A.), Perth, 1992.

Williams, I.R., and Sofoulis, J., *Prince Regent and Camden Sound, W.A. 1:250 000 Geological Series: Explanatory Notes*, Bureau of Mineral Resources, Canberra, 1971.

Worms, S.A., 'Contemporary and prehistoric rock painting in central and north Kimberley', *Anthropos*, no. 50, 1955.

Index

The scientific names of plants and animals are set in italics; bold page numbers indicate illustrations.